THE LAST RALLY

To Tom T., with sincere thanks.

CHARLES II
The Last Rally

by

Hilaire Belloc

"I came, I saw, God conquered." —KING JOHN III, 1683

Norfolk, VA
2003

.

Charles II: The Last Rally.

Copyright © 2003 IHS Press.

Charles II copyright the Estate of Hilaire Belloc.

Preface, typesetting, layout, and cover design
copyright IHS Press.
All rights reserved.

   Charles II was originally published in 1939 by Harper & Brothers
Publishers of New York and London. Cassell and Co., Ltd., of London
issued an edition the following year, which edition forms the basis of
the present edition. The spelling, punctuation, and formatting of the
Cassell edition have been largely preserved. Minor corrections to the
text have been made in light of the earlier edition.

ISBN: 0-9718286-4-4

Library of Congress Cataloging-in-Publication Data

Belloc, Hilaire, 1870-1953
   Charles II : the last rally / by Hilaire Belloc.
      p. cm.
Originally published: New York : Harper & Brothers,
1939.
   ISBN 0-9718286-4-4 (alk. paper)
   1. Charles II, King of England, 1630-1685. 2. Great
Britain--History--Charles II, 1660-1685. 3. Great
Britain--Kings and rulers--Biography. I. Title.
   DA445.B38 2003
   941.06'4'092--dc21

                                              2003042384

Printed in the United States of America.

Gates of Vienna Books is an imprint of IHS Press.
For more information, write to:

Gates of Vienna Books
222 W. 21st St., Suite F-122
Norfolk, VA 23517

TABLE OF CONTENTS

Charles II in Coronation Robes

An oil painting by J. M. Wright, 1661

INTRODUCTION

This book, one of the last that Belloc wrote, appeared in 1939 when he was 69 – three years before a stroke that ended his literary career. Its theme and message did not depart from that of his many popular biographies written in the 1920s and 30s. Those works were all based upon the same premises that characterized his general approach to and understanding of European history. Foremost among those premises is the notion proclaimed in his 1920 work, *Europe and the Faith:* "The Faith is Europe. And Europe is the Faith." That meant that European civilization was the creature of Catholicism and to the degree that Europe departed from Catholicism, she would loose her identity. And if that happened, "Europe" would come to signify just a geographical area or – as seems the case today – a mere economic and administrative unit, lacking any spiritual or cultural basis.

Belloc saw as providential the link between classical Roman Civilization and Christianity. The Church was able to employ the structures and the thought of Rome for its own development while preserving Roman Civilization, making it, in baptized form, the civilization of Europe. This view contrasted strikingly with that of Gibbon and other Enlightenment-era thinkers who blamed Christianity for Rome's decline.

And what of the barbarian invasions and the so-called "Dark Ages" that followed the political collapse of Rome? Belloc viewed the barbarians not as conquerors, but as immigrants, themselves aspiring to be part of Rome. Administrative and economic weaknesses in the empire enabled the newcomers increasingly to assume authoritative roles, but as Roman officials, not as conquerors. These quasi-Romans also accepted Christianity, which had become the religion of the empire. That religion, especially through its monastic orders, preserved the classical heritage during the disorderly centuries that ensued, when socio-economic structures had become rather primitive, and when the territory of the old empire faced invasions by non-Christian Vikings and Islam.

CHARLES II: THE LAST RALLY

Belloc certainly did not accept the popular view of early medieval English history, which held that the inherent self-governing abilities of the Anglo-Saxon settlers had enabled them to prevail over the Celtic Britons and the few surviving Roman-Britons. Rather, he saw Anglo-Saxon success in dominating England as having come from their acceptance of the Christian message of St. Augustine. In his analysis of later-medieval English history, he emphasized the reforming and civilizing role of the Norman kings and their successor sovereigns in promoting law, parliament, and the general development of civilization. This view contrasted decidedly with the popular notion that the "democratic" Anglo-Saxons were conquered by the Normans, and that British constitutional history since then is simply the story of the Anglo-Saxon effort to restrain the encroachments of the Norman monarchy upon popular freedoms.

Naturally, Belloc regarded the Reformation of the sixteenth century as the disastrous disruption of European unity. He thought the Reformation need not have endured, as much of it consisted of localized, reformist zealotries prompted by serious grievances and abuses. It was made lasting, however, when England was lost to the Church. That loss was closely linked to the rise of a landed oligarchy, enriched at the expense of the Church, and which over a century or more fatally weakened the monarchy that had favored that enrichment. The last hope for blocking that oligarchic ascendancy existed during the reign of Charles II. Hence, "the last rally."

Belloc's "unconventional" historical vision has to be understood in large part as a reaction against the historical views prevalent when he came of age in late nineteenth-century England – the era in European history labeled by the late historian Carlton Hayes as the "Generation of Materialism." Then popular was an intellectual progressivism that regarded the latest age as the most intelligent, and which expected human progress on the basis of scientific development to be inevitable. Central to this scientifically determinist materialism was Social Darwinism, which interpreted human relations according to the Darwinist explanation of the evolution of species. Prevailing historical attitudes worked hand-in-glove with this progressivist determinism, as seen, e.g., in the already mentioned "Anglo-Saxon" myth about the inherent self-governing ability of the forebears of the English-speaking world.

INTRODUCTION

Also common to that era was what historian Herbert Butterfield labeled "Whig History": the tendency of historians to write favorably of the winners in historical confrontations, especially if the winners were Protestants and/or liberals (but not necessarily revolutionaries, like the French Jacobins). Such seems the case in modern British history, which has an historical vision running as follows: the Reformation in England was the victory of religious liberty against Papal despotism; in succeeding centuries the monarchy that had brought on the Reformation was itself brought under control by the parliament; and parliament itself, over time, became more and more democratically controlled. Events of the later nineteenth century worked to confirm this Whig-Progressivist vision, as the Protestant and industrial societies seemed to prevail over Catholic and/or agrarian and traditional societies, e.g., the North in the American Civil War, Prussia in the struggles with Austria for the unification of and domination over the Germanies, Lombardy-Sardinia against the Papal States, the relationship between England and Ireland, and the defeat of Emperor Louis Napoleon in the Franco-Prussian War (which started two days after Belloc was born).

British Imperialism had reached its peak in Belloc's early manhood. By that time it had been transformed from a pattern of purely diplomatic and military involvements in distant lands for limited, specific objectives, to a popular ideology endorsing the extension of the British flag to the four corners of the globe. Another now-forgotten but then-fashionable intellectual trend in England was a strong Germanophilia, whether in neo-Hegelian philosophy, the racial identification of the Anglo-Saxons with the modern Germans, or simply an admiration for the technical, administrative, and economic ability of the Germans in terms of education, public service, and industrialization.

No wonder, then, that young Belloc considered himself an outsider when a student at Oxford between 1893 and 1896. He was a Catholic, his father was French, and he himself had retained his French citizenship, even fulfilling his required service in the French army. (His being an "outsider" did not prevent him from becoming President of the debating society – the Oxford Union – even though, however, he aggressively labeled himself a "Republican," to the consternation of his predominantly Conservative, Imperialist, and upper-class colleagues.) Belloc even felt out-of-place in secondary education, at the Oratory School in Birmingham founded by Cardinal Newman who, although elderly, still resided at it. Most of the students there were from the aristocratic, Catholic recusant families, who had retained the faith for centuries at great cost in terms of denial of privilege, but who had not let their Catholicism dent their English identity, patriotism, and conservatism. In contrast, Belloc was not only the son of a Frenchman, but his mother was a convert who had come from a long tradition of political radicalism. Her father was Joseph Parkes, a radical publicist active in the promotion of the Parliamentary Reform Act of 1832, and her great-grandfather the politically radical scientist Joseph Priestley. Belloc had little contact with Newman, and in his young adulthood he identified much more closely with the populist and ultramontane Archbishop of Westminster, Henry Cardinal Manning, who had especially concerned himself with the hundreds of thousands of Irish Catholics who made up such a large component of the lower classes in 1889.

Not surprisingly, Belloc, drawn to the study of history, would virtually turn inside-out the prevailing views, downplaying the qualities of the Anglo-Saxons, applauding the Normans, disliking the Reformation, and celebrating the French Revolution.

The last attitude might startle readers having only a superficial understanding of the man. After all, wasn't he the champion of the English monarch against the parliament, calling Charles II's struggle to retain his power "the last rally"? His first two biographies, however, were favorable treatments of Danton and Robespierre, the Trotsky and Lenin of the French Revolution. But his explanation and justification of the revolution had a reactionary character: "It was essentially a reversion to the normal – a sudden and violent return to those conditions which are the necessary bases of health in any political community." He lamented the fact that the privileged classes of France, having lost faith in the institutions formed in the Middle Ages, nevertheless continued to take advantage of them to enhance their own position. Belloc saw them as having "used the name of the Middle Ages precisely because they thought the Middle Ages were dead," but then, with the revolution, "suddenly the spirit of the Middle Ages, the spirit of enthusiasm and of faith, the Crusades, came out of the tomb and routed them."

INTRODUCTION

Belloc did not see "a necessary antagonism between the Republic and the Church," but believed the differences that existed were the result of a miscalculation about the Church by the Republic's leaders. The Civil Constitution of the Clergy, which nationalized Church property and officialdom, was not based so much on hostility but on the idea of the inseparability of the church from the national society. On the other hand, many of them were not believers and looked upon the Church as a declining institution that should be nursed like a dying person. Hence the hierarchy and the clergy were to be publicly salaried.[1]

This unusual interpretation of the French Revolution can be read as compatible with sympathy for the Stuart kings of England and even for Louis XIV of France. Belloc read the violent uprising as an organic development of a society returning to normality and rejecting artificial institutions. No doubt this vision was quite different from that of Edmund Burke, whose conception of the gradualist, organic development of political society led him to see the French Revolution as the apotheosis of political evil. But Belloc's temperament, which allowed him to see value in both the thought of Jean Jacques Rousseau and the career of Napoleon Bonaparte, was quite different from that of Burke, which was one of Whiggish conservatism. Instead, Belloc's was a radical conservatism that could understand violent upheaval and the role of strong political leaders.

The same temperament fostered his disillusion with parliamentary politics, after he served for five years (1906–1910) in the House of Commons as part of the radical wing of the massive Liberal majority. He turned his back on what he called "the Party System," for he came to regard both major political groupings – Conservatives and Liberals – as the collaborating servants of plutocratic oligarchy. The issues between the parties were ruses used to enable periodic changes of power. That oligarchy, with its political servants, was in fact the object of many satirical novels he wrote at the time. By the early twentieth century the oligarchy had broadened beyond being landed and had come to include capitalists in its ranks. The sense that this privileged oligarchy was about to use the engines of the state to

---

[1] Cf. Hilaire Belloc, *The French Revolution* (London: Williams & Norgate, 1911), and John P. McCarthy, "Hilaire Belloc and the French Revolution," *Modern Age,* Vol. 35, No 3 (Spring 1993), pp. 251–7.

protect its interests and inhibit popular dissatisfaction prompted Belloc to write his *Servile State*.[2]

He came to advocate the strengthening of monarchy for Britain and elsewhere as an alternative to plutocratic parliamentary politics. For him a strong monarch need not be a hereditary figure, but could be a strong President or executive. In the 1920s and 1930s he saw the likes of Franco, Salazar, and Mussolini as corrective alternatives to plutocratic and ineffective parliamentary regimes. The Catholic character of the regimes of the former two, and the nominal adherence of the latter to Catholic values and its allusion to classical Roman heritage, made them attractive to Belloc. On the other hand, his consciousness that Germany had never been part of the Roman Empire, and his suspicion that the Northern Germans (the Protestants) had never completely absorbed the message of Christianity (which fact was apparent to him in observing the Bismarckian Second Reich) made him immune to the neo-pagan and scientistic message of Hitler and Nazism. He also had no sympathy for the essentially unhistorical doctrine of Marxism, about whose ultimate success he was correctly doubtful.

But let us return to the subject of *Charles II*. As a young king, replacing a "Protectorate" that had executed his father, Charles had to tread very gingerly in maintaining his position. He had been brought to the throne by the same parliamentary forces that rebelled against his father twenty years before, because they realized that toppling the monarchy in fact ushered in an arbitrary dictatorship. They understood the paradox that parliamentary liberty required a king. Most in the parliament had also come to the conclusion that the maintenance of the established Church of England was as similarly linked as the monarchy to the maintenance of English liberty. They viewed the Cromwellian dictatorship as an inevitable consequence of dissenting Protestantism. For this reason they were more orthodox than the king in insisting upon a code expelling nonconformist clergy from the National Church, and inhibiting the meetings of Nonconformist congregations. The appreciation of the connection between the

---

[2] Belloc believed that since the insecurities linked to industrial capitalism were liable to bring on socialism, the ruling circles would seek to save their own position by drawing on the language of reformers to sell a "Servile State." In that system individual freedom would be forsaken in return for security and economic sufficiency, but the oligarchy would also retain its profits and position. This was the central thesis of Belloc's seminal tract, *The Servile State,* originally published in 1912.

monarchy, the High Church, and English liberty (the essence of what would be called Toryism) explained the willingness of parliament – however reluctant – to accept Charles II's brother, James, a convert to Catholicism, as his successor in 1685. It was feared that any tampering with natural, hereditary succession would open the door to "republicanism" and its logical consequence, dictatorship.

Charles had tried to get around the parliamentary dominance of his revenue by accepting subsidies from King Louis of France, in return for foreign policy concessions and for a promised improvement of the position of English Catholics (a shrinking minority at the time, but towards whom Charles was well disposed). When the subsidy was discovered, Charles then had to concede changes in his ministers and the imposition of restrictions upon Catholics. Within a few years he even had to endure an outrageous anti-Catholic frenzy inspired by Titus Oates, which saw numerous Catholics martyred, including St. Oliver Plunkett, the Catholic Archbishop of Armagh.

These excesses led to a reaction against the Whigs, who were seeking further restraint upon the monarchy and who wished to prevent Charles' Catholic brother, James, from succeeding him. The Tories, supporters of the king and of his brother's succession, effectively argued that an effort to prevent the hereditary succession would open the door toward elective kingship, which in turn would lead back to Republicanism and ultimately dictatorship. Better a Catholic as king than risk that. In this case it would be an especially worthwhile gamble, since James' second wife, a Catholic, was considered unlikely to have a child, and his successors would be his Protestant daughters from his first marriage. However, the birth of a son to James' wife, Mary of Modena, along with his rather impolitic awarding of religious toleration to his co-religionists and to the dissenting Protestants, turned the Tories away from him and towards an alliance with the Whigs. His daughter Mary and her husband, William, the Prince of Orange, were invited to replace him as monarchs of England. That *coup d'état* constituted the "Glorious Revolution." Along with the new rulers came their acceptance of a Bill of Rights, an increased frequency of parliaments, and religious toleration (but continued exclusion from office) for dissenting Protestants (but not for Catholics). A side effect of the victory of the Whigs, considered by them to be a major step in the advancement of Anglo-American liberal constitutionalism – much like the American Revolution – was the defeat of James' allies, the Irish Catholics, and the imposition upon them of near-genocidal Penal Laws by the Protestant Establishment in Ireland.

Belloc's view on this period is a useful antidote to a simplified, black-and-white version of history, and enables us to appreciate the complexity of causes and effects in historical developments. To Belloc monarchy was more popular and democratic than oligarchy. He saw the seventeenth century not as the advance of constitutional liberties, but as the struggle of popular sovereigns against wealthy interests. His interpretation of the reign of Charles II was quite different from that of the Whig historians, for he saw the King "faced by the inescapable conflict between the Money Power and Monarchy," in which struggle the Monarchy ultimately failed.

And Belloc analyzed Whiggery itself. He defined it as the "political force which in its growth foreshadowed the English Political Revolution from a monarchy to an aristocracy." It was a combination of "the liberal theory of the state: freedom of the individual, an inviolate rule of law[, and] the equality of all citizens before that law," with the contradictory conception "that the wealthy are the natural leaders of the community." The seeds of Whiggery were at work in the reign of Elizabeth I and grew during the English Civil War. The Revolution of 1688 was "Whiggery triumphant and enthroned." Popular English history took all the Whig presumptions for granted and regarded opponents of the Whigs "as exceptions or oddities." The Whig mindset fostered the Anglo-Saxon myth, disregarded England's dependence upon Roman and Catholic roots, depreciated continental society, and saw the problems of Ireland as a consequence of "the exceptional incapacity or exceptional dishonesty of the Irish people." What Whiggery was fighting at the time of Charles II were the ancient principles of "royal Catholicism," which principles, Belloc noted, constituted the tradition of the "great kingdoms of Europe": namely, the Holy Roman Empire, Spain, and France.

While historians may quarrel with Belloc on particular issues and might note imbalances or over-emphasis on some matters, his capacity for a grand view remains unsurpassed, and valuable. He also possessed a capacity for prophetic insight based upon his historical perspective. For instance, less than two years before the publication of

INTRODUCTION

Charles II, he noted how, until recently, the Western World had "taken for granted, and acted upon, consciously or unconsciously[, the] main doctrines inherited from the Catholic past." These included: the existence of a personal God, the immortality of the soul, the institution of Christian marriage and monogamy, and the Christian view of property. But by Belloc's own time, these were "not merely questioned by a few but wholly denied by numbers so large as to form a formidable body in our own civilization."[3] Alas, in our time that formidable body has become the dominant force. However, Belloc also saw the Church in the modern age as playing the same civilizing role that she played in earlier centuries, and that in one matter in particular: the defense of the sanctity and permanence of marriage. Noting that the Church had condemned the marital breakdown of the upper classes in Ancient Rome along with the absence of marriage among the substantial slave population, he maintained that her insistence upon the permanent character of marriage turned things around. In his words:

> The Church, therefore, today is where it was sixteen hundred years ago in the days of the Christian emperors, fighting a running battle in which it had no civil backing save in a few places, preaching by example and affirming the true doctrine of marriage, but not able to impose it upon the civil laws; for the great mark of our time is the return to paganism.[4]

Unfortunately, there is today a shortage of vigorous and courageous champions like that which the world had in Belloc.

John P. McCarthy
Professor Emeritus of History, Fordham University
October 13, 2003
Feast of St. Edward the Confessor

---

[3] Hilaire Belloc, "The New Departure," *The Sign,* October 1937.

[4] Hilaire Belloc, "The Story of Marriage," *The Sign,* September 1938.

The Restoration of Charles II

DRAWING BY J. GILBERT, *ILLUSTRATED LONDON NEWS,* JUNE 1, 1861

THE LAST RALLY

THIS BOOK IS A SEQUEL AND COMPANION TO MY BOOK UPON Louis XIV. To that book I gave the title "Monarchy," as my theme was the eternal conflict between One Man Government and the Rich.

Napoleon said it: "The only institution ever devised by men for mastering the Money-power in the State, is Monarchy." It is obviously true and is the most practically important of all political truths. The Government of the United States, with its large development of presidential powers in modern times and the present struggle between those powers and plutocracy, is a very good example in point. A still more forcible example is to be seen actively at work before our eyes: the new governments calling themselves "Totalitarian" are essentially extreme monarchies at issue with the plutocratic rule in the older world around them: to a large extent in France and obviously in Great Britain.

As I dealt in my former book with the leading case of Louis XIV of France as a monarch standing up to the Money-power (and, upon the whole successfully), so in this book I deal with the parallel and complementary case of his contemporary and first cousin, Charles II, Stuart King of England.

He also found himself faced by that inescapable conflict between the Money-power and Monarchy; but, unlike his cousin Louis, Charles failed. The Money-power was too much for him. So long as he lived he managed to fend it off though not to tame it; but immediately after his death, in the less competent hands of his brother James (the last real and active King of England, as also the last by hereditary right) Monarchy went down. The Monarch was driven out and the powers of Government in England were taken over by a Governing Class of wealthy men which class has remained in the saddle ever since. For England in this our day is the one great example of aristocratic government in the Old World.

CHARLES II: THE LAST RALLY

It is essential to affirm here, at the outset, that the conflict between Monarchy and Money-power is *not* a conflict between good and evil. One may legitimately prefer government by the wealthy to government by one man, which is the opposite of, and the corrective to, government by the wealthy. In the particular case of the English monarchy its breakdown after Charles II had struggled so manfully to maintain it did not involve the ruin of England: quite the contrary. The aristocratic government which then succeeded to monarchy proceeded from one triumph to another. It expanded the English Dominions beyond the seas. It laid the foundations of a vastly enhanced position by the acquisition of India in the face of French rivalry; it triumphantly maintained the power of England against European rivals. It produced an unrivalled fleet which at last, after a century of aristocratic government, obtained (in 1794) complete mastery of the seas and was largely instrumental in defeating the French Revolution and Napoleon the heir thereof.

Meanwhile during those two and a half centuries of aristocratic government the commerce and wealth of England perpetually increased, and increased enormously. So did the population after Charles II's time. Even at the end of the reign, in 1684, England had not much more than six million inhabitants; at the end of the next century (1800) England had twelve million inhabitants. Today Great Britain, as a whole, has nearer four times as many inhabitants as it had then.

Further, under class government and the direction of the wealthy, England began and developed the "Industrial Revolution": modern machinery, especially modern transport, to a large extent modern armament, and all the rest of it. Those therefore who prefer aristocracy or class government to monarchy, those who would rather have a state controlled and directed by the rich than directed by the will of one man, have a great deal to say for themselves on the material side.

They have also a great deal to say for themselves on the moral side. For though aristocratic government degrades a people by neglecting human equality and human dignity, yet it does foster individual liberty. All aristocratic or plutocratic protests against monarchy have used this argument and have been at least half sincere in using it. On the other hand, government by the rich in England destroyed the independent farmers of which the English State had formerly consisted. Whether we call them peasants (the Continental name) or yeomanry (the specifically English name), such a body of free men was at the basis of all English society until the rich destroyed the English Monarchy after the last effort of Charles II to maintain it.

The English after 1600 were generally transformed from a comparatively small nation of independent agricultural men, shopkeepers, individual traders and sea captains owning or part-owning their ships, into a vast mass of proletarian men existing upon a wage, their livelihood more and more dependent upon a few masters who controlled all the activities of the State. Today the life of England has fallen almost wholly into the hands of monopolists, especially the monopolists of credit under the banking system.

This new book of mine, "The Last Rally," being the episode of Charles II and his reign, deals mainly with the development of a struggle between Monarchy and Money-power; but it has to speak of other things, some almost equally important.

First among those is the personal figure and story of the man who took up the challenge and attempted to make monarchy supreme over the great merchants and financiers of the City of London and the great landowners: Charles II himself.

The character and adventures of this king are of a dramatic interest beyond the ordinary. His boyhood began in the splendour of a Court wherein he was unquestioned heir to authority and glory for the future. Suddenly, abruptly, all was changed. The Royal boy, ten years old in 1640, becomes the lad who, in his teens, shares in the defeat and shame of his house. At twelve he is under the shadow of Civil War, at sixteen he is a fugitive and at nineteen he shudders, in exile, to hear of his father's murder.

All the formative years of his life, from puberty to his thirtieth year, were passed either in the atmosphere of the Great Rebellion or in wandering misery. First when his father Charles I was desperately trying to save the throne; next, after his father's execution in 1649, Charles is a hunted man in recurrent poverty and distress – often extreme destitution.

From the end of his teens until his full and mature manhood in his thirtieth year Charles Stuart knew no repose, little luxury and even less security. His contemporaries all believed that the English Monarchy had come to an end for ever and that the House of Stuart had fallen to be replaced by a sort of military republic, the symbolic head of which was Oliver Cromwell.

CHARLES II: THE LAST RALLY

Mazarin, the great statesman who was ruling in France in those early years of the young King's tragedy, took it for granted that he must ally himself with Cromwell, and turned the impoverished and ruined Prince of England out of France.

Charles Stuart is driven from pillar to post, now in Holland, now trying to retrieve his fortunes again in France, now in Germany; hoping for succour from here, from there, and never receiving it.

His mother, the aunt of the young French King, does her best to maintain him but can hardly do so. Up to the very end of his ordeal he himself could hardly believe that he would be restored to the throne. Contemporary Europe did not believe it for one moment.

Yet restored he was by a singular and most arresting chain of circumstance, chief of which was the presence in the English republican army (inherited from Cromwell) of a determined, ambitious, secretive, thoroughly disreputable man, the once Royalist, later republican, soldier Monck, who again betrayed his side. It was through General Monck's abandoning the English republican cause and suddenly rallying to that of the young King that Charles was able to return to England.

Then followed that illusion of a shining recovery which "Restoration" provoked. The English were delirious with joy at the return of their national monarchy and of their legitimate royal line. The hatred men had felt for the oppressive years of the Commonwealth, with their intolerable taxation and their even more intolerable series of confiscations and robberies, had grown explosive under the last restrictions before the whole top-heavy tyranny broke down; and immediately on the King's return in 1660 men imagined that the old state of affairs before the Civil Wars would come back again and that a young, powerful King, restored to his righteous authority, would lead England into some happy and glorious future, immediately to hand.

As I have said, all that was an illusion, and here again appears one of the most dramatic contrasts in European history: the contrast between the imagined Restoration of royal power founded on popular loyalty, and its *real* supplanting by a new government of mere wealth. The great landowners who formed the two Houses of Parliament (the House of Commons and the House of Lords) proceeded not only to enrich themselves at the expense of the people of England but to fight the Monarchy: sometimes with conscious intent, sometimes instinctively, but throughout all the years of the reign increasingly.

With them also there worked the powerful and rich guild of lawyers who were by this time inextricably mixed up with the landed families. Many of the wealthier fathers had put their sons into the law, and the new Governing Class had allied itself and was soon identified with the lawyers, who more and more enjoyed large public salaries and great offices as well as the high revenues of their trade in advocacy.

A further element, which became at last the most important matter of all in this struggle, was the City of London; that is, the mercantile and financial centre of the country.

The rise of London at this moment from no more than a large town to a great capital of world-wide importance, is another of the major marks of Charles's reign. The very stones of London – or rather, its brick and wooden and plaster houses – suffer or enjoy a material Revolution at the same time. It is the period of the Great Plague (fifth year after the Restoration), of the Great Fire (sixth year) and of the complete reconstruction of the town and of the port. London came before Charles died to deal with three-quarters of sea-borne commerce, and that commerce was expanding out of all knowledge.

Meanwhile the banking interest of London was growing rapidly and was beginning to rival that of Amsterdam. It got the King thoroughly in its grasp. Charles was constantly and hopelessly in debt to the financial interests, which grudgingly advanced him for purposes of the national government credits on which he had sometimes to pay as much as ten per cent., and nearly always at least eight per cent., while arrears would often run on at compound interest. Against such crushing burdens it was impossible that the monarchy should, in the long run, win.

But Charles II put up not only a very gallant fight but a subtle and pertinacious one. He was the next best diplomat and politician of his day, only second to his own cousin the King of France who excelled in all forms of negotiation. Charles was able to play off the rich men of the House of Commons and the House of Lords against the threat from the military strength of France and the commercial and financial rivalry of Holland. Whenever the power of Parliament had almost swamped him he obtained secret advances of money from the King of France. When the King of France would next have used this power to make English policy subservient to himself Charles deftly swung over and left his new ally in the lurch; and all the while Charles continuously supported and expanded, relied upon and increased, the *naval* power of England.

The splendid fleet, which began under his father Charles I (built out of revenue provided by the wise, direct, tax of Ship Money), had been trained under the Commonwealth through the accident of long service, not designed but imposed by the necessities of war. A body of professional sailors thus arose. Charles and his brother James, who ruled over the Admiralty, started a permanent corps of officers out of which a regular naval service could and did develop. The same diplomatic talent by which this King played off the French against the Dutch and both of them against the encroachments of the English wealthier classes in Parliament upon the English Crown, was used to counterbalance Dutch naval power with the new English naval power.

Charles is himself, of course, the central figure in all this. His very tall, dark figure, his easy, courteous manner, his concealed tenacious energy, the personal devotion which he inspired, his successful struggle against the depression which early misfortune might have bred in him, his firm hold upon what was left of his rights and upon anything that could benefit the future of the Crown – all these are like the grasping of a helm, and that passion for the sea, that possession of his soul by the sea which came to him in early youth, provides a metaphor for all his course. The reign of Charles II is a passage through peril and storm under a great captain, a great sailor, and his story is the story of the Fleet, side by side with which go two matters later of paramount importance – the new English Colonies in America and the vast growth of trade and of the Port of London.

It was a period during which the future of English Religion lay in doubt. The country was predominantly anti-Catholic and the newly established church (hardly a hundred years old) would now certainly remain of a Protestant complexion; but there survived a large Catholic minority – very much larger than our official textbooks would give us to understand.

Those who were in varying degree sympathetic with the old national religion were still, until the end of the reign, something like a quarter of the population. That point must be insisted upon as clearly as possible, for it is at once ill recognised and of determining importance.

It was part of the political skill of Charles II that in spite of his own conviction of Catholic truth he never joined himself with the large Catholic-minded minority of the English people as they then were. He would not be formally received into the Catholic Church himself until the very article of Death. During all his reign he attempted to hide his sympathies. He sacrificed the Irish people and the lives of his own innocent fellow countrymen to his one fixed object of restoring the Throne.

Not so his brother and heir, James. This brother and heir was converted to the old religion by the influence of that remarkable woman his wife, Anne Hyde. She thought and reasoned herself into the Church, and after her death James could hesitate no more. His open profession of Catholicism, the knowledge that Charles was in secret sympathy with him were, between them, the reason that the English monarchy fell; for not only had most of England by this time lost its old Catholic tone but a very large minority – and that by far the most powerful part of the nation – the richest, the best organised and most tenacious – had become vigorously anti-Catholic, whether from inherited vested interests in Church lands, or from new religious family traditions recently acquired; or (still more) from a novel mystic passion for the Nation itself which had long become the lasting object of general worship in men's hearts: and such it still remains. "Patriotism is the Religion of the English." France close at hand, the head of the Catholic culture, highly centralised, far more numerous and with a much larger revenue, was an ever-present contrast and incentive to eager resistance against all Catholic forces within the State. This very difficult interplay of religious sentiment during the reign must be made clear, because legend and myth upon it have warped all our historical teaching.

This double conversion, public and private, is the capital event of 1660–1685 for it decided the future of England.

But the colonial story is also of great moment. It was the Stuarts who made the colonial empire of England; the North Atlantic seaboard of America they gradually reduced to one complete English-speaking whole. It was Charles II who negotiated for and conquered the exception, which had cut the English-speaking colonial shore in two – the Dutch settlement at the mouth of the Hudson. New Amsterdam became New York, taking its name from the Duke of York. That also determined the future not only of England but of the New World.

With this colonial expansion of England under Charles goes the long struggle for religious toleration among the various Protestant sects; an idea always associated with the Stuart name, ultimately failing upon the English side of the ocean though later more rapidly established on the American. It achieved the moral unity of England: necessarily at the expense of English Catholicism which was virtually wiped out in the next century.

The end of the reign rises, as befits any dramatic episode, to a climax of interest.

The King appeared before he died to have won his battle. He had got the people mainly in support of him against the pretensions of the rich to supplement the Throne. He was free of the big land-owners, bankers and merchants of the two Houses of Parliament. He governed single-handed. The revenue of the Crown and the wealth of the people were rapidly increasing.

All seemed to be well, at last, with the Monarchy – when the curtain fell and King Charles died, somewhat suddenly and too early, not yet half-way between his fiftieth and sixtieth year.

On that side of the King's life which has been a great deal over-done in the past (I mean the long string of amours, the illegitimate children, mistresses and the rest) I can put no more than the due emphasis. It was not *these* which gave its character to the reign; though they must be understood, both for a right reading of the King's own self and for an appreciation of his time. It was impossible for him to have legitimate children by his submissive effaced wife, on account of her physical disabilities. He married his nieces, the ultimate heiresses to his throne, in what he thought was the most popular manner to Protestant princes, a policy which he thought would best preserve the imperilled succession of the English Crown. They did not inherit his political genius; and their father, the King's brother, had no such genius in him either – nor could he dissemble, nor could he judge men.

Therefore after Charles's death the ship he had so skilfully steered through so many perils foundered. What worked the wreck? This: that she had struck a sunken reef in mid-passage and sprung a leak. That sunken reef was the personal call of the Faith which had claimed both Charles and James. It would not be denied – and it was at issue with the new fates of England. The ancient English Crown, stretching back to the Dark Ages, was cast down with the expulsion of the Stuarts not four years after their apparent triumph.

THE TASK

THE STORY OF CHARLES STUART IS THE STORY OF A TASK UN-
dertaken. It was his life's business to restore the English
throne: that is, to re-establish active and real monarchy in
control of the English polity as it had been in the days of
his childhood, before the Civil wars, and the military despotism which
followed, had first shaken and then cast down that throne.

Why did he find this task imposed upon him? And why did he
undertake it with such continuous determination in the face of such
difficulties?

There were three main forces at work.

In the first place, it was his duty; it was the work incumbent
upon him as a matter of honour. All those around him who felt as
vividly as he did the point of honour took this task for granted. No
man could escape from a surrounding moral atmosphere of that intensity, least of all a man in the family tradition of Charles.

In the second place, Monarchy was still, in those days, of the very
stuff of England. The interlude of the Commonwealth had been in
the eyes of the average Englishman an enormity, something unnatural;
and, from the very structure of English society and its past, a republican and military experiment was doomed to a rapid disappearance.
Men could be enthusiasts at the moment for some republican ideal or
some military authority; but they could not remain in that mood.

In the third place, the general instinct of the populace reached
out to meet the king as though to reclaim a possession of their own.
Charles setting out to re-establish the throne was not only, nor mainly,
fulfilling a personal duty, nor even in the main following only the
minds of those who had surrounded him in childhood and youth. He
was mainly occupied with meeting a national demand; with playing
the part expected of him by his own people, to the governance of
which, by all the ideas of the time, he had an hereditary right. He felt
of the thing as the mass of the English felt of the thing, and they felt

as one feels about the restoration of a lost or stolen property. The property to be so recovered, though personal, was still more national than it was personal. It is this last point, by far the most important, which men of today, especially in England, are most likely to miss. The strongest surviving political conception in the seventeenth century was still that monarchy belonged to the very soul of the English people. By so much as personal monarchy is now forgotten, by so much was it then alive. Not only were its benefits taken for granted as a matter of popular experience and habit, but its disadvantages seemed to most men nothing but necessary evils or passing strains which could be adjusted. Even those who had most violently rebelled against the novel taxation of Charles's father had not envisaged the ending of kingship.

A republican doctrine was certainly held by enthusiasts and was interwoven with memory of victory under arms; but it was not normal to England. So much was this felt that when the substance of monarchy was withdrawn by the wealthy oligarchy five years after Charles's death, the successful rich plotters of 1689 dared not withdraw the name of king.

At first, of course, in Charles's boyhood, the task, while the battle was on in the field, was no more than the military affair. The battle must be won. When that battle began to waver in the lad's fourteenth year, when it was obviously lost in his sixteenth year, there still remained the simple task of bringing back peace and a modified kingship by some compromise, and all the while Charles was too young to have a policy, though his eagerness for the end before him which that policy should reach was great.

By his seventeenth year the outlines of the task which destiny had set him were clear and thenceforward he pursued it unremittingly. Mere practice in the pursuit of it developed his activity and skill as practice develops ability and skill in every trade. After they had put his father to death the task became consecrated. It did not change in character but became inviolate and a shining vision.

It is difficult or impossible for the men of our time to experience by an effort of imagination the horror caused by the murder on the scaffold outside Whitehall. One of the best places in which to catch the air of the time is a brief passage in the writings of Hyde. It is of special value because it comes from a pen always critical of the Cavalier spirit and essentially opposed to it. Yet that pen, which was not only unsympathetic with all strong emotion but particularly with the lyric emotion of loyalty, writes with sudden violence on the matter of that killing. It loses all restraint, and you could not have a better example of how the impossible tragedy affected the English mind of the day.

Between the killing of the King his father (from motives of fear – fear of reprisals for rebellion was the dominant note) and the return of Charles himself to England, was somewhat over eleven years; and during all that time of distress, and nearly of despair, the task remained simple in the extreme, mechanical as it were; a mere business of replacing a new and uncertain thing by an old thing well known. One might almost say that the task had become a formula. But from the moment Charles landed at Dover, and even before that, when he was negotiating for his restoration and framing the beginnings of a positive policy, the second and far more difficult phase of the King's task had opened.

Hitherto, it had been an aim at a distant target, a trajectory sketched out in the void. Henceforward, it was to be commanded, modulated, interrupted, endangered by immediate circumstance. He had now to work in continual contact with reality and reality meant in this case the infinite complexity of politics and religion, combined in Restoration England with the privileges and strong power of the great landed families whose presence had become for Charles a dim memory and one with which he had lost touch for all these years.

Reality meant also the great merchants of the City of London, the incipient banking system, the building of the fleet and the making of its organisation afresh. It meant a comprehension of, and continual contact with, the warring interests of the Continent. It meant, above all, the struggle for an income adequate for the work to be done.

Charles in 1660–1680 was the only executive head of any European nation who found himself with great national duties to perform and no income with which to perform them. He was wholly destitute. He would be dependent upon what not *his* government but another body altogether, the Parliament, the rich squires and merchants and lawyers meeting at Westminster, might choose to provide.

When I say "destitute," the word may be protested as a rhetorical exaggeration. There was a tiny fragment of capital left to the Crown; a remaining fragment on which the King could still put his hand. There were rents and a few other forms of hereditary income still surviving. But the amount all told was not more than five per cent. of the bare minimum required for public life, armament and policing of England. Charles at the Restoration was like a man of thirty coming by inheritance into a great house with all its domestic establishment and park and the rest, after being excluded for ten years, and then, on asking his man of business what his investments are producing receiving the answer that he has but a shilling in the pound of his family income left intact: one twentieth and nothing more. The establishment needs £5,000 *a year* to keep it going and in repair. He has a capital remaining to him of £5,000 all told! It will yield him not £5,000 a year, but only £250. For the balance he must go cap in hand to men who are not even trustees, but who regard themselves as equals of independent fortune with himself, but are good enough to keep him going by their voluntary assistance: an assistance which they grudge him and so cut down that his embarrassment can but increase.

Remember that with all this the expenditure upon all public services, and especially upon armament (which meant, for the bulk of it, the Navy) was expanding continually. The ships and guns were more and more expensive and their number had to be continually increased.

There was yet another large factor in the situation which seemed to render the task impossible; the value of money was consistently and almost uninterruptedly falling; the price of everything was rising, and continued to do so throughout the whole period of the great experiment.

Charles, therefore, was not really like a man who needs for his establishment and fixed activities £5,000 a year, and finds himself with only £250. He was more like a man who should have come into that £250 a year in a moment when it was shrinking to become at last worth little more than half its face value. At the moment in which I write these lines we are living through a similar period, the English pound of 1914 is down to 11s. – and falling.

Consider further something equally difficult for the modern reader to grasp: the England of that day, the England of 1660 to 1680 and beyond, was in its own eyes and those of Christendom an actively revolutionary country. England, which has become under the effect of aristocratic government the most stable and united, the most homogeneous of the European States, was in the seventeenth century transition between monarchy and aristocracy the most changeable and disturbed.

A true restoration, in the sense of putting back what had been there before the troubles, was manifestly impossible. Restoration is always difficult, even after a brief interval of breakdown. The longer the interval and the more thorough the changes established therein, the more hopeless is the effort to return to what had been. We see this in case after case in history. We see it in the return of the Bourbons after the French Revolution; we see it in the failure of the Pagan reaction after the conversion of the Roman Empire; we even see it in the Counter-Reformation, which, though it set out to restore a Church which was by its own claims immutable yet had to modify one element after another of the old clerical organisation.

Not only do new institutions take root in these periods of violent change, but a new generation supplants the old. The younger men may be as keen as you like, as romantic as you like, in their desire to recover a lost society; they will not wholly recover it. They are the creatures of their own time; their fathers are already ghosts.

Consider what had happened since the last Parliaments of James I and the return of his exiled grandson to England nearly forty years later. The first revolt of the squires and lawyers of Parliament had been heard muttering over the expenses of that Spanish War which they had themselves insisted upon. James's son had seen that muttering grow into a whole new constitutional theory. After James's death Charles I had had to face open refusal of supplies. Then came the murder of the new young king's right-hand man and great representative friend, Buckingham; a frank repression followed; then came the explosion of the Civil War. By 1660 English life had been turned upside down for eighteen mortal years, while English religion swirled about like the whirlpool under a cataract.

The execution of Charles I had been the central and most striking event in that astonishing moral chaos. Men had had to accept the despotic authority of an upstart commander-in-chief. They had witnessed the apparent dissolution of the political fabric on which

England had through so many centuries arisen. Those who had been first conscious of these things as young men in their 'teens, at the first quarrel with James I in 1625, were now, in 1660, growing old. Men whose years marched with the century had passed through all these things and were coming to the close of human action. And still the turmoil went on.

It was on such a scene of such memories that Charles II's effort was to be made.

The stress was the greater for the fact that all over Europe elsewhere outside England things were returning to the normal. By 1660 the French monarchy, the main central institution of the Continent, was fully set up again after the rebellions of the lawyers and of the blood royal. The unfortunate Germanies, bled white by half a lifetime of horrible religious war, had become stable again since 1648 – that is, for the last dozen years. The Papacy had increased its central authority over the reduced area which it still spiritually governed. Spain, in spite of declining wealth and population, was well established in its highly centralized royal scheme. Even the Emperor at Vienna, having failed in his bid for supremacy over the German states and cities, was secure in his hereditary lands. The very wealthy Dutch merchant oligarchy was increasing its wealth and fairly sure of its position under the especially rich Calvinist group which administered it, for Spain had admitted the independence of the Seven Provinces. The return of her King to England might have made men think that a period of special unity and peace was opening for his three kingdoms also. On the contrary, what was opening was more than a quarter of a century of struggle between the Crown and its wealthy subjects, only to end in the destruction of the monarchy. England under Charles II was regarded in Europe as revolutionary while, all around her, reaction against revolution had triumphed.

There were four points on which the delicate and masterly steersmanship of this man, who was at heart the handler of a ship, would turn.

He must unite as far as possible on the point of *religion*, or, to be more accurate, on the point of the quarrel between the various Protestant sects, this energetic people of his whose recent distractions had turned so largely on theology.

He must unite them as far as possible on the exceedingly difficult matter of compensation for the brutal robberies which had accompanied the Great Rebellion.

He must deal, meanwhile, with the increasingly strong Moneypower (in practice a rising oligarchy), the name for which was now, in England, "Parliament."

He must deal with a permanent major cause of disunion, today so little understood: the survival of Catholicism in the England of his time.

Let us look at these four points in their order, remembering always that the last is by far the chief problem of those which Charles II had to meet: the chief obstacle which he had to get round if he were to achieve his end, leaving to posterity at the end of his effort a country united under the common rule of its hereditary and rightful King.

I.—He must attempt to make peace between the warring Protestant sects.

I have used the word "unite." He could not' "unite" his subjects (in the full sense of that word "unite") where Protestant opinion was concerned. He must try to lead them or persuade them into a sort of common Protestantism which they have, long after him, achieved, but which in his time seemed beyond hoping for. This effort (maintained by Charles with so much suavity and patience, bungled by his brother) was arduous indeed.

It was in the very nature of Protestantism, from its vigorous origins long before, to refer the ardent aspirations of the soul to the individual judgment. Indifference, a disease of the Catholic mind, was abhorrent to the eager spiritual aspirations which had arisen in outbursts of energy under the surface of the corrupt ecclesiastical control of the later Middle Ages. These outbursts had broken down the Universal Church in Europe and had produced the turmoil which we call "the Reformation." The mass of men would, from the beginning of the trouble, have been content to follow ancient custom: but in these things it is not numbers but intensity of conviction and a consequent, sometimes delirious, always violent, determination to achieve and impose a doctrine which work the most in the communities of men. No people had fallen into religious enthusiasm more vigorously than the English. The mass at first desired the customs and the consolations of their fathers; but the mass was lethargic as it always is; and the separate enthusiasms, which had been white-hot for so long, were, in 1660, still dangerously heated.

The Calvinist influence, a very definite creative thing, establishing a counter-church in Scotland, had profoundly affected many of the middle classes in England, and a sufficient proportion of the wealthier people, the squires and the lawyers, to influence Parliament. The alliance with Scotland during the Civil Wars had planted a sort of experimental Presbyterianism in England. Church livings had been handed out to many of Presbyterian conviction, not a few of whom were of the strict Presbyterian discipline. London had felt the influence strongly, and much more than London. These formed numerically the bulk of the enthusiasts. They were a minority, of course, of the nation, but, I repeat, we are not concerned with mere numbers here; we are concerned with energy. The Presbyterians were determined, they were convinced, they had allies beyond the Border. They still believed that the future was with them and they intended to inherit that future.

Next came a number of particular sects. Important had been the Independents, whom Cromwell himself led and who had pervaded the commissioned and non-commissioned ranks of the triumphant rebellious army during its recent victory over the mass of Englishmen. The main tenet of these men was that each Protestant congregation was an authority of itself (the modern Congregationalists are their descendants). They held a position rationally deduced from the general principle of private judgment, though they had at the back of them dogmas which are certainly not of private institution. They held, for instance, very firmly, to the Divine authority of Holy Writ which they had inherited from Catholic times. Note also the Friends, called under a nickname which has survived, "Quakers." Heroically opposed to arms, professing a singular charity, and remarkable for awaiting the inspiration of the Spirit in their reunions, these men were formidable because they lived by passive resistance and would not be shaken in their conviction of a moral and political system to which they had become individually but intensely converted. They were distinguished by an abhorrence of forms, descending even to the form of taking off one's hat. Yet they were amiable, as their worship of charity would presuppose.

Then there was the remnant of the old Anabaptists, detested as anarchists by most of their fellow Protestants, and originally, indeed, somewhat anarchic in temper; so far as a common temper can be ascribed to them, it was an extreme demand for spiritual autonomy, even in social action by the individual. They had, therefore, had a communist savour about them. That stream was drying up by 1660, but it still trickled.

There were other minor sects. It would be tedious to analyse the list. Over against them all was the Established Church, the Church of England.

Now here we have a problem almost peculiar to England. I have written "almost" because in the nature of things the Government had had to organize religion in the new Protestant part of Europe everywhere. It had at least to ally itself with religion (as with the Calvinist scheme in Scotland, Holland and the Palatinate); government had had at the very least to define its attitude towards religion, even where that religion was in rebellion against the government and at the most to take over religion bodily. Therefore, the problem of an established Protestant Church, faced by the individual and corporate separatism of Protestant sectarian zeal was to be found everywhere outside those societies which had kept the unity and discipline of the ancient Church.

Certain points must be noted about the Establishment if we would explain its struggle against those who would not conform with it.

In the first place it *did* now stand in 1660 for the bulk of the nation. Since the settlement of this religious institution under the creative genius of William Cecil and his subordinate friend Parker, 1560–1570, the Church of England had been especially *national*: national in its determination to break away from the common religion of Europe; and the strength of this breaking away from the general religion of Christendom lay in the vast economic revolution which had transferred the old Catholic religious endowments of England to the land-owning squires. The Church of England was national also in its liturgy, using the national language everywhere and using it in a united form. It was national in its social organisation, coalesced under the national crown as a symbol of national religious independence and everywhere in the thousands of village churches which were the spiritual habitation of the English people and in those days constantly attended; it was bound up with the village squirearchy and all the organisation of English country life.

Always remember when you read of the English seventeenth century that though London had begun to grow and was to become vastly more important in wealth and political power in the latter half of that century than it had been before, yet England remained throughout agricultural in the main. London by the end of Charles II's reign held, with its suburbs, nearly one tenth – certainly more than one-fifteenth – of the total population, and there were a few large port-towns on a much smaller scale – notably Bristol. Still, during the reign of Charles II and long after, the English people were a people of villagers, farmers and squires, as they remained within the memory of those whom we of this generation can recall. And in the villages the Church of England was everywhere the one organ of public worship save perhaps in a few exceptional and isolated places (as in parts of East Anglia).

To reconcile the Church of England with the Nonconformists was that part of Charles's task which, after his dealings with the Catholics, was the most arduous. The elements of Anglican dominion over Nonconformity were very strong. There was tradition, a tradition of liturgy and habit a hundred years old at the Restoration. There was social feeling – the sentiment that the Establishment meant social order and regular habit and so much as could be achieved of spiritual unity. There was the influence of words; for the names and offices of priest and bishop had been continuous. There was the possession (now restored to them) of the cathedrals, colleges, all the official external things, and the village churches. Perhaps more important than these was the memory of cruel wrongs suffered by the established clergy during the Rebellion and after it; as also some desecration and mutilation of ecclesiastical buildings – though these had not been in England on a scale comparable to the iconoclasm of the Continental religious conflicts, especially in France.

It is a formidable list. The varied quarrelling Protestant thing that Charles had to soothe had many heads; their multiplicity alone was enough to give the peacemaker pause, and between them convinced Anglicans and convinced Nonconformists, including the sympathies with Calvinism, made up at least three-quarters of the whole nation.

THE TASK

II.—During the Great Rebellion – which had involved the Irish rising and the violent and barbaric treatment of Catholic Ireland – confiscation of lay property, partial or total, had taken place on a scale never dreamt of in England before; not even during the confiscation of lay property, or repressions of Catholic rising and plot under the Cecils.

The original transfer of land after the looting of the monasteries, hospitals, colleges, grammar schools and the rest, was, of course, at once the origin and the greatest example of the whole affair. Certainly more than a fifth, perhaps a third of the rental values of England had gone either to enrich further men already rich, or, more commonly, to build up quite new vast fortunes, such as those of the Russells, the Cromwells (Williamses), the Cavendishs, the Wriothesleys, and fifty others.

After the first rush of the loot, between 1536 and 1556, there continued a considerable series of further confiscations, to which must be added the eating away of ecclesiastical revenue attached to bishoprics, deaneries, canonries, prebendaries and minor endowments. This especially marked the period of the Cecils, which coincided with the official reigns of Queen Elizabeth and James I.

Then came the very large transfers of property from the original legitimate owner to some other favoured person, which went on during and as a result of the Great Rebellion.

To give two examples out of hundreds. The brother of John Milton the poet had a substantial town house on Ludgate Hill. It was taken from him by the Parliamentarians and he had to buy it back at a cost of one-third of its value. Lambert, the last commander of the Parliamentary army before the Restoration, was found in possession of one main slice of the Queen's dowry – and he had many companions in that piece of "transfer." The successful rebellion took the occasion of its victory to fleece or beggar those who had supported the constitutional government of the King.

By far the greatest case of wholesale seizure took place in Ireland. Even before the Cecil regime the Irish estates in the hands of native families with tribal traditions or English families of the French-speaking governing class that had come over and intermarried and acquired lordships in the twelfth century had begun to be supplanted by new owners from beyond St. George's Channel. This idea of "colonising" Ireland (as the German historians call it) was as old as the impact of the feudal civilization of the Middle Ages on the old tribal tradition of Ireland. English political overlordship was affirmed and on the whole accepted when a new spirit altogether rose with the Reformation. The confiscation of monastic lands in Ireland passed without great friction, but the attempt to impose the new Establishment never worked. Under Elizabeth there had been all manner of intrigue, rebellion provoked or spontaneous, corresponding repressions with confiscations following; but a turning point came when, under James I, a serious rising in the north and the flight of its leaders gave an opportunity for systematic plantation, though this had begun even before the reign of Elizabeth.

The main shock came when the quarrel between Charles I and his Parliaments, added to the conception of recruiting an army in Ireland, changed the relations between the island and England. The Protestant English Crown being in difficulties with its own subjects at home, there was a partial rising of the Irish Catholics, who remembered the tricks and worse by which they had been despoiled of their land. That rising was accompanied by a massacre of a certain number of Protestants which number is disputed. Probably the number of people actually killed was about two thousand; but with the temper of English Protestantism at that time those numbers were, of course, exaggerated out of all knowledge. The victorious Parliament commissioned Cromwell to lead an army into Ireland. With this force he completely subdued the kingdom and on his victory there followed such a rape of Irish land as had no parallel in the past. It seems probable that before that milestone in the history of the two countries (marked by the massacres of Drogheda and Wexford and many other horrors of zealous Puritan revenge), half the cultivable soil of Ireland still remained in the hands of men descended from the original owners. After Cromwell had done his work, perhaps a twentieth in value so remained; though rather more in acreage. It was a complete revolution. The land was parcelled out among those who had financed the expedition (including, of course, the City of London), and Cromwell's own officers and soldiers.

When Charles had to deal, on his return to his kingdom, with the losses of those who had been loyal to his father's crown in England, he was unable to restore the greater part of the lost estates to their original owners; but he restored a considerable proportion who had behind them a strong public opinion. The main Irish robbery, a thing on a far greater scale, he condoned. The nature and effect of that error I deal with on a later page. It was all part of his determination to stabilise the Crown by an appeal to English public opinion, which was in the main indifferent to Irish claims.

III.—The opposition of the Parliament was a thing of gradual but rapid development.

On the King's return, the gentry, with their sprinkling of lawyers and merchants who formed the Commons, were for the most part filled with the general public enthusiasm for the Restoration; and the House of Lords (which meant, in practice, the greater landowners), though there was opposition among them, were much in the same vein. The squires and the Commons and the Upper House as well, stood out as a whole against a reconciliation between the Established Church and the dissident Protestant bodies. But there ran through the whole of this aristocratic class, whether the Upper or the Lower House, an instinctive desire for the subordination of the Crown to themselves; and the instrument whereby such a tendency might effectively work, even when it was not fully conscious, was the revenue.

We have seen how the nominally restored power of the Crown was in effect dependent for income – that is for life and for any real executive strength – upon supplies voted in Parliament; for the capital values remaining to the King, the Crown lands and the rest, supplied but a twentieth of the annual sums needed even so early as this for the armed forces, the maintenance of the Court, and the administration of the country. A Parliamentary Committee was nominated to examine the total revenue immediately received and fixed the amount at £1,200,000. Such a sum was insufficient and it was not received in its entirety. At least one-sixth, or perhaps rather more, disappeared before it reached the Treasury; and the continual fall in the purchasing value of money, the continual and inevitable rise in the expenditure essential to the maintenance of national affairs – especially the Fleet – necessitated continual borrowing at high interest from the money-lenders of London. With every year that passed, the executive found it more and more difficult to make both ends meet, and fell more and more deeply into debt. There was no end to the process and Charles was powerless to arrest it.

He could not appeal to the Parliament as to the people. For they were not the people; and even if they had been representative, the principle of voluntary grants made the sufficient increase of revenue impossible. The main difference between the financial position of Charles and his cousin Louis of France lay not in what many moderns used to mistake for a representative body voting supply in England and an arbitrary government imposing public contributions in France; it lay between a fiscal system which was in England capricious and in France regular. The French King could levy at will, upon all but a privileged minority of his people, tribute which was much the same in principle (though far less justly apportioned) as a modern income-tax. He could directly rely upon an assessment made as we make it today by public official action, without consulting any more than we do today the convenience of the payer.

I have said that the House of Commons in those days was not representative, as we understand that term today. The habit of reading the present into the past has made this term "House of Commons" mean something very different from what it really was. It was composed after a fashion little connected with numerical proportion. Each county returned two members. In law those might help to choose members at the polls who owned land to the value of £2 a year – say, £5 or £6 rental of today's money.

The number of those who owned land in small amounts was already beginning to shrink at the date of Charles's return and shrank rapidly throughout the whole reign with the decay of the yeomanry. Further, the great mass of those entitled to go to the polls neither did so nor desired to do so. Nor at first were there generally contested elections. County "representation" meant in practice the sending up to Westminster of two men from the greater landed families, or men under the protection of the greater landed families. The counties being of every sort of size and population, county membership would not have been representative, even if it had been what no one desired or pretended it would be, an emanation from a general vote.

But this anomaly was only the beginning of the hotchpotch. The agricultural county population, the great mass of the people, stood for about twice as many members as there were counties, whether the county were Rutland or Merionethshire or Yorkshire. Side by side with these were a far larger number of borough members. A borough with a charter to that effect would return two members. Some were towns large for the time, like the principal ports; some were market-towns; many no more than villages, to whom for their own convenience governments had extended in the past the right of sending two burgesses each to Parliament. In some there were but a handful of men who might if they chose go to the poll. In others almost every family might in theory have a say. In others the mayor and corporation decided what should be done. In all, the great moneyed interests, principally the big landed people, determined who should go to Westminster. Meanwhile London, with three-quarters of the foreign trade of the country in its hands, sent only double the number of burgesses returned by the smallest and most insignificant borough.

When the system came to an end (thoroughly fossilised) in the nineteenth century, you had a London returning four members by the vote of the freemen, Gatton in Surrey returning two by the vote of *three* gentlemen resident in that hamlet, Old Sarum returning two without any resident electors at all; and cities like Birmingham and Liverpool not even counted as boroughs.

To think and speak, therefore, of the House of Commons in 1660–1680 as representative of the English people numerically is nonsense; but it would be an error to think of it as unconnected with any representative quality. The squires who sat there came from countrysides the general opinion of which they could, though imperfectly, reflect; the burgesses, even though dependent on the great landed interests, were not unanswerable to local feeling. Those who talk of the result of a general election even in the later seventeenth century as "the voice of the country," as though a general vote had been cast by the mass of Englishmen, are saying something quite unreal. But it is still true to say that the House of Commons as a whole, especially when it showed great majorities or something near unanimity in moments of popular excitement, was national and worked as an English thing: an institution which was in extreme cases capable of general public expression. The most of its action was the action of a wealthy class which more and more proposed to rule the country.

IV.—The survival of Catholicism in the England of the Restoration, the England of Charles II and his brother James, was the most important single element in the make-up of the community.

To under-estimate it, as was universally done by our official historians of the nineteenth century, is to misunderstand the time altogether. How large it was, why it was in opposition to the mass of the English people, how it was divided against itself and deprived of effective action, how nonetheless on account of its numbers and ubiquity it was a permanent irritant to most men and permanently regarded as a latent public danger, we shall see further on. It is enough to remember here that Catholicism in 1660–1680 was formidable in England. It was not formidable through its unity, its energy, or its direction. It was negative, divided and morally weak; but its numbers must be remembered; and those numbers though continually decreasing, were before the end of Charles II's reign at least one-eighth of the population – if we count only those who were willing to make a great sacrifice rather than conform. They were anything from one and a half to twice that number, anything from one-sixth to a quarter of the population, if we count all those who had remaining sympathies and connections with the old religion.

The presence of so very large a body at issue in varying degrees with the rest of their fellow-subjects and either actually or potentially subject to rigorous exclusive laws was, though a neutral and passive, yet a dominant element in the problem which the restored monarchy had to face. For the national monarchy could not be fully re-established till there were some approximate social unity on which to found it and against such unity a large minority of sympathisers with the ancestral faith and conservative in their memory thereof was an obstacle and a menace.

*****

Such is the plan of the field of action which Charles had to appreciate, reduce if possible to a common kind, and manœuvre to the general interest by the refounding of the Crown. It would seem a prospect before which any man might despair of achievement. He did not despair; he all but achieved his end.

THE FORMATION

W E ARE DEALING, THEN, WITH CHARLES STUART AS THE man who attempted a task which seemed beyond human power, the restoration of the English national monarchy for the guidance and strengthening of the English people against the power of wealth. This task he pursued with singular aim during all the most active days of his life – from the age of thirty when his first opportunity for decisive action came, till his death at fifty-four.

I have said that he seemed, at the very end, to have succeeded; so close and tenacious had been his pursuit. As a fact he had failed, though his failure was not seen till four years after he had left the arena of this world. He took the helm in the spring of 1660. Before the spring of 1685 he was dead in full career and had failed to found a second, secure establishment of the English Crown. Indeed he had rather inaugurated its approaching ruin. In place of a King there arose, fully armed, an oligarchy of rich men under which for two centuries England prodigiously increased in wealth and dominion as in the area over which she exercised her might until it covered a vast portion of the Globe.

The complete success of the new Aristocratic thing was the more thoroughly confirmed by the retention of the *name* of King for his successors, the Hanoverians, aliens and despised. These were to be the creatures and the puppets of a Class Government which had destroyed the real Crown. The name of King remained as a title, and the office, surrounded by majestic trappings, was preserved as a symbol – not without great use in the maintenance of national unity, but of no effective value in action. In this our own day, when the title is no longer despised but revered, it still stands to the great advantage of the commonwealth: but no active power has been restored to it nor is even the idea of an active monarchy so much as remembered in England.

CHARLES II: THE LAST RALLY

Charles's "last rally" covered not quite twenty-five years. Their interest is unique for us today, for we live in a time when an extreme form of monarchy, at Rome and Berlin, has arisen to challenge Money-power, while the particular rivalry between England and Nazi-Germany is essentially a conflict between the opposing political ideals of monarchy and Class Government; so in watching the fate of Charles we watch the inherent chances of victory and defeat on either side.

*****

Preliminary to this struggle came two successive periods in Charles's life. The first was that of early youth, when his character was formed and made consonant for the work by which he should ever be remembered.

This first period lasted into Charles's nineteenth year when he first made a decision on policy, which, baffled for the moment, bore ultimate fruit.

The second phase, following such formation of the man for his life's work, was one of unceasing trial; exile, poverty, wandering – a wider and wider experience of men only to be gained by the wise, and best learnt in adversity. This second phase, which I shall call "The Ordeal," dragged on for near a dozen years until, fully matured, and filled with that mixed experience and suffering and irony which most inform and fill a man, a sudden change of fortune put him upon the ruined Throne of his inheritance. He, by rare skill and tireless application tried to re-erect that throne and make its structure permanent. But during that great labour there was still weakness in him which marred it, and which also had its roots both in the early years of his formation and the later years of his ordeal when all seemed hopeless.

What was he? What were the soul and body so deeply engaged in so desperate a hazard?

Physically Charles was a Medici.

Let not that word confuse us. The royal families of Europe have come of every European stock, especially in the later development of their various houses. There is to be found in the royal family of France (the most national of them all) blood from every source, even Russian: and ultimately descent from Alexander the Great. There are to be found in the royal family of England strains of Scottish,

Iberian and Italian ancestry from all over Christendom. There were many other strains in Charles than the Medicean. The physical type a man exhibits may come, fantastically enough, from some ancestor not immediate. Such "throwbacks" we may see around us in private life upon every side. Sometimes we even find, to our astonishment, that a famous ancestor (whose portrait still hangs on the walls of one of those rare houses which have preserved historic continuity) is startlingly reproduced in the features of a modern descendant. The Medici face is to be discovered now here now there, often at long intervals, in those descended from the wealthy ancestors who became masters of Florence and whose posterity was sought in marriage by foreign Courts. It is first fixed for us in Vasari's famous contemporary portrait of the Great Lorenzo, which anyone may see in the Uffizi. It is one of the most striking pictures of the Renaissance.

That unmistakable concavity of outline, as if the profile were modelled on a crescent moon, that extreme swarthiness of hair and skin, those deep furrows running across the hollow cheeks and framing the corners of the mouth, that peculiar length of the nose and that strong narrow chin – all these features in Vasari's portrait forcibly recall the Stuarts of the later seventeenth century. We feel as we look on it, especially if we be unprepared, a sort of shock at such resemblance.

Nor does the resemblance lie only in the outline or the colouring; there is also the keen intelligence of the eye and I think one may say its reserve, in spite of its brilliance. They are stamped on the features not only of Charles II but more fully and less sharply upon the proud mask of Louis XIV. Both men had it through their grandmother, Mary of Medici, the wife of Henri IV of France. Her daughter, Henrietta, it was who married Charles I of England and whose sons were the last two Stuart kings, Charles II and James.

Henrietta Maria, Queen of England, the heroic companion of that husband who was destroyed by the Great Rebellion, did not herself show very markedly the Medicean type but her brother, Louis XIII of France, the father of Louis XIV, showed it markedly. After Louis XIV it was, I think, lost in the French royal line; but at the Court of England this "Medici face," this "unmistakable outline" abnormally long, concave and determined, was seen in the Duke of York (James II). The last appearance of it with which I am myself acquainted in the Stuart descent can be seen most vividly on the severed head of Monmouth. Visit the National Portrait Gallery in London and look on that singular thing! It is the only picture I can recall of a royalty painted after a violent death. Seeing it you can no longer doubt the truth of Monmouth's claim to be Charles's son. Indeed it astonishes me that this claim should ever have been disputed, however virulent the opponents of the King, and however strong the motive of James II's supporters to dispute Monmouth's parentage.

I say that this reference of Charles's peculiar face to Lorenzo de Medici may at first sound extravagant for it is unaccustomed – but it is true. Charles's prototype in Italy was two centuries apart from his day. For common ancestor to both in the male line you must go further back still, to the early fifteenth century: to Lorenzo the Magnificent, the first cousin to that Julian, the great-great-grandfather of Mary de Medici, whose daughter was Queen of England and mother of Charles. But we must remember that this Medicean type crops up in the course of the centuries though the more famous of the Medicean names do not recall Lorenzo's concave profile. There is no sign of it, for instance, in Leo X, his nephew, but the famous blood now and then still produces it and a shadow of it is seen in certain of the Dukes of Tuscany and now and again in one of the bastards of the Bourbons.

In the same way, the Hapsburg lip most markedly appears long after Philip II, the mighty lord of the Spanish Empire.

He showed from early childhood another physical character more general than his inherited facial type, and that other physical character was vigorous health. As he grew up it appeared in his capacity to bear fatigue, in his enormous power of work, in his rapid stride and long journeys in the saddle, in his aptitude for games, notably tennis, in his endurance of the sea (the influence of which on him I shall mention in a moment). It went with a strong dark presence enhanced by great stature (he was over six feet, perhaps six feet three or four before he stopped growing). It went with his close-knit, spare frame: muscles always taut and strong. This unfailing health supported – though it did not cause – a sweetness of temper in him which made him, during his reign, the best loved public man that ever dealt with English affairs – and loved especially by subordinates. Such health he carried all through life till the last sudden breakdown in his fifty-fifth year.

He inherited also from his mother the vitality of the House of Navarre, of which his own grandfather, Henry IV, he of Bearn, gives the most famous example.

Whatever the effect of heredity, one thing is certain from our observation of ourselves and of others: that two main influences go principally to the moulding of a character while it is yet in formation.

The first influence is the ill-remembered but profound and permanent impressions of early boyhood, the years when the man is still a child, the years before puberty. The second – different in character – is the more conscious influence of human association and of personal habit in the second half of youth, of immaturity from puberty to very early manhood. This second phase of a man's formation is longer or shorter according to the first experience of responsibility in active life. It ends, often abruptly, at the moment when the young man first has to undertake public action, to act unguided, and to decide his life for himself.

Of these two periods in the formation of character the first may be said, in the case of Charles, to have ended in his twelfth year. It ended at the same time as his earlier experience of princely grandeur and ease. It ended with his last experience of his father possessed of real power and at the head of a great Court. It ended with the beginning of the Civil Wars.

It must always be remembered in estimating the later character of the man, that these strong, very early impressions – a few of which are so vivid, but no series of which form a connected story in the mind – were a continued reception of kingship. Kingship was all around the child as a matter of course. He saw his father in power. He heard echoes (which he could not have understood) of snarling opposition to authority, but the obvious external thing with which always, daily, he came in contact was the secure grandeur of the Crown.

He felt it the more because it came to him as full heir. All those whom he met (particularly that old nurse of his who had so strong an attachment for him), all the servants of the Palace, all those guests whose chance conversation fell upon his ears, treated him as something different from the rest of mankind. He was the first Prince of

Wales for generations to have grown up, breathing this air of sacred and complete privilege.

His father had not been so trained. Charles I had been a very sickly, neglected child, hardly able to walk until he was more than three years old, stammering and not even brought to Court in his first years. He had been quite overshadowed by the popularity and splendour of his elder brother Arthur, whom everybody took for granted to be the next King. That older brother had died 1612. The child who was to be Charles I, was suddenly and, as it were, unnaturally thrust into a new position to which he had not been born and to which it took him long to accommodate himself. He did so by perseverance, and that tenacity which marked all the Stuart blood. He had forced himself to become an accomplished horseman in spite of his disabilities. He had studied carefully for the part he would have to play. But it was not as though he had been the acknowledged inheritor of England from the beginning and those very first years may well have set their mark upon a man who was afterwards to be, not a vacillating, but an anxious ruler. They may well have weakened in him the full self-confidence required for the regal office. James I had never enjoyed admitted heirship to the Crown of England. Cecil intended him to be the successor of Elizabeth and Cecil had put him on the throne; but James was already thirty-seven years old in 1603 when he came to England and acceded. He was a foreigner and not a popular foreigner at that. Elizabeth was illegitimate in the eyes of certainly more than half her subjects and of all Europe. Her youth had been passed in doubt of its future. Mary's youth, before her, had been still more harassed and still less given any royal due, at least during the years that counted. Her own father had proclaimed her illegitimate. You have to go back more than a long lifetime, nearly a hundred years – to 1547 – to find a Prince who was admittedly and from birth heir to England, as was Charles II in 1630 when he began to live. After such an introduction to life, such security and such surroundings of majesty, the second phase of Charles II's formation comes with an abrupt shock in 1642. The boy is in the midst of armed rebellion. He is surrounded by perils; the future is dark and all his environment is in turmoil.

He is present at the first battle of the Civil Wars, Edgehill, in his thirteenth year. Thenceforward, till after his seventeenth birthday when he first has to take responsible and independent action, that is when the period of formation is over and he has entered active life, the whole story is one of flight, concealment, distress, increasing peril. It is an experience of defeat with the ever-growing menace of final doom which shall destroy his House and all that to which he had been born. So abrupt a change, so violent a contrast between the childhood and the boyhood of the man account for very much of what we are about to read. It was an experience of a kind which does not come to one in a thousand: it was of a kind especially rare with the wealthier classes. It made him – just in those years when a lad is looking about him and comparing, that is, learning the real world – fully acquainted with the harshness which that word "real world" contains.

Further, there was no influence of family upon him in the years when such influence naturally launches a boy out of childhood into the beginning of life. His father was in the midst of a mortal struggle all during his teens. His mother was fighting half the battle herself, the right hand of her husband. All the senior influences affecting the growing character were thus of secondary authority not primary: not the influences of the parent, let alone of the parent with the authority of royalty upon him, but the influences of men deputed first to the guardianship and afterwards to the counselling of his youth.

There had been, while he was yet a child, a sort of grand official functionary to look after him, chosen for his great birth, Newcastle. He had given Charles advice some of it consigned to writing: not unwise advice, for he insisted on the importance of experience rather than book-learning in a ruler, and he insisted on the maintenance of the externals without which authority cannot be maintained. This same Newcastle was not, however, of the stamp which should preferably have been chosen. He was not by nature a conductor of the young or of anyone. He was a subject only to his own pride and he abandoned the Crown in its most critical moment after its first great defeat at Marston Moor.

The next official tutor or guardian proposed for the training of Charles was worthless. He was admittedly vain and foolish and imposed himself by mere reiteration and pestering, added to his fortune and position. It was Berkshire. He had very little effect on the making of his pupil's mind, unless it were that negative effect of making him somewhat too early seek to stand alone and to feel inwardly contemptuous of command set over him. But among those with whom Charles was in continual contact in that second phase of rapidly maturing boyhood there was one character to whom history has always given especial attention. This was Edward Hyde – later to be Earl of Clarendon.

If anything, the importance of Hyde in English history and therefore on the life of Charles Stuart, has been exaggerated; but we should make a worse historical error if we were to underrate that influence, to underestimate its value or to misunderstand its character. Edward Hyde has been over-praised, but for more than twenty years his was the figure which took the first place in Charles's surroundings. He had the most to say on Royal policy when first that policy began to be recognisable. He was the chief counsellor in the years of exile and ordeal. He could not but be retained by the King after the Restoration, and though his influence naturally and rightly dwindled, until at last it was lost altogether, no other character came so much in contact with the King.

Hyde's age, when he first came across the boy familiarly, was suited to enhance his influence. He was twenty-one years older than his charge, for he was born in 1609 and therefore just of age at the moment of Charles's birth. He was a staid man of over thirty when he entered this career of counsellor to Charles Stuart, which may be said to begin as early as the field of Edgehill itself, for he was present there in care of the twelve-year old Prince of Wales and his brother during the battle – but another saved them from capture.

It is to be feared that his own account of what he did on that famous occasion is doubtful. Indeed it is one of Hyde's defects, common to autobiographers, that he suppresses and invents in his own favour. But take it all in all the very long and detailed *History of the Rebellion* is far more valuable a contribution to true history than the bulk of such works. He is especially good at analysis and description of character, and in this connection note the chief effect he had upon the development of the King: *He taught Charles how to watch and understand individual motives.* This great political and social advantage which Charles used so thoroughly all his life he got from Edward Hyde.

Hyde's advice was especially valuable through his knowledge of the Protestant temper. Charles was never fully familiar with this: in spite of his upbringing and his father's strong feeling against everything foreign (which included, by this time, the Roman Church),

Charles had few familiar contacts in youth with the Protestant mind. Edward Hyde not only sympathised with the Protestant mind, but had it so fully in himself that he thoroughly understood the Establishment, as well as the Nonconformists. He knew the strength of Particularism, sectarian feeling and personal religion with the whole of the Protestant body throughout Europe, but especially in England: the tendency, often passionate, whereby private choice in religion forced men to join religious bodies unconnected with official and State organisation. He even knew or instinctively recognised the truth that the tendency to nonconformity would grow and might in time become so powerful as to destroy within the nation that unity of religious opinion which had for long been taken for granted as a necessity. Therefore he could and did warn his young master against the fatal danger of withstanding that tendency.

If Charles early understood the policy of compromise with the independent Protestant bodies in England, he owed that early comprehension mainly to Hyde.

Charles, then, was taught by Hyde to follow men's thoughts and to know what was going on behind their faces; not so James, who saw of Hyde much less.

In this lay the chief practical contrast between Charles and his brother James. Charles, by the time he was thirty, knew humanity inside out. James never knew it – not to the day of his death. It is true, of course, that Charles co-operated with Hyde's influence by using his own eager, receptive mind while James's mind was closed; still, but for those early days with Edward Hyde, Charles would not have reached the pitch of excellence he did in the art of knowing men.

Yet Hyde bored Charles, and bored him more and more as the older man's years increased. The fatigue of Hyde's company was due to certain defects native to that type of mind (and especially that type of religion). He was pedantic, his motives were mixed with greed, and he tended – especially after 1660 – to domineer. But these drawbacks appear rather at the end of his life: in its mid-portion he was vigorous in judgment and reasonably broad – though always too much on the anti-Catholic side to understand Europe properly.

For the purpose of understanding the *formation* of Charles it is the earlier years that count most: and during these Hyde certainly did much to instruct and guide.

CHARLES II: THE LAST RALLY

He remained in perpetual contact with the boy and young man from Edgehill in '42, the lad's thirteenth year, until Charles was long past thirty. His influence, therefore, was not only great from its own weight but from its continuity and no one can understand the story of Charles Stuart without giving to Hyde's connection therewith a capital importance. He is at Charles's elbow during nearly all his minority, either at his elbow or within call during all the strain of poverty and exile, advising him and largely moulding his policy on the turn of the Restoration and still in a sort of control for some years onwards.

Edward Hyde had all the qualities required to impress his pupil or ward (whichever you like to call the relationship). There was a difference in age and, what always counts with a vivacious mind (such as was Charles's), there was that ponderated (I had almost written ponderous) element in Hyde's make-up which invariably impresses youth: indeed it impresses youth rather too much as a rule, for in the long run youth finds it out.

Moreover, Edward Hyde was a gentleman in just the sense of that word which made a gentleman influential in the training of the Heir. By his first marriage he had become a connection of the Villiers family. That is important. When you mix with the great it is useful to your converse with them to have some other relationship than that which is merely individual and personal. They like to connect you in their minds with their own gang so that you can bring with you, however much attenuated, something of the "one-of-us" feeling. The average squire of Edward Hyde's moderate though growing fortune (what we should call today "a few thousands a year") would not have appealed to richer men as did one who could talk familiarly of Buckingham and *his* crowd. For Buckingham had been so rooted in the Court connection that an association with his memory was like the savour of an onion in a dish. The savour of the Villiers connection made all the difference.

But there was another quality about Hyde which further enhanced his suitability for the post and his exercise of influence there. He was extravagantly national. That was exactly what Charles I wanted in his servants, for it was in his own tradition. Charles had reacted violently at first against the Spanish Court, later, in his early married life, against the French influence. He never would talk French himself if he could help it and he went so far as not to have his son and heir taught a word of the language! The boy's own mother, the sister of the King of France, the Queen, always had to speak to Charles, and in early youth usually to write to him, in English. Edward Hyde's nationalism, reinforced by religion and class feeling, took among other forms the form of deep antipathy for the French court and nation – language, temper and all. This, then, is the first point to seize in the matter of Edward Hyde. He was fitted in every way to influence and impress the heir to England, and being a great public servant as well – Charles I's Chancellor of the Exchequer – added to his prestige.

Hyde has for history another great interest: he was one of those who are in tune with the future of their time; who are already in sympathy with that which is about to be.

Such an attitude is often called foresight. It is in reality a mere accident, especially in times of acute division such as was the mid-seventeenth century in England. We none of us know what the future will be and least of all can men say what it will be when all is in conflict, confusion and undetermined. If, for instance, Communism tomorrow be the ruling force in Europe, the Communist of today will seem a forerunner and a true prophet. If it be defeated he will seem futile and of ill judgment.

I say that this quality of sympathy with that which does in fact come to pass is accidental, but it is of great effect upon reputation. Most of Hyde's high place in the estimation of posterity comes from the fact that he backed up the things which posterity was to embrace. He was all for the greatest leniency towards religious rebels within the Protestant scheme, and toleration on this model won the day within half a lifetime of Hyde's death. He was all for the repression and extermination of the Catholic minority in England, and that policy also within half a lifetime of his death won the day. He was all for directing English policy against French power, and within half a lifetime of his death English policy had become permanently so directed. Those who were later to be the moderns feel of Edward Hyde that he was one of their own. He obtains thereby a repute for wisdom, especially among those (today the great majority) who think of the political processes of history as inevitable. Nonetheless, as time went on, Edward Hyde's advice was to be less and less useful to Charles. He had no talent for "steering." The complexity of foreign policy grew to be more than he could deal with. He was inflexible upon too many things, notably the relations with Louis XIV, and, as he grew older, that inflexibility increased.

To this first memorable force in Edward Hyde add another which was of great effect upon the history of England. It is this: though devoted to the Monarchy and to the Monarch's heir, Hyde instinctively and at heart belonged to that very large opposed body which generally combated the Stuarts and at last brought them down: the country gentlemen.

He was a squire of the squires and he was a squire of the kind at that moment outstanding in its influence on Government and society – the squire who was also a lawyer: a combination much commoner in his days than in ours. After the early death of his first wife he had married the daughter of a great lawyer, Sir Thomas Aylesbury, prominent also himself by the fortune he had acquired and a support for his new son-in-law at the Bar.

At the Middle Temple, which was his Inn, Hyde would also meet the Chief Justice, and that Chief Justice was his uncle, Sir Nicholas Hyde. Being a squire, and a lawyer-squire, of this kind he was naturally in Parliament and as naturally joined in the growing claims of his class against the King. He was not violently upon that side but it is important to remember that it was his native environment and that he retained this tradition all his life.

He was also closely connected with the Merchants of the City through his legal work. He had piloted through and perhaps drafted that petition. But it is characteristic of him that he was equally in touch with the other side of things. Laud had a great opinion of him. He had sat in the Short Parliament of 1640 for Wootton Bassett in his own county. According to his own account he tried to mediate between Charles and the rich men of the Parliament in the growing quarrel of that critical moment. I say "according to his own account" for we must always keep in mind in whatever we read of Edward Hyde that he was not only an advocate by trade, but a strong advocate for himself and therefore, as I said above, not very trustworthy in the personal parts of his narrative. For instance, he certainly helped to prepare the impeachment of Strafford and he as certainly lies when he says that he tried to save Strafford's life. But he *did* go orthodox on the point of Episcopacy in '41 and he *did* join the King at York in June, 1642. It is nonetheless characteristic of the man that he advised against the dismissal of Essex and he even advised against the King's challenge at Hull.

This point is very important for the understanding of Hyde himself. The governorship of Hull, a fortified and garrisoned town, a port whence munitions could come from oversea and one lying on the flank of any advance towards London from the North, had been given by the Parliament to a man for the moment at their command. He ratted later, as so many did on one side or the other during the struggle of the Civil Wars.

When Charles demanded entry into Hull and was refused, the King was challenging something of vital importance to his throne and executive power. Yet Hyde was not only afraid to do anything that looked like challenging the wealthier classes in Parliament, but also disliked provoking them because of that social feeling I have spoken of – his own instinctive sympathies were with the average Parliament man, that is, with his own class.

You see the same thing in the summer of the next year, when Bedford, the head of the chief Reformation millionaire family, the Russells, vacillated between the King and the rebels. Hyde sincerely lamented Charles's failure to propitiate this most wealthy of wealthy men and others of the same sort. He thought the failure to conciliate Bedford and keep him on his side was Charles's chief error; and Hyde was the author of that policy whereby Charles called Parliament at Oxford.

Roughly speaking, in the whole story, Hyde, whether suggesting the Parliament at Oxford or advising against this or that special claim, was leaning heavily against the traditional powers of the Crown and towards the transfer of that power to the wealthy. But there was no conscious hypocrisy about this. It was the natural action of one of his class in his day.

We must think of him during the whole of that long life (born in 1609 he did not lose power till the latter part of 1667; he did not die till the very end of 1674) as a man of cautious, guarded speech and of a presence the less impressive from his countenance, which was of the cherub type, round and too full. It is often so with men of good judgment and the opposite is also true. Your hatchet face, clean cut, eagle features, often go with lamentable imbecility.

We must think of him also during these years as a man who accumulated wealth.

That was natural enough: anyone exercising political power in the seventeenth century would be deep in the pursuit of money. Richelieu was notorious for it, so was Mazarin. But Hyde was remarkable in having begun to accumulate long before he had political power of any kind. As a young man, when he inherited his father's estate through the death of a brother, he still added field to field and we shall find him at it all his life long.

Can we call him corrupt? I will discuss that point when we come to the sale of Dunkirk after the Restoration. There is certainly no trace of corruption in the earlier part of his career.

Before we leave him we must emphasise the main point of all: the power of the word. Hyde wrote. Had he not written he would still be a great figure in English history. But having written, he is much greater. Hyde's history of the Civil Wars, which were to him "the Great Rebellion," has dominated all our historical tradition and somewhat warped that tradition. It presents difficulties to the modern reader from certain ambiguities of phrase, but it is still by far the most important document we have of that time. As he aged, his mind, never very broad, narrowed. It became what is today called "a one-track mind." He grew pompous about his grandeurs, autocratic with subordinates, touchy about his privileges. Long before the first five years of the Restoration were over he was becoming difficult to deal with. It is one of the best examples of Charles's political wisdom that he dropped Edward Hyde, Lord Clarendon, before it was too late. The King had already long ceased to follow the old gentleman's advice, and two years later, in September of 1667, Edward Hyde left his country – the only land where he could be himself, the only air he loved. His departure was a flight. He lived in exile on French soil.

But all this belongs to the later pages of this book; for the moment let us retain the image of him as a jealous guardian of Charles in the disastrous later years of the Civil War, always resisting the influence of the Queen Mother, always attempting to keep the lad in England, and, when that was no longer possible, combating the influence of the French Court and especially of the exiled Queen.

So much for the chief personal influence exercised upon the formation of Charles's character. But the truth is that in that formation personal influence was not the major force at work. The boy had largely emancipated himself and he had rapidly learnt from unhappy circumstance the art of standing alone. He had also learnt the folly and perfidy of men, their inability to forecast the future, their necessary errors in policy. It was, I say, a group of external things, not personal, not the advice of counsellors, which had most to do with the development of Charles's mind and the direction of his will during the later part of his adolescence up to that moment in his seventeenth year when he first acted on his own initiative and behaved as master. Of those external influences, the first by far – the thing that colours his whole life – was his knowledge and love of the sea.

The sea in those formative years did more for the making of Charles Stuart than any human companionship did. Unless we get a good hold of that main truth we understand neither the man nor the time nor the reign.

It was under Charles II that the English Colonial Empire beyond the Atlantic took root. It was under Charles II that the endurance of this Empire and its consolidation were made possible by the conquest and occupation of the Hudson Valley and its mouth – the decisive strategic point of New York. It was under Charles II that the carrying trade of the world gradually began to fall to England and that London caught up with Amsterdam and passed that market and centre of exchange. It was under Charles II that the Fleet, which his father had so wisely conceived and made possible through the excellent stroke of ship-money, became the prominent and increasing weapon of English power and the special note thereof. It was under Charles II, therefore, that the SEA came into English life as the master motive which until then it had not been. He was to fail indeed in restoring the Monarchy to England. The oligarchic government, which was to take the place of Monarchy, inherited all this maritime affair and developed the Colonial Empire, the carrying trade and sea-power to the highest point; but Charles, and his brother James stand at the origin of that capital turning point in the story of England. It was not Drake and Hawkins and their like, it was not piracy and the slave trade that constructed English sea-power. It was the Stuarts.

It will be found in the life of every active male that some exercise of the body, some contact with nature and natural forces through physical activity, some hobby or rather passion of this kind, implanted in those years which are the only years of freedom in a man's life, determine that life for good. With some men it is the rid-ing of horses, with others the discipline of a great game, with many it is an early apprenticeship to arms. With Charles it was the sailing of boats: a thorough marriage with salt water, its waves and the winds that blow thereon.

Here is that field of trial, adventure and exaltation which, when it has been entered in early youth, captures a man and never leaves him again. It has been said (and unfortunately truly said) that Charles never loved: the chance never came to him for one strong affection, nor did he love any of human things. But of inanimate things he loved and was loved by the greatest, which is the Sea.

He first came across the meaning of that word when as a boy, pushed further and further West by the victories of the Great Rebellion, he had been taken to the coasts of Cornwall and had heard the Atlantic thunder on its cliffs. He crossed to the Scillies and thence – a desperate refugee – had reached Jersey at last, beyond the broad of the Channel.

In that voyage which must have stood vividly in his mind for ever, that cruise of his seventeenth year, he had been himself, on his own demand, hour after hour at the helm. He was, after a fashion, though so young, the captain of the adventure. And that adventure reminds one of what his ancestor did, the young Plantagenet, Edward of York, when he was for grasping the throne of England, which was his right; for he, too, steered the boat by day and by night across Channel and up Channel in a flight from enemies in arms.

The chief demand of Charles during the brief and perilous leisure in Jersey was for further sea-faring. It was provided for him on such scale as was possible in a new two-masted boat built in St. Malo, and brought over for his delight. He learnt to sail it also in those very difficult waters. He tasted the sea again abundantly during the desperate effort to save his father's life.

Thenceforward, though he snatched every hour he could for that special individual delight which was in the very heart of him, the opportunities were few, but he renewed them as often as possible and all his life long the mere sight of a tall ship moved him and in spirit he was moving with the wind and tide.

It is wise to compare his masterly skill in the avoidance of obstacle, the management of opponents, the whole conduct of those difficult twenty-four years, to the steering of a boat. All his life Charles was a helmsman.† No man who knows his own life and who knows the effect upon it of even a brief interlude of strong physical experience in the opening of manhood can doubt that this interrupted glory of seamanship shone upon him to the end.

*****

The Vigour of the Sea thus met and enhanced the young man's exultation on the threshold of life. By a particular accident of which we know very little – not even the mother's name – this adolescent was a father in his seventeenth year. She was of his station it seems and presumably, from the common character of such affairs, some years older than he; but still quite young. For he has left a beautiful and pathetic line in which he tells us they neither of them meant any harm.

*****

There is one side of a man's life which is today grotesquely exaggerated: sex. It is exaggerated through the loss of that which both explains and regulates human life: Religion. The chief mark of our age is the eclipse of religion, that is, of one fixed and consecrated Philosophy which shall make a man understand his own nature, provide moral sanctions for his acts, and see his various functions in their right proportion. In the absence of such a flywheel our machinery "races." Emotion masters reason and appetite occupies the mind. Since sex is, with men, a strong recurrent and permanent motive, a society lacking religion, as does our own today, will give sex far too great a place, but a conventional avoidance of the subject would render it impossible to understand the life of any man, and especially of such a man as Charles Stuart, at once precocious in development and very strong. The part that sexual experience played in the formation of this man must be known or we shall never understand him.

From that very early first introduction to such things Charles knew them everywhere. Thenceforward there is no interruption to his amours. Outside books, in real life, such promiscuity is rare. Why so abnormal a story for a man eminently normal and sane?

---

† He might have taken for a motto in the worst of his bothers with plutocracy: "Do not talk to the man at the wheel."

CHARLES II: THE LAST RALLY

There were many convergent causes. Puberty, in which the whole being changes, came on him at a moment when all external rules and supports were wrecked in the sudden upheaval of the Civil War. The violent experience of battles strikes him it once. The thunder of cavalry charging right home around him: the shouts of counter attack: the deafening crash of ordinance close at hand and cannon balls shocking the ground at his feet – he had known such novelties in his thirteenth and fourteenth years, the months when lads of his nature are commonly under careful ward and inspection. The man deputed to protect him proved, in his first action, unequal to the task. Thence onward as the tall figure so rapidly strengthened and grew it had a life of ceaseless strain and flight and alarms – when those of his age should be schooling and at games.

In that same time there was no home for him. The valiant little mother was as much a wanderer and in peril, not even a companion still less a guide. His father, whom that mother succoured and re-armed with such gallantry, had not a moment for the training of his son. It is thought probable, and may be true, that the attached nurse of his childhood who saw him not infrequently, fostered and condoned his vagaries. Later his ceaseless wanderings, his rootless life, the degradation of poverty quite bereft him of familiar habit. He had no hearth. He never learnt to need constancy nor to acquire it by use. It was his tragic loss, but a loss he could not feel, for he had never known possession of the thing he lacked all his life: home

THE ANNEALING

CHARLES MAKES HIS FIRST DECISION AND ACTS FOR THE FIRST TIME alone and as a man very early indeed; when he is seventeen. This early start was part of his precocity of development in everything, but it was also a result of his "timing" – that is, of the relation between his dates, of birth, of maturity, etc., to the dates of the violently disturbed world around him.

He begins that most exceptional set of adventures, which may be called his ordeal, so early as this age of seventeen. He does not conclude them till he is just on thirty.

Now it was this unique and prolonged experience which determined his character and explains why he was what he was after coming to the throne. That experience which no other ruler came near to having makes one understand his approach to victory over his opponents, but also makes one understand the prime cause of his ultimate failure; for that prime cause was the perception of Catholic truth, a conviction which he could not hide completely and which, in the nature of the human mind, he could not abandon. No man can abandon a conviction, he can only at the most betray it or act against it. This conviction of Catholicism came to Charles in and through those years of the "annealing." And we should particularly emphasize this, that this faith came to Charles after a fashion which made it firm beyond the ordinary and buttressed by an experienced contempt for its opponents – particularly the most direct of its opponents, the Calvinists.

One may generally notice when one watches a process of conversion – no matter what sort of conversion: a conversion, for instance, from dislike of a foreign nation to admiration and affection for it; or a conversion from some irrational but strongly rooted religious myth to a rationalist materialism (a common process nowadays, especially with Bible Christians who have read Outlines of Science, Mathematics and – heaven help us! – History) – one may generally notice, I say, in any essential turnover of doctrines, in the abandonment of one set and the adoption of another, a certain sequence of *weaning*. There is a necessary and human reluctance to leave the old for the new and a persistence in the earlier emotions even while they are fading and giving place to their successors.

For example, many a man will abandon in disgust what is called "public life." He comes, not perhaps until after years of politics, to be so nauseated by the wickedness and folly around him that he tears himself up by the roots and chucks the whole affair. I have seen that happen a dozen times before my own eyes. Nevertheless, the attractions of the nasty thing survive that virile decision. A chance public meeting, a chance return as a friend to a debate in Congress or the House of Commons revives something of the old false "ambition" – unworthy of so noble a name.

Commonly, this lingering attachment to what has been abandoned is especially strong in the major case of all: the acceptation of Catholic authority.

Men who have passed through this great experience from origins say Anglican or Agnostic or Jewish (these last make the strongest converts of all), are still moved for years by the sounds and objects which recall the time before the change. They cannot forget what was once their home. And this nostalgia haunts them, even though it be lessening, to the day of their death.

Now mark this carefully: *such a "weaning" process was never part of Charles Stuart's experience.* Until he was twenty-one he had never come across the spirit, the personality of the Catholic Church at all. He had been in contact with its externals, of course, and that largely; for in England of the seventeenth century one came across it on every side. But to come across the Catholic Church from the outside is a completely different thing from an experience of the thing itself: a growth of the illumination from within. This fell upon Charles II in one particular chance moment of his life, as we shall see a few pages further on. It was like the planting of a seed or the catching of a contagion: a special sudden transforming force appeared. After that unique accident, conviction grew in him regularly and unchecked.

So it has done with a myriad others. But with those others there was a non-Catholic or anti-Catholic home to be remembered. Charles Stuart had never had a home since his mind began to work actively.

With others there is already stored in the mind, on the approach of manhood, a considerable body of reading, un-Catholic or anti-Catholic in spirit. Charles Stuart was full of no such reading for he was full of no reading at all. With others there is a continuity of social experience which creates rooted habits of mind and such continuity is particularly to be expected in the wealthy and leisured classes. Charles Stuart had never known those influences at all. He had been condemned in the midst of his boyhood to vagrancy and destitution.

Above all, there comes to nearly every man some strong experience of affection very early in life and the converts have nearly always known this tug at the heart through the love and influence of some soul attached to their youth before they had come across the Faith. It was Charles Stuart's heavy misfortune never to have known any such appeal. He loved none and had been loved by none until, already in early manhood, he came across the familiar conversation of that much younger sister, whom he adored and whose loss was the only tragedy of his life: a tragedy profound and shockingly sudden. Now that gay, that lovely, that charming child was wholly Catholic from birth and by every habit. A sudden deprivation of intense spiritual companionship stamps the whole being with its memory. The influence is far more deeply impressed and more clear-cut than if it had continued uninterruptedly. Death stamps. So it was with the influence of Minette on her brother; and that influence came when he had already begun to understand the change of religious conviction within him.

There was another factor. I have said that a new conviction is confirmed by contempt for its opposite. Well, Charles Stuart was violently inoculated with such contempt during the most vivid months of his life. He was plunged into a bath, as it were, of seething Calvinism in the great attempt he made, during his twenty-first and twenty-second year, to recover his throne by arms. And from another direction an active distaste for the counter-church or anti-church came to him through the insults and neglect of the Dutch merchant oligarchy, whose anti-Catholic religion, less pure and fiery than that of the Kirk, was, in his eyes, even more contemptible, because, by his standards, more vulgar.

This mention of the Dutch merchant oligarchy, with its strong anti-Catholic atmosphere, brings me to another factor of the highest importance for understanding Charles Stuart's Annealing and the way in which it fixed his character for ever; he learnt under that Ordeal the spiritual meaning of money; he learnt to appraise Wealth at its true – and base – position in the scheme of real things.

Here again, with most men of any rank and with nearly all men born into the wealthier part of society, such a vision of Mammon (a most impressive repugnance!) is not granted. We – and when I say "we," I mean those whose upbringing has been sheltered and comfortable as are those of most well educated men – receive unconsciously all the illusions of Mammon. Some few of us may have discovered the truth that culture and good breeding and all the necessary furniture of our lives are rooted in, and would be impossible without, some measure of wealth. Most of us have not even that abstract truth to guide us. We simply take all those secondary effects of wealth as final; as part of the nature of things; a matter of course. With the less fortunate, with the poor, a converse process is at work. At the best they revere, at the worst they envy, those things in human society which are the product of wealth in their superiors, Thus the illusion of wealth, or at any rate of sufficient comfort and security, permeates all society high and low.

Charles was stripped of that illusion early and at once at a blow – he experienced real poverty; poverty not relative but absolute. When he landed for the second time as a lad from the boat which he had steered down Channel, he found in his pockets French money to the value of 4s. 6d. When he was already mature, he and his mentor, Edward Hyde, often lacked the wherewithal for a fire in freezing weather. Their clothes were threadbare and on occasions disgraceful. From time to time they would have to run up a bill for weeks with disgruntled landladies, from whom with difficulty they obtained the mere necessary daily food. In the interludes, when there was sufficient, that sufficiency was paid for by humiliation and servitude. The Court of his aunt, the Princess of Orange, which housed him for a while, housed him as a dependent. If grudging aid came from the French Court to his mother, a Princess of France or later, to himself, it was spasmodic and utterly inadequate; and could be and was, now and again, suddenly withdrawn. That mother had even to render him strict accounts of the wretchedly small expenses which his presence in her household had cost her. He was thrown at the head of his cousin, the Grande Mademoiselle, the richest heiress in France, and felt himself forced into a ridiculous wooing, during the first experiment in which he could not even talk to the young woman (two years older than himself) in a language she could understand. Luckily for him, the marriage did not come off – mainly, I think, because she foolishly hoped to catch her cousin and his, the young French King.

Towards the very end of this searing but formative trial, when he had stooped to beg the hand of Mazarin's niece, another heiress, he had seen himself thrust off by the millionaire Cardinal with all the irony of pretended deference to his nominal royalty.

If ever a man had tasted fully at the gates of life the bitter mixture of rank and destitution combined, it was Charles. Nothing more thoroughly teaches a man the truth that money rides all human affairs, and should be hated for the thing it is – though necessarily sought.

Even had he come into affluence at last and ceased to feel the spur and the curb of money, save as a memory, that memory would have burnt itself into his very soul for ever; but he had not even that good fortune. Become King, his revenue was kept by his wealthy subjects deliberately below the level of an English King's mere State necessity. He must for ever be in the hands of money-lenders and reminded daily that even such income as he had came from the contemptuous permission of the landed and mercantile fortunes called "Parliament," or, more grandiloquently, "The People."

Is it not a marvel that under such unceasing and torturing strain he kept his aims clear to the very end and held one course after the Restoration until he died? Is it not a marvel that amid such distractions he could still steer? It is. And that marvel was made possible by those annealing years of misery and exile.

It is a still greater marvel that the experience left him as it had found him: the best-tempered man of his time; the most courteous and the most gay.

*****

Now with this almost unique experience of what money really is to men there went another experience of profound educative value – alas! Promiscuity with women.

It is an experience which either ruins character (and this it more often does) or very rarely, fits them for political design by depriving them of domesticity. Thus Promiscuity, *can,* in exceptional fashion, act like its opposite Celibacy, and train a man for consecutive action by depriving him of what is best in human life. For Charles, whose far too early introduction to amours we have seen, became, from the moment of first introduction, promiscuous.

Now promiscuity may rot a man. It commonly does so when it follows upon an earlier innocence and a single flame. The debauchee (as such an one is called) is absorbed by sensual pleasures to the increasing neglect of all else. With Charles it was not so, nor did any one of his too numerous mistresses affect his judgment. The conversation of some – of one especially, the Keroualle, delighted him and became a custom; the wit and vivacity of another – even the kindness of a third. But in all that harem (the term is here justly applied) not one had real effect for good or evil on his spirit – because he had never connected affection with the mere corporal enjoyment of such things.

What his life was under such a regime will be seen when we come to talk of those women. The point to remember here is that promiscuity which in the vast majority of men debases and even destroys them had with Charles Stuart an effect of segregation from disturbing influences of special passions and personal appeals. It left him free to pursue one political aim undeflected and uninfluenced. In these promiscuous years of exile one of innumerable women, Walters, bore him a son whom he later cherished and who is remembered under the name of Monmouth.

*****

Two matters stand out in this period of "annealing." First the young man's acute experience of Calvinism; second that brief, that momentary, flash of revelation on Catholicism which came to him quite unexpectedly; isolated, intense – lasted not an hour, yet deflected his whole life, and, coupled with his brother's later but open profession of the old Religion, ultimately sank the Monarchy of England. Also – but not till he himself was dead – it undid all Charles's untiring labour to bring back popular kingship to England and to master the Money-power.

Each of these things – the experience of what Calvinism was, and the sharp and sudden discovery of Catholicism, of that which the profound influence of Calvin worked to destroy – came in the same year, when he was twenty-one: a year which could not but determine all the rest of his life.

His experience of the main anti-Catholic force in Europe, the Calvinist ideal came to him through his appeal to Scottish armed force for the recovery of his throne. England was firmly grasped by the victorious rebellion, Ireland had been conquered and occupied by Cromwell. There remained only Scotland from which to act and only the chief organized political energy in Scotland, the Kirk, for Charles to appeal to.

The skill shown by Charles in his efforts to attain Scotch support for the recovery of the Crown is especially remarkable when one remembers how young he was.

The comedy played between him and Scottish fanatics did not require high diplomatic talent, for it was patently conventional on both sides. Neither party believed for a moment that the young man felt at heart the absurd professions which he had to make by way of ritual. To the hardly sane clericalism of the Calvinist ministers it was a matter of profound import that the ritual should be carried out. Charles had to pretend to a covenanting temper as intense as their own. He had to profess the full Calvinist philosophy by which his new allies so sincerely lived – to the horror of those not in sympathy therewith.

It was even essential to the ritual that he should particularly condemn his own father and his own mother – the one for having opposed the Saints in arms and fostered the abomination called Bishops in the State church; the other for her papistical idolatry.

It is always foolish to confuse ritual with genuine emotional action: each is necessary in human life, but they do not overlap. One need waste no time therefore on the absurdity of these solemn professions, renunciations and comminations. Bat Charles's dramatic talent in all this is worth remarking, the more so as no more than the same talent on the stage was it intended to deceive. It was intended, like play-acting on the stage, to be consonant with the situation and no more. Meanwhile, we must remember that this same ritual was insulting and that the insult was bound to be remembered. A man may use a form of words condemning his own father in order to recover that father's inheritance, but if this unnatural form of words has been imposed upon him he will not forget the occasion. It is probably true that Charles Stuart did not suffer a permanent reaction against any of the innumerable attacks he had to bear save in this one case. All the rest he took as the inescapable blows given and received in battle; but that he should have been required by clericalism run mad to take such oaths and make such public protest against his own blood, as he did in these days in Scotland, was a thing he never forgot and, one may fairly say, never forgave.

If there was a talent remarkable for a young man of twenty in the role he played for the benefit of the Kirk, there was soon to appear a talent far more remarkable in a thing more practical, the matter of arms. For, immediately succeeding upon his submission to the Kirk leaders, his coronation at Stirling and the rest, came the only active military episode of his life. He showed during this brief passage a knowledge of leadership sufficient to make one muse on what his fate might have been had he had the chance of putting the task of his life to the issue of battle. His attempt to act independently of his jailers (for one may properly call the Scottish clerical leaders "his jailers") failed. He was brought back after the abortive effort, known to history as "The Start," and subjected again to their control. But the universal truth that reason is the master of human affairs, was to give him his opportunity through the utter unreason of those who held him captive.

The leaders of the Kirk, living in an unreal world – the world of their enthusiastic deluded minority – were convinced that numbers and quality in the field were disregarded by the Lord of Hosts. They got rid of the best fighting material in their army by their insistence on orthodoxy and in particular they lost their most efficient officers through such "purging." The Scottish soldiers of fortune, gentlemen and others, had learnt much of war in their Continental adventures, especially those on the Protestant side in the German religious struggle; yet such as were suspected of the least divergence from the iron Calvinist code were got rid of. The Covenanting army had its cadres increasingly diluted and ruined by this attempt to ride two horses at once. It is not true to say that Dunbar was the result, for Dunbar was, like most equally-matched actions in war, mainly accidental. But the element in Cromwell's victory at Dunbar was the sharper initiative and earlier movement on the English side and these we may probably put down to the insufficiency of the new officering among the Saints.

THE ANNEALING

Cromwell's unexpected victory at Dunbar put the south-east of Scotland at his feet, save for Stirling. It put the Covenanting party into moral disarray. They could not believe that their strange Moloch God had deserted them, but they had to admit that He was visiting His people with severity – perhaps for their sins. Charles took up the situation at once and began to plan, upon the basis of this situation, the re-establishment of his throne by arms. It was now no longer possible to exclude from those Scotchmen who would fight upon his side the men who were in sympathy with the older traditions. It was no longer safe, with a shattered army, to exclude any element having a military value. It was therefore with a large body – perhaps nearly 20,000 strong – that he set out to cross the Border.

The campaign of Worcester is made up of one or two very simple elements which we must see clearly if we are to understand that decisive action, which closed the English Civil Wars.

The main elements of a strategical position are usually thus simple and clear to the commonest intelligence (hence the interference of politicians with wars). It is the carrying out of a plan that requires special talent and discovers the soldier. Anyone could see in 1918 that the Dardanelles were a key point, but the problem was: "How should that key point be seized and held." Not "anyone" could solve such a problem. It was a matter not for professional politicians but for soldiers, for a united command by sea and land, acting early, secretly and suddenly with exact co-ordination and synchrony.

Anyone can understand the strategy of Sedan. It was the separation of two enemy forces by a rapid advance into the gap between them. But not anyone could have taken immediate advantage of the chance information which the German General Staff obtained on the eve of the battle.

Anyone can understand the strategies of 1812. The campaign was a pair of pincers. But the pincers failed to meet because Napoleon's brother was not Napoleon, and lost three days at the start from Warsaw on the right wing.

In the same way anyone ought to understand the particularly simple campaign of Worcester. It was no more than a case of one man faced by two men, but hoping to get help from a friend so that when the fight was joined the issue should at least be equal. The one man stands for young Charles's command, the two men stand for Oliver's total command on both sides of the border. The campaign of Worcester was nothing more complicated than an army under Charles racing down southward in the hope of getting help in England, while an army under Cromwell, growing far superior and gathering reinforcement as it went along, raced after. Charles had skilfully given Cromwell the slip and obtained an initial advance of three days, which made his lightning march into England possible.

Charles made that march with the object of doubling his forces before the end of it by the inclusion of English sympathisers in numbers at least equal to his own. Lancashire was full of such, and he hoped that Lancashire would rise. Everything turned upon that hope and it was disappointed. He received only a comparatively small contingent from Lord Derby. For the rest, what should have been his allies south of the Border never moved. Therefore, when the issue was joined at the end of that violent effort, when the young King had halted and accepted battle at Worcester, he was faced by forces more than double his own.

The main reason of the failure of the English Squires in the north to support their King was the fact that the Scotch were, in the English eyes of those days, foreign invaders. There would be reluctance in any case to risk what was left of a man's property by further resistance to the victorious Rebellion. The loyal gentry who had stood by the constitution of their country and the cause of their Sovereign, had already been bled white. Further, there was no unity of command, no one leader for so dangerous an effort. There was no sufficient accumulation of arms and munitionment. There were no garrisons. But in spite of all this, if Scotland had been to England what Scotland is today, there would have been no hesitation. But Scotland, to the Englishman of 1651, was a foreign country and a Scottish army south of the Border was an army of invaders. That was the main reason for lack of English support and therefore for the disaster that followed.

When you have an advantage of two to one over your opponent you may make military use of that position in a number of ways. The simplest and most obvious is to hold him with one half of your force and to manœuvre round him with the other. That was what Oliver did at Worcester. The remaining 16,000 under Charles were contained while a marching wing walked round them beyond the river and attacked from the farther side.

It was a foregone conclusion. The fine defence put up by the loyal Scotch with Derby's contingent, and the active street fighting could not save the battle, nor could Charles's own conspicuous courage and vigorous ubiquity. The young man, a lean, very tall figure was seen first rallying one unit, then another, heading the desperate charges which attempted to stem the tide. There was just as much success as permitted the struggle to be kept up to the last of daylight. It was dusk; a rout had begun, and through that mob the mounted King thrust his way out amid a handful of followers.

There followed that most dramatic of modern English historical episodes, the successful concealment and flight of the King across country to the Channel till he found the ship in the eastern dead water of Shoreham harbour, near the then mouth of the river and not far from the last houses of Brighton. It was six weeks after the battle that he found himself aboard a loyal ship, on the deck of which he could declare himself, and was carried thereby to Fecamp on the further shore. Worcester had been fought on the 3rd of September; Charles landed on the Norman coast on the 16th of October. He had before him those nine years of poverty, perpetual wandering and abandonment which might well have broken his spirit had he been another. But throughout he maintained his purpose and at last it was rewarded.

They were the years in which a man in any station commonly founds the solid achievement of his life, those years between twenty and thirty when full manhood is entered and full experience at last used. They were the years in which a young man of the wealthier classes learns to use the advantages of his leisure and of his instruction. But those years for Charles were years in another school, the school of adversity which, with strong characters, breeds wisdom in the reading of mankind.

*****

In the midst of that half-miraculous escape there fell that very brief but capital second episode which was of equal moment to the future of England and of Charles himself.

CHARLES II: THE LAST RALLY

Luckily we have this most important hour in the life of Charles described by two eye-witnesses. Here are their words as they were later printed with the names of the writers, Thomas Wit grave a gentleman of Staffordshire, who was present, and John Hudlestone the secular priest, later a Benedictine. They are in a tract called by the authors, *A Summary of Occurrences,* etc. The scene is the little chapel at Moseley Hall, and the hour late on the night of Tuesday, the 9th of September, 1651.

> "His Majesty spent likewise some time in perusing Mr. Hudleston's books, amongst which, attentively reading a short manuscript written by Mr. Richard Hudleston entitled *A Short and Plain Way to the Faith and Church,* he expressed his sentiments on it in these positive words: 'I have not seen anything more plain and clear on this subject. The arguments here drawn from succession are so conclusive, I do not see how they can be denied.' He took a view of Mr. Turbervill's Catechism and said, 'It was a pretty book,' and he would take it along with him."

That is how things happen in human life. It is the *"Tolle-Lege"* of St. Augustine: the chance happening which determines a mortal destiny and an eternity.

The seed was sown and grew. That which arose from it branched out till at last, during the tragedy of half-despair and the long eight years of baffled hope, it burgeoned; until in mid-life and the fullness of external activity in the restored activity of governing and apparent power, it flowered; until it bore fruit; until, in the very article of death, that ripened fruit was garnered.

In the King's thirtieth year, that is with the early summer of 1669, it was apparent that things in England were falling into confusion. It was believed abroad that the republican system would stand. Men understood, indeed, that Richard Cromwell was no substitute for his father. They heard of the domestic difficulties and differences, but these they took for granted, as things inherent to any republican system conducted by a military head, when such a head is for the moment absent. Perhaps if one could have got the private opinion of the best judges one would have heard it in intimate conversation that the whole system was cracking up, and some few might have made sure already that there would be a demand for the return of the King, which demand would grow in volume until there should come, as there did come, the sudden change of the Restoration. But after all Mazarin had on his now ageing shoulders (ageing in health, not too advanced in years; he was barely fifty-seven years old) the best political judgment in Europe; and *he* would have wagered heavily a few months earlier against what was to happen. We have seen how he rejected the proposal for marriage between Charles and his own niece, on a mock plea of the unworthiness of his family, but really because he put no faith in the fortunes of the Stuarts.

What was happening was this. The personal and reluctant despotism of Cromwell had been maintained by the still vigorous discipline of the army, because that army had, what all armies must have to be of any value, one visible head. A further support for the Commonwealth was the prestige of victory, confirmed by successes abroad. The English regiments had done very well on the Dunes in front of Dunkirk, the English navy under Blake had done very well at sea. Moreover, there were multitudes enjoying new fortunes which they feared would be imperilled by any further political change, and there were many more drawing good pay as soldiers, which income they feared to lose for the same cause.

The real reason of the break-up was that feature universal to power merely military – jealousy and competition between various commanders.

Of these there was one who had special advantages, the adventurer Monck, whom Cromwell had appointed to rule by the sword in Scotland. His special assets were these: first his own character, an unpleasant, secretive character, and base in its association (a ridiculous, base marriage†), but through its very vices, especially its lack of principle and its sly silence, excellently fitted to do the decisive thing in a time of confusion.

Next, his command was the farthest moved from London. The garrison in Ireland was also far removed but it was growing roots and would be difficult to transfer. It had got hold of grants of land all over the place in Ireland; many of the soldiers were married there and expecting to settle in their new country – quite foreign to them but promising a regular income.

---

† Mrs. Monck was the daughter of a blacksmith and the cast-off of another blacksmith. She was a slut and a scold.

Next, the only possible dynasty alternative to the Common-wealth was a Scotch dynasty, whose claimant to the throne had a large personal following north of the Border and had been actually crowned there.

Next, though Scotland was at the moment a conquered country and an alien one which Monck's garrison held down by force, yet that garrison would be partly removed without much danger. There were bonds of sympathy, partial and contradictory, but still bonds, between the two Protestant kingdoms. There were no such bonds between England and Ireland. It would be possible in the future to amalgam-ate the governments of Scotland and England without violence. That would never be possible with Ireland. The only alternatives were, either to keep Ireland down by the use of a large foreign garrison, or to suffer the consequences of Irish rebellion with separation from England following upon it.

Put all this together and understand why salvation for Charles Stuart was to come from Monck.

Meanwhile the repeated futile, and indeed ridiculous, wobbling of authority in England produced among the exiles in Holland, and especially in Charles himself, an expectation of change. The wretched remnant of the Long Parliament, the Rump, the pretensions of Lam-bert (the general who was most in the public eye), the uncertainty of all things, and the whole hotch-potch emphasised by the very silence of Monck in his distant security (obviously able when he chose to march south) filled the air with a double murmur: the murmur for calling a free parliament and the murmur that "if there must be the rule of one, why not the rule of the one whom most men would ac-cept – the King?"

Monck marched on the 1st of January, 1660. He crossed the Tweed with 7,000 men, not all of whom were needed, and advanced on London at a regular and soldierly pace. The marches were not ex-cessive but they were sufficiently well spaced. He entered the capital on the 3rd of February, having covered just under three hundred and twenty miles in thirty-one full days. His force arrived intact, united and well in hand.

The man whom we know on positive evidence – his own letter – to have spotted Monck quite early as a probable ally was John Cole-peper, the irascible, wayward, courageous, most intelligent companion of the King. Even as early as the first news of Cromwell's death Cole-peper pointed out that Monck had less motive than any other general for refusing to help a restoration *and* was also that one of the competing general officers who held the best and most disciplined command. But it was not till the next year – in July '59 – that Charles himself moved, by sending a letter through Monck's brother Nicholas. When Monck heard in October of the Parliament's fall he at once made his plans like a soldier, putting garrisons into Edinburgh and its port and into Berwick, a "bridge head" for his eventual advance into England. In March, Monck had sent his connection, Sir John Greville, to the King, but (characteristically) he would put nothing in writing: all had to go by memory and word of mouth – but Monck's recommendations to the exile were much what Charles adopted in the Declaration of Breda (whither Monck had suggested that Charles should proceed). That important document was of the date the 4th of April.

On the 25th of May Monck stood on the shore at Dover to meet the landing King whom he had restored.

*****

Superficially it might appear that Monck's march was the most important thing that had happened in the fortunes of England at that moment; but if we look a little more deeply into the motives of men and women it was not so.

The most important thing that had happened during that winter to the future fortunes of England was the well-calculated action of Edward Hyde's daughter, Anne.

The winter drew to its close, Edward Hyde was giving advice, on the whole sound enough, to the young man now approaching his thirtieth birthday, and himself now so well schooled by adversity and travel, so well experienced in the nature of men. The principal decisions had been sketched out: the Declaration at Breda, the private inheritance of the Orange family, where Charles and Hyde and the others had been given hospitality by Charles's aunt, the Princess of Orange, widow of the head of that family and mother of the sulky, sickly little heir at her side. Those decisions included promises of appeasement for the violent religious divisions in England, schemes for settlement of the claims to sequestrated property: the whole programme which was in fact carried out for the most part and in detail, when Charles had returned to his inheritance. All this was important enough and takes the first place of course in our textbooks, because it is obvious and because it is political. But, I say again, another thing, very far from obvious, and only indirectly political must be reckoned as of still higher importance to the English story than the compromises and appeasements and overtures that were being worked out by Charles and his advisers with Edward Hyde at their head.

I repeat that the more important thing was the well-calculated action of Hyde's daughter – Anne.

I shall return on a later page to this remarkable woman who left so profound a mark upon the fate of the Stuarts and with them on their national popular monarchy in England. Anne Hyde had exercised a powerful attraction upon James, the brother of the King. He had attempted some time before to satisfy the desires she aroused in him, but that was before any sign of the Restoration had appeared above the horizon, and Anne, though she was continually in his company as maid of honour to the Princess of Orange and as her father's daughter, kept the gallant at arm's length. She was strong morally as well as physically, her large mouth was a decided one, so was her step and every gesture of hers. There was no getting past that obstacle, and James must remain disappointed, despite the tenacity of his nature. The door was barred against him – *until the news of Monck's march shot back the bolt.* At some date near, and not later than, the 20th of January (old style), 1660, she admitted the Prince to her favours. It may have been earlier, it can hardly have been very much earlier. It would seem probable that the crucial date was coincident with the news that Monck was on the march for London. Even beating up against the wind that news might have reached Holland from some north-east British port well before the end of the first week of January, 1660. Before February was out Anne knew that she was with child and the father of that child was the heir presumptive to the Crown of England.

FIRST GRASP OF THE HELM

HE FIRST MAJOR ACT OF CHARLES STUART AS KING (PER-
formed in his first year of power) was a well considered,
well balanced though daring piece of clemency. It was
an act of appeasement between the two violent factions
which still divided England. No one but a king could have accomplished this in the England of that day; it is, therefore, an act which
strongly illustrates the value men must always attach to monarchy.

There were, of course, in the first months after Charles's landing at Dover any number of public decisions, notably those which
registered rather the will of the new governing class in Parliament
than the will of the Monarch. But the subtle and yet exactly guided
policy of appeasement in this first year was especially the King's own.
It was done in the very teeth of those violent factions into which the
governing class was divided, and yet without any exaggerated appeal
to popular support. Popular support is the very essence of Kingship.
Charles before his death was to use it exaltedly against the Rich in
their revolt against him and attempt to murder him. But it can play
no part in deciding between popular factions. Between these the King
must stand as arbiter and superior to all.

In order to understand the value of what Charles did we must
take ourselves back to that intense moment, feel as Englishmen then
felt, and thus appreciate how a common supreme authority, independent of and above the warring moral claims, could work with creative
effect.

The country in 1660 was only just rid of a prolonged and increasingly hated despotism, commanded by armed fanatics. The most
of men were still filled to saturation with the memories of insult, of
degradation, of robbery, of murder – there had been nothing like it
before in the story of this island and, of course, there has been nothing like it since.

CHARLES II: THE LAST RALLY

The Civil Wars had been but one chapter, the opening chapter in that exceptional business. They had concluded with the complete victory of one party over the other and that party the party of a *minority*. This victory of a *minority* – and a Puritan one at that – had rankled the more with the mass of Englishmen subjected to it because the iron grasp had not seized them at a blow but only after repeated abortive efforts to free themselves from the stranglehold. The mere memory of oppression so detailed, so intimate, and so vivid, would have been enough to make reconciliation impossible. All the native amenity and comfortable air of England had been poisoned; all the common habits of Englishmen, their recreations, their intimate domestic life, had been outraged. We live today in an England when Puritanism, though it still affects the general mind, has spread much wider and therefore has been diluted out of all knowledge.

It is true that those who thus violently oppressed their fellows were numerous. The Puritan minority which had triumphed was a large minority. Still it was only a minority; and being at acute issue with its fellow citizens Puritanism in power had proved itself odious and intolerable.

It had committed what was at that time in the eyes of most contemporaries within the country, and of all Europe outside, an almost inconceivable crime. It had put to death an anointed King.

We must remember also that these moral injuries were given substance and vigour by material injuries on an enormous scale; and because these are insufficiently emphasised in our official histories it is essential that we should grasp them here.

In the first place came that universal grievance already mentioned; landed estates of all kinds, large and small, had been violently confiscated. The thing had gone on all over the country, and because it had been most striking in the case of the wealthier families it had been the more advertised.

The Stanleys are an example: The head of the family, Lord Derby, had supported the King. The Puritans not only killed him but (as they thought and hoped) ruined his family by robbing them of his good land and leaving them little but the barren coast of his county.

To have supported the King's legitimate Government was a natural cause for reprisals by the victorious rebels; but there were other more despicable causes at work. There was the greed of the Parliamentary leaders and of the chief officers of the army. There was private vengeance. There was the satisfaction of family feuds. There was what its victims certainly felt to be sacrilege; for the endowments of religion had been sacked right and left – such as remained of them after the original enormous loot of a hundred years before.

Then there was that worst element in any civil quarrel – the division of families. Perpetually as you read of the Great Rebellion you come across in private letters, in occasional notes and diaries, in chance references, the universal prevalence of this strongest of all incitements to vengeance; this most rooted of all the emotions which forbids the forgiveness of an enemy; the family quarrel. Fathers were against sons, mothers against daughters, husband against wife, even lovers had been broken asunder by divided loyalties. Strangers ruled as masters in rooms of ancient inheritance and many had tasted exile.

Such a potential of hate had accumulated that nothing but a miracle, it seemed, could prevent a catastrophic reaction when the oppression should be relieved.

It was as though an accumulating weight had been poised upon a platform more and more insecure and overhanging prospective victims below, so that when it toppled over it could not but crush and destroy.

Here was the King home again. He was the Justiciar who should set all to rights and take due and final vengeance for so much wrong. He was the supreme governor of the Church, and he was the incarnation of the nation with which the Church claimed to be identified, and the Church of England had suffered especial wrong.

Charles, now restored, was the son and successor of a father whom the revolutionaries had put to death to save their own skins. He had been of an age to see the beginning of the whole tragedy in the indecisive battles of the early war (when he was already entering his teens), in the later defeats of the Crown, in the military disasters of his early manhood. He had suffered personally in loss of place and prestige more than had any subject. His cause had seemed hopeless. For years it was taken for granted that the Royal House of England was destroyed. The King had been turned into an exile and a wanderer; he had been robbed of all he had, and exhibited by the victorious rebels as an object of scorn for Europe and for his own countrymen. He had often lacked the bare necessaries of life; he had never known a moment in which he could feel secure of the immediate future in money, housing or goods.

Might not the now victorious party feel certain that the King would do justice to the full?

It is true that under duress, before his return, he had promised mercy in general terms, but surely these would not count against the necessity of restoring once and for all the ancient peace and full settlement of England.

Had Charles himself obeyed the natural inclination of the populace he would have been a man of less foresight than he was. It may be argued that had he taken full vengeance and done what the mass of Englishmen certainly desired him to do it would in the long run have saved the throne. But such effects were far too distant for any practical calculation. The ultimate reaction against even the most just severity would have inflamed at last the wounds which it was the King's business to heal.

Charles's whole object was to restore the national health by restoring the national kingship: for that purpose it was the very core of his policy to reduce the fever. He did all that could be done to prevent a prolongation of the strain. Therefore he determined to prosecute as few as possible and to leave the living as much as possible undisturbed.

It was necessary indeed to make a visible effect. The outward sign which symbolised the illusion of a full royal restoration must obviously be – could not but be – drastic and impressive. There had to be a public sacrifice of the regicides. There had even to be physical readjustment of the revolutionary symbols such as the semi-royal funerals of the usurper and his kin. But it is notable that the opening steps of restoration involved no immediate loss of life; only a solemn and spectacular act to undo, physically, as it were, the acts of usurpation and to recall full monarchy to life by the magic of Death – but of death in simulacrum.

The corpses of Cromwell, the real and personal author of the King's death, of his gloomy son-in-law Ireton, of Bradshaw the lawyer who had presided (to his own enrichment) as chief judge over the mock trial of Charles I and had passed sentence, these were pulled out of their graves, drawn to Tyburn on hurdles as though they were criminals still alive, hung from the gallows on that triple tree from mid-morning to the setting of the sun. Their mummied corpses were then cut down and beheaded and their trunks cast into the quicklime of a common pit, dug under the instrument of death.

The roaring traffic of modern London passes the accursed spot on either side, for this last sepulchre of Oliver and his companions lay in that narrow triangle of wall (as it now is) where the Edgware Road falls into Oxford Street. It is the parting of the ancient Roman roads; the one to the north-west and to Chester, the other to Bath and the Severn estuary. Since imperial days at least, and probably for long before history, such a meeting of ways outside the City was the normal place of public execution, and at Rome the ancients so ordered it: thus may you see today St. Paul's Outside the Walls marking the place of the Apostle's martyrdom.

This solemn and dramatic act of reparation, the exhumation of Cromwell, was performed upon the anniversary day of Whitehall: the 30th of January, 1661. It was a day which had already been set apart as a public memorial of the martyrdom for all time – that is till the nineteenth century; for two centuries are an eternity to modern man.

In the autumn, after time had been given for the new sheriffs to take office, the ten regicides who had been selected were led out to suffer – that there were only ten out of so many conspicuous men still surviving and notoriously responsible for, or glorying in, the execution of the King's father was due to the fixed policy of the King himself. On that there can be no doubt. No other authority had the weight required to enforce such leniency; the policy of no other man not even of Edward Hyde (Clarendon) was consonant with such an extreme restriction of justice.

The victims were sacrificed on separate days amid the execrations of the people who had assembled in vast crowds.

The bravest among them was Harrison. That soldier declared loudly at the foot of the Tree that all he had done was the work of God. Even as the hangman groped in his vitals for the heart in his half strangled body, before it was quartered, the butchered soldier sat up and caught his tormentor a sounding buffet on the side of the head and so died avenged.

The most shaken of the men thus destroyed was the vehement insulter, Peters, that oddly inspired, half lunatic Puritan divine who had ridden at the head of Charles's escort in the Via Dolorosa from

Hampshire to London reviling the defenceless King. He had also preached the most extravagant sermons against this prisoner in the toils, and no man was more hated than was Peters. It was the knowledge of this public scorn and disgust that weakened Peters at the last hour. But he rallied from his shaking, helped, I am glad to say, by a draught of strong waters.

For the rest there was in England, Wales and Scotland no very violent redressing of the moral balance destroyed during and since the Civil Wars. With Ireland indeed it was far other, as we shall see in a moment.

Much the most remarkable example of Charles's policy in this critical time was the tacit amnesty of John Milton.

It is not possible even for those who least understand the nature of Charles's aim to deny that here the King's direct personal influence was at work. It was Charles Stuart who saved John Milton and it was among the wisest of the many wise things he did.

Be it remembered that Milton was the most guilty of all the intellectuals of the time and among the most guilty of the politicians of the time – if any guilt there were in the thing that was done on the scaffold at Whitehall.

John Milton had been the mouthpiece and penman of Oliver. No man had been more certain or more emphatic. His was the chief literary support of what Oliver had called in that famous ghostly scene (passed in a darkened room), "cruel necessity." But Oliver had only killed Charles I as a cruel necessity, a personal necessity, a piece of killing but for which Oliver himself would sooner or later have been tried and executed as a traitor. It was a pity, for Cromwell saved not ten years of life and of the wrong end of life – nine years, of which the last were a breakdown and misery of the body, not worth saving. But certainly Oliver was not of the type that would rejoice in such a deed as Charles's murder. He was often nervously excited against a religious opponent, rarely against a political one. And Charles was a strong Protestant. But if Oliver were at heart reluctant to kill the King, Milton had been exultant and ferocious in that business.

Milton (since the transformation of his character by domestic misfortune) was certainly of the type that rejoices in the putting to death of a victim. That pen – the pen of the Prince of English Poets – had registered the reply to Salmasius (the *Defence of the English People*), and had transfixed the "Eikon Basilike." Milton it was who stood before all Europe as the chief protagonist in the course of that trial and execution which it was thought (when Milton wrote) would never be avenged.

That Charles II fully foresaw the future stature of Milton in English letters is not probable. It is very rare that the degree, the quality or the basis of literary fame are understood by contemporaries. Moreover, though that epic was on the stocks, *Paradise Lost* had not, by 1660, yet come completed into public view. But the man was already sufficiently famous as a poet and prose writer and Charles, like his father before him (and more than his father before him), understood the part played by writers in the greatness of a nation. He knew what it was to have had Milton for a subject.

By a very happy accident, then, due to the political wisdom of the King, Milton was spared and with him was spared our inheritance of certain lines such as the opening of the fourth book of *Paradise Lost*, the "airs vernal airs," the superb invocation to creative light and all the splendours of fantasy, rhythm and classic strength which shall enrich us – I had almost written "for ever": but there is no earthly for ever; no, not even for high verse, the most enduring of mortal things.

*****

When Charles on the eve of his return had discussed (with Hyde principally, but also with others in his company) the conditions of his restoration, he had to consider three main settlements for the union of English society, the gradual extinction of hatreds and that stability of his own throne which occupied all his thoughts. The first was the settlement of landed estates, the second was the settlement of religious endowments, the third was the settlement of the limits to be fixed to religious toleration under a newly re-established active monarchy.

As to the first of these, the estates in land, the problem was as follows:—

There had been a very wide and revolutionary transfer of land (far and away the most important form of property at all times and in those days overwhelmingly the most important).

In Ireland the native population had been robbed wholesale. The "settlement" there effected I will present a few pages further on. In England the robberies had been of another sort. They comprised estates confiscated in their entirety (this was rare), under the plea that those who had fought from loyalty against the rebels had proved to be themselves in rebellion against a *de facto* Government. The plea was obviously false but on that plea the victors took their stand. Next came estates of which some part only were seized; often a third, sometimes (as in the case of Derby) very much more; hardly ever much less. The victims compounded with the Commonwealth authorities and sold fields or stock or borrowed at usury to pay what was demanded of them. The change-over was enormous and the losses gigantic. Crown lands, including the dowry of the Queen, had been grabbed wholesale, and a considerable acreage thereof had been transferred lock, stock and barrel to individual supporters or officers of the victorious side.

In pure justice the robbers should have been compelled to disgorge. But the King had to consider something more than pure justice. He had to consider the peace of the country.

It was now eighteen years since the opening of the Civil Wars and more than eleven since all restraint had been thrown to the winds after the killing of the King and the supposed extinction of the Monarchy: the final submergence of the loyalists. There had been sales and resales, leases and subleases innumerable, deaths, inheritances, etc. A Settlement cutting clean through all this would have been a still worse disturbance and would have left behind an even more violent discontent than the original confiscations had done. The principle at last adopted was a compromise not without wisdom and insofar as it may have been suggested by Hyde (and Monck) it was to the credit of both. Where there had been mere loot of the original possession, particularly in the case of royal property (including the Queen's dower), the looted wealth was taken back by the Crown without compensation. But where the victims of this tyranny had theoretically condoned it by paying the fines demanded, the new arrangements were allowed to stand.

To give an example which I have mentioned elsewhere, the brother of John Milton the poet – a lawyer who had loyally followed the fortunes of King Charles I – could only get back his London property by paying out to the Masters of the day a large part of its value. He now, in spite of the Restoration, could not recover the sums so filched from him. He was deemed by the new settlement to have transferred his land and wealth of his own free will. The loot was made similar in law to a voluntary gift or sale. Naturally there were loud outcries against such conclusions, which destroyed or crippled ancient estates all over England; but they were thought the only way to prevent disasters greater still.

All up and down the country today you come across farms and parcels of land and woods whose names dimly recall this most extensive redistribution.

In the matter of the Church endowments the same rule was followed as in the matter of the royal property. Those who had seized the revenue of these endowments to swell their private fortunes were made to restore their ill-gotten wealth. It was advanced that there had been a considerable leakage – as one may well believe – and that a good deal of the stolen acres stuck to the hands of the despoilers. But at any rate that was the principle of the settlement in this department.

The settlement in the matter of toleration involved two decisions. First, what should be done about the benefices into which had been introduced Presbyterians who refused to accept the constitution of the Church of England. Second, what forms of public worship should be permitted by law.

The immediate details of these connected settlements do not directly concern our matter, which rather is Charles's character and aim. Where they do concern this our matter is through their impingement upon, and their being conditioned by, the underlying policy of religious toleration which was the special note of the two last Stuart reigns, those of Charles II and his brother James II.

There is no point upon which our textbooks have less appreciated the nature of the times, the character of the two Kings, and even the principle of toleration itself. The truth is beginning to be told and to be more widely known, but there is a time-lag in these things and the vested interest in official history, from universities to elementary schools, is so enormous, the profits made on textbooks is so very great and so continuous, that the reform of that abuse and the rewriting of true history is a formidable undertaking. I can go no further in this, here, than to state in general terms the outlines of that truth. And first, let us begin with the nature and meaning of toleration.

In Victorian days men talked of religious toleration as though it were a positive virtue, like Chastity or Honesty. They never thought out the first principles that lay behind this astonishing presumption.

I remember once in the House of Commons a worthy old professional politician laying it down as a self-evident doctrine that the views and actions of no religious body should be subject to civil restraint! Amid the murmurs of assent which this strange pronouncement evoked there was one sharp exclamation by a wag from the back benches, and it was very much to the point. He cried *"What about thugs?"* Thugs (as even the House of Commons knew) were an Oriental sect who murdered people to the glory of their goddess.

Now in that interjection you have the whole philosophy of prosecution for religion. Any religion productive of acts intolerable to the morals of the community, or to its safety, must be restrained by the civil law, its propagation as far as possible prevented and its fruits in action punished. The principle should be self-evident to any thinking man.

The analysis of religious toleration resolves itself into two simple questions. (a) What are the doctrines and therefore the consequent morals, and therefore the consequent acts, which are at issue with the moral sense of the community? (b) What measure of evil doctrines, and consequent morals and acts, may be permitted lest worse evils should follow upon their suppression than the evil of their presence? On this last point, the very word "toleration" turns. We *tolerate* an abuse, we tolerate an evil thing, only when the forcible suppression of it would lead to worse evils. For instance, we tolerate in a free country arguments in favour of a potential or past enemy in time of peace, because to interfere with natural discussion of policy is to destroy the soul of freedom in a State. But we do not tolerate an express attitude of this kind when the country is fighting for its life in a great war.

Civic freedom should permit an Englishman to say, at the moment in which I write these lines (July, 1939), "I am all for strengthening the Third Reich and I will do my best to help Berlin because it is the only force that can keep the peace in Central Europe." But Englishmen would not tolerate such an opinion and such a recommendation of policy were the forces of the Third Reich present as invaders.

It is even now being debated in what is by far the freest of European polities, the Swiss Confederation, whether Communism may be taught, let alone organised and professed. So far the Swiss forbid and punish the thing. Communism is not *tolerated*, because the community will have none of the fruits in action which they fear would follow from its toleration.

Now the later seventeenth century in England, from 1660 onwards, was a period and place in which not only killings and confiscations and destructions had been actually seen by most men then living to follow upon certain doctrines, but also was a period and place in which there still threatened catastrophies of the same sort. So long as vehement enthusiasm for doctrines which the State and the mass of its citizens thought subversive should continue, so long toleration of those doctrines would seem perilous.

But the trouble in the particular case of seventeenth-century England was that you had no general mass opinion of one kind. Most men in 1660 were averse to Catholicism, but there was a large Catholic minority, which would presumably live peaceably with its fellows of the majority if it were let alone. A much larger number were devoted to the idea of a national church, and disliked dissent, and knew by experience that the opposing parties might be got to live peaceably together.

The Stuart brothers, successively Kings of England, desired a peace of this kind, even as early as 1660. That was with them a first principle. Later, this principle was reinforced in their private consciences by, in the one case, a sympathy with Catholic doctrine, in the other a declared profession of it. But quite apart from the effect of this Catholic bias the principle of general toleration, on very broad lines, inclusive of all (except perhaps declared atheism), was an ideal clearly and simply held. And the great example of that spirit in action was the attachment of both Charles and James to the remarkable character and Colonial policy of William Penn, with whose effect I will deal when we come to the one Colonial achievement of Charles and his brother.

All his life long, from the Declaration of Breda to his death, Charles II worked unceasingly for the widest form of religious toleration. He could never succeed in carrying that policy through Parliament. At first Parliament meant the squires and the Church of England, violently hostile to the other sectarian Protestant bodies at whose hands, after the sectaries had captured the victorious army, they had suffered such cruel injustice and loss. Later, from dread of a Catholic succession, but also and much more as an opportunity for pulling down the power of the monarchy, the squires and the City-Capitalists swung round from a front opposed to dissent to a front more and more opposed to Catholicism alone. How this happened we shall see when we come to that crucial date, 1670. But whether in the earliest phase or in the later one, whether in anger against dissent or much more violent anger against the Catholic Church, there was always the same difficulty of realising on this side of the Atlantic the principle of almost universal toleration.

On the other side of the Atlantic, in the Colonial Empire which we owed to the Stuarts, there were here and there rare examples of this toleration; and of these the constitution of Pennsylvania, following on that of Maryland, were the most remarkable, as we shall see when we appraise their effects on American development.

As to the benefices enjoyed by the Presbyterians at the moment of the Restoration, those who so enjoyed them were expelled if they could not bring themselves to accept the Constitution of the official Church, with its episcopal hierarchy and its fixed liturgy. There was admitted a very great latitude of interpretation on church doctrine, but none on church structure.

The number of those who refused to conform was large. Perhaps two thousand altogether were dispossessed of their livings. For full toleration here the King himself could not act. It had to be one thing or the other, and the Church was made, officially at least, universal throughout the realm.

IRELAND

In the midst of these first acts of the reign – acts which were characteristic of its aim and of Charles's special aptitude for achieving that aim – there fell what was also the first of his blunders, I mean his abandonment of the Irish people.

At the appearance of this word "blunder" I must define and explain lest it be misunderstood.

The one great business of Charles Stuart being the real Restoration of the Monarchy in England, was he not justified in sacrificing *anything* to that object? If he were so justified, then the abandonment of Ireland (which was directly connected with his determination to re-establish the active and national Crown) was justified, as were the two other blunders (as I shall call them) which also marked his career, the postponement of his conversion and the abandonment of Stafford. All three are directly bound up with the business of religion. In all three he sacrificed to the interests of a political task what he knew to be the true and only spiritual reality.

He abandons the Irish immediately after his return to the Throne because the interests of Catholic Ireland are violently at issue with the inherited anti-Catholic policy of England. He postpones to the very last moment of life his own reception into the Church because the announcement of that act would have seriously shaken his position as King. He sacrifices the victims of the Popish Plot, of whom Stafford is the last and most typical example, for the same reasons. To save the innocent from death is surely the first duty of any ruler, but it would have put his throne in jeopardy.

How can we call any of these three major acts "blunders" since they served his major political object? Only in this sense: that it is always unwise to sacrifice the greater to the lesser. However clear the goal which a man has put before himself as the object of his whole life and work, however important that success to himself and to the commonwealth, there is one thing more important still which is integrity.

Now it is obvious that complete integrity cannot be preserved in the pursuit of any political object. Every such pursuit, especially every realisation of such an object, involves perpetual sacrifice in details of the truth, of sincerity and of that full agreement between the inside and the outside of a man which we call integrity.

But there comes in here, as in all human affairs, the element of degree. There are minor sacrifices of integrity which are unavoidable all day long if human life is to be conducted at all. There are major departures from it which are also necessary if, upon full consideration, the ruin of one's main object by intrigue and make-believe would be a tragedy outweighing the evil price paid for it. But there always comes a point after which no temporal object whatever, *no* worldly consideration should hold against the Eternal. If indeed all conviction of eternal things be an illusion then justice itself may be sacrificed to a temporal need, but if the great virtues (among which justice stands so high, and bearing witness to a conviction upon divine things higher still), if these are to be put first, then one must, in any temporal task, come to a point where the defence of justice and faith have a claim superior to everything else, however important: even one's country, even one's public functions – and of public functions the highest, indistinguishable from the good of the country, is sovereignty.

Those who are confused upon these difficult issues and who are ready to complain of anything which a great actor on the stage of this world performs against justice or against his own conviction of truth, should remember that they themselves and all other men are perpetually compelled to make such sacrifices. For instance, during a war men of the strongest integrity will perform what is called today "propaganda," that is deliberate falsehood for the good of the nation. My point is that there is a limit, and that limit should not be passed. In my judgment Charles passed this limit in three cases: that of Ireland, of his refusal to proclaim his intimate religious convictions, and of the Popish Plot with its leading case of Stafford.

It may be superstitious to remark, but it is of curious interest, that commonly when men do so exceed the permitted limits of concealment, falsehood and denial of right, they miss the very reward for which they pay so terrible a price.

It is not true that wrongdoing involves loss or suffering in this world to the perpetrator of the evil deed. It is, as we can all see by the most superficial acquaintance with human life, generally the other way. The wages of heroism is death. But in the major examples, when right-doing is too violently reversed, there does attach to the wrong an apparent Nemesis and that would seem to be especially the case when the wrong is done by those who are in general of right mind and instinct and who are untrue to themselves in going contrary to that mind and instinct.

In the case of Charles it was certainly so. He allowed a monumental wrong to be done to the Irish nation. He lived a whole life in contradiction with his profound perception of religious truth.

He sacrificed the victims of the Popish Plot in general and Stafford in particular. He was guilty of all these three major evil deeds for the sake of restoring their Monarchy to the English: and he did not restore it. He paid the highest possible price for that which he legitimately desired, and failed to obtain what he had thus thought to have purchased....

*****

On its largest lines the issue of Ireland between 1660 and 1663 was as follows:—

Five hundred years before, in the heart of the Middle Ages, an effort had been made by the English Crown to incorporate its Irish province with the general feudal system of Western Europe.

This Plantagenet effort seemed legitimate enough. The Pope, who was then the universal moral arbitrator, sanctioned it. It seemed reasonable, natural and almost inevitable that the accepted political system of the time, the feudal system, should extend to all the lands and subjects of a feudal monarchy.

But the organisation of the Irish people was tribal, not feudal. The hierarchy and succession of their local rulers did not follow the feudal rules. An heiress did not by her marriage convey lordship of her tribal lands to her husband. A chieftain did not inherit the right to rule by mere primogeniture. Rather was he chosen by his own people, from among a small number it is true, but not by the mere feudal rule of descent. Hence, from the beginning of the direct connection with England under Henry II in the twelfth century, arose a deep-rooted misunderstanding. What seemed just and normal to the higher material civilisation of Plantagenet England involved what shocked the moral sense of tribal Ireland.

So long as Western Christendom remained united there was no outrage to Irish tradition in these things. There was pressure against it and intrigue against it, often successful, but it was not merely and brutally attacked with the object of destroying it.

When the Plantagenet inheritance was disputed in the later Middle Ages, the Irish tradition recovered its vitality. The great feudal families settled in Ireland acquired the Irish tone in political organisation as in language and in everything else. During the great family quarrel of the Plantagenets at the end of their rule (the Wars of the

Roses) which coincided with the end of the Middle Ages, in the last century before the Renaissance and the Reformation, Ireland became almost independent, though of course still acknowledging the sovereignty of the Kings of England. This was also the moment when the military power of the Crown was increasing very greatly everywhere and artillery was beginning to tell against the feudal castle. Oddly enough it was not the Reformation which created the first step in what was to prove so fatal a development, the planting of Irish land with aliens, the effort to "colonise."

The first false step of this sort was committed during the very reaction of Catholicism against the Reformation, that is, under Philip and Mary, and the old names of King's County and Queen's County bore witness to it. Henry's break with the Papacy, even his suppression of the monastic orders and loot of Church endowment of every kind, including hospitals and schools, provoked no Irish rebellion. But when the fundamentals of religion were changed, when the Mass and Sacrament of the Altar were proscribed, when the reign of the Cecils began, then indeed open and unending war had been lit and the fire has raged ever since to the devastation of Ireland itself and to the apparent destruction of the Irish Nation.

All the power of England from Elizabeth onwards was devoted to a gradual conquest of Ireland, as of something alien and hostile to England itself. The process was confused. Irishmen were themselves divided on it, but upon the whole, what with confiscation for rebellion, acts interpreted as treason and the rest, about half the land of Ireland had been lost by, say, 1625 to those of the Irish blood and faith whose fathers had possessed the whole. In the early part of Charles II's reign the Irish tradition was in English eyes an enemy tradition. The Irish in full succession to their fathers still holding about half the rents of the island were now despised as barbarians, and a little later – say by 1660 – much more hated than despised as members of a religion which had by this time become foreign to some appreciable majority of Englishmen, and actively detested by a large Puritan minority of Englishmen.

Then came the first mutterings of rebellion against the King in England, the failure of the Scotch war, the necessity for Royal armament against the danger. The age-long truth that misfortune to England was opportunity for Ireland vividly appeared. There was a violent

partial rebellion of the dispossessed, who avenged their well-remem-
bered and bitter wrongs by sporadic murder and destruction. This
"massacre of Protestants" was grossly exaggerated. Not only popular
rumour but solemn official pronouncements multiplied it by at least
ten. But the excuses for these excesses and the exaggeration of them
must not blind us to the effect of the horror upon Englishmen of all
kinds. From that moment the Stuart cause was associated in the minds
of a large English minority with the murder of Englishmen and the
robbery of their goods and the destruction of their homes, and in the
minds of nearly all Englishmen with alien attack. The inherited personal monarchy of England was tainted by this memory.

After Charles Stuart had lost his battle in 1644, when the rebels
who had defeated him put him to death in 1649, their chief soldier,
supported by the organised wealth of the City of London, crossed
the sea to put an end once for all to the Irish menace. The trained
army of Oliver swept over the island. Its success was accompanied by
reprisal and massacre, but above all by wholesale confiscation of the
soil. The soldiers were rewarded, the English financial backers of the
campaign were repaid, by large transfers of land, covering nearly the
whole island. The dispossessed were driven in great numbers to the
most barren province, Connaught, beyond the Shannon. The great
majority of those who remained on their ancestral land were now
subject to the new masters, working for them and deprived of what
had been theirs from immemorial time.

The Irish religion was of course stamped out as thoroughly as
the means of the day permitted. There had been loot enough and
transfer enough of English land from the defeated Royalists to the
rebellious victors, the economic revolution in England had been on a
very great scale, but it was nothing to what had happened in Ireland.

With the restoration of Charles the iniquities of the English
transfers were in some part repaired as we have seen. On the analogy of this reparation it was thought that a similar reparation would
be effected in Ireland. At least half the land would of course have
remained in the hands of foreign intruders, but the wholesale loot of
Cromwell would have been undone.

With that critical date 1660 an opportunity had appeared, not
indeed for settling the endless problem of Ireland, but for making the
relations between the two nations tolerable.

CHARLES II: THE LAST RALLY

The choice lay personally with Charles – whether he should risk the partial restoration of the Irish to their ancestral land or not. There were many counsels, divided policies, but in the main it was for the King in the flush of his Restoration to decide. He decided against justice in order to make his new throne secure.

The story has been told in all manner of ways – as might be expected of a story concerned with conflict of race, conflict of religion, and national hatreds carried on with increasing intensity to our own time. That story has also been warped by the many and acute divisions among the Irish themselves upon the national and the Catholic side, and even upon the anti-Catholic side, insofar as it was Royalist. There were Protestant Irishmen who had had lands in Ireland given to them as invaders and aliens in the first part of the conquest, long before the Great Rebellion. These lands they had lost because they had loyally taken up the cause of their lawful King against the rebels. They were as anti-Catholic as anyone but they had been ruined by the Puritan victors of the Civil Wars and they clamoured for the restitution of their property and their rights. There were Catholic rich men who had had their land taken away from them because their families had joined in with the Rebellion or because there was proof of some correspondence, however slight, between them or their fathers and the National Committee which had attempted to restore the independence of Ireland, and especially the practice of the national religion. These all cried out that what they had inherited had been seized by force and they clamoured for reinstatement in their fathers' lands and for redress.

Then there were a vastly larger number of rank and file who had lost their petty holdings in masses because they were known to be in sympathy with the national cause or because they had taken it up actively, or even because they had done no more than to live quietly under the administration of the National Government while it was in the saddle. The just but confused and much too manifold claims were not simply refused; Charles's abandonment of the Irish people was not a mere refusal to do right. It was the denial of justice in fact rather than in theory and a denial of justice by perpetual postponement, perpetual revision and by allowing the discussion to drag on interminably so that those actually in possession remained in possession at the end.

A common interpretation of Charles's action has laid it down to his indolence, the error of our older historians when they deal with this reign. It certainly was not the indolence of the King that abandoned the Irish. It was not fatigue with the length of the debates or the intricacies of the legal arguments. It was clear policy – for Charles all his life followed policies clear in motive, however tangled they might be in action. The clear motive of Charles here was that leading motive of his whole life – to save the Crown. Had he proposed full justice and the restoration of their lands to the Catholics and to the Loyalists as a whole, he might have provoked a new rebellion. He was faced with large numbers of men still armed, men with strong military traditions and capable of reforming rapidly in military organisation – for the bulk of those who stood between the Crown and the just settlement of the Irish claims were the soldiers planted by Cromwell, or their descendants.

It was certain, moreover, that a liberal and just policy in favour of the Irish Catholics, the overwhelming majority of the island at that time, would have provoked a violent reaction in a great part of English opinion. It was Charles's one thought, in this as in every other problem before him, to avoid such a reaction of English opinion. He determined not to challenge the risk; and therefore, a just Irish settlement, which might have borne fruit down to our own time, was sacrificed.

I have said that the three great blunders (of which this was the first) were blunders because the peril, rather than face which Charles yielded, was not so great as he took it to be. There would have been heavy friction, had Charles done right, but there would have been no more. There would hardly have been armed rebellion; there would certainly not have been an organised army in the field against him. On the other hand, by doing justice as his every inclination prompted him to do, Charles would have acquired for the English Throne an element of strength which was now lost for ever. We feel the effects of that loss today and we shall probably feel it increasingly throughout the future. There might have existed an Irish Catholic landed class solidly established and bound by every tie and interest to strengthen the Protestant English throne. The triple title of "The Three Kingdoms" might have become a reality and the King of England would have been King of Ireland as well as King of Scotland, his whole position firmly based and with a better chance of endurance from the power he would have had to play the opposing elements one against the other.

As it was, Charles's abandonment of the Irish worked within one not very large but very intense field for the weakening of England and of the English Crown. It is true that in the succeeding generations after Charles's false step the numbers of those who could have opposed England from Ireland diminished. It is true that the Irish nation as a potential enemy to England was ruined and that the very race of the Irish was almost destroyed. When the crowning wound of the famine was delivered in the middle of the nineteenth century, a leading English daily paper could write in triumph that the Irish had now "'gone for good." But Ireland was not quite killed. It was thought to be dead. It was in our own time hopelessly diminished and impoverished. Its rising from the dead in the future will almost certainly show that the heavy spiritual sacrifice which Charles made by his surrender was made in vain.

In the island itself only some two-thirds of the people remain in full possession of their ancestral tradition and religion. An alien corner of the north-east is still maintained on English subsidy as a hostile element in the midst of Irish things. It is a policy which our leaders have long come to regret and one of which our naval and military authorities have pointed out the peril in case of war. But nothing has been done to appease the friction.

Many would say that the danger arising from Charles's blunder in those early years of his reign can never be effaced. The proportion of Irish income to English income has dwindled since Charles's time from perhaps one-third to some tiny uncertain fraction – certainly less than one-twentieth. The total population, even including the alien and hostile element, has sunk from being perhaps half that of Great Britain to less than one-tenth thereof.

But those who estimate problems of this kind numerically rather than organically make a grave political error. Ireland, through that fatal false decision, became from 1660 onwards more and more, for generation after generation, the strategic danger on the flank of England and, what is far more important, the spiritual menace to the opposing spirit of England.

THE FAIR RUN

E HAVE SEEN THAT CHARLES RETURNED TO HIS COUNTRY in the spring of 1660. He was then in his thirty-first year. He overthrew the revolutionary movement of his opponents, that is, of the Squires and Merchants when he dissolved the Oxford Parliament in 1681. After that date he was indeed King until his death three and a half years later.

These twenty-one years – 1660–1681 – are divided into two almost equal periods by that decisive event, the Treaty of Dover in early 1670 when Charles entered his fortieth year. During the first half of his action, the first ten years, 1660–1670, he was pursuing without too much peril his course towards the full restoration of the English Crown and the ultimate success of Monarchy against Oligarchy.

I have compared his action throughout his life to that of a helmsman. The craft which he steered was, during those first ten years, running in normal weather. There were bad gusts – the Plague, the Fire, the Dutch in the Medway; there was often the necessity for beating up against the wind, there were checks and delays; but taking it all in all, these years of his life, when he was in his thirties, were the holding of one course with what appeared throughout a reasonable chance of reaching his object and restoring the throne. But round about the year 1670 – from mid-1669 to early 1671 – there fall, in surprising unison, in a whole succession of increasing perils and shocks, a number of things which change all his earlier security into a growing threat of shipwreck. The second ten years, those between his forty-first and fifty-first year, 1670–1671 to 1680–1681, are a series of increasing storms from which he and the craft he commands hardly escape.

It is essential to the understanding of his apparent success at the end of that passage – which is also the end of his life – that one should appreciate the difference between the first and the second part of his reign. Those two periods were, I say, divided by a series of adverse events coming all in an assault together, in a crowd, and changing all his chances.

These were: (1) That very important and neglected matter, the introduction of divorce into English law, the first omen of his disputed succession. (2) The further insistence of the squires in Parliament upon religious persecution. (3) The change-over in the relations between England and France from hostility to alliance, and therefore, the origin of that triangular play between Charles, Louis XIV, and the Dutch which the King of England conducted with such singular skill. (4) The death of Minette, his younger sister, the only character that ever swayed his judgment through affection.

All these, together with the striking economic policy of the moratorium – called "the closing of the Exchequer" – and the arrangement for the subsidies from the French Crown, would of themselves have begun some new chapter in the story of the reign; but much more important than any of them was the contemporary thing, which lay at the root of all that followed and in the long run destroyed all that was left of the National monarchy. This – far and away the greatest matter in that brief pivotal period which turns on 1670 – was the open conversion to Catholicism of the Duke of York, the heir to the throne, from which change all the rest was to follow – down to the destruction of the dynasty and, with it, of the Crown: the transformation of England from a realm still under a king to an open oligarchy under a governing class, the ultimate triumph of the Money-power which Charles had devoted his life to repel.

Those first ten years, when the course the King was steering could be held without too much fear for the future, contained, of course, much more than the main policy of Charles. They were the years in which the struggle for sea-power, for colonies and for the carrying trade was at its height between London and Amsterdam. They were therefore the years which saw the first confirming of English colonial power beyond the Atlantic, and the principal maritime victory of England under the Duke of York as admiral. All this I shall treat separately before we come to the capital turning-point, the Treaty of Dover. For the moment I will confine myself to the main sequence of the ten years: the last of the reprisals against the Great Rebellion, the Braganza marriage of the King, the last phase in the premiership of Edward Hyde, including the sale of Dunkirk; the attempt of the King to establish religious toleration and his failure therein, the Triple Alliance, and the three heavy disasters, plague, fire and invasion, which the monarchy then survived and of which one, the Fire, worked strangely enough in favour of the Royal power.

As for the last of the reprisals, these were marked by the execution of Vane, more than two years after the return of Charles. Vane amply deserved the fate that befell him. He deserved it in his own character, he deserved it by custom and law, as an avowed and unrepentant traitor. He was the man who had, more than any other, compassed the death of Strafford by his secret strategy (which had included theft); and he was the man who had openly proclaimed the theory that the Parliament – that is, the two committees of wealthy men, the House of Commons and the House of Lords – were the rightful possessors of sovereign power over their fellow citizens. It was not a question, with Vane, of obeying a *de facto* government such as the Rebellion had set up under the name of "Commonwealth": it was a question of a doctrine and the proclamation thereof. In presenting the class to which he belonged as having the right to supplant the King, who stood for the whole community, Vane deserved death at the hands of that community and its King. He died with courage on that same Tower Hill which had seen the death of his victim Strafford twenty-one years before. It was the end of that long series of attack and counter-attack, revolutionary action, and reprisals, which had continued unceasingly since Charles's eleventh year and the opening of the Great Rebellion.

Until the execution of Vane, in all the earlier series of punishment imposed upon the regicides, Charles, as we know, had erred on the side of mercy. It might have been better for the English Crown, and therefore for the English populace, had he been more vigorous. But he was convinced of the principle which Monck and Edward Hyde, who had both restored him, both held – the principle of appeasement.

We have seen a further remarkable example of this in the King's saving of John Milton's life, though there the high Stuart appreciation for great verse and great art of all kinds played a personal part.

But when it came to this last case of Vane, Charles was persuaded, and rightly persuaded, that to compromise upon the matter would too much weaken his office. Vane was symbolic of the whole thing from the beginning. He was steeped in the blood of Strafford, and had declared himself an enemy to the English kingship and a champion of its destruction.

The Braganza marriage is one of the most debatable points in policy of all Charles's decisions – insofar as it was his personal decision (for in this as in so much else he was still influenced by Hyde).

Catherine of Braganza, Princess of Portugal, was, of course, a Catholic. It would be an error to exaggerate the importance of this, but it was not without effect. The Catholicism of the late Queen, Charles's mother, had been a continual weapon of offence in the hands of the Crown's enemies, and though the conversion in the previous generation of Anne of Denmark, James I's Queen, was not widely known, it is remarkable that for more than a hundred years every queen of England had been baptised and brought up a Catholic or had died one; for one must count Elizabeth in that list, apart from the fact that she strongly acclaimed Catholicism under her sister's reign.

The Restoration might have seemed the moment for breaking this series and arranging for Charles a marriage into one of the Protestant Courts of Europe. The strongest immediate reason against it was the repugnance felt by Charles himself for a German wife. He had seen the petty German courts during his exile; the nature of their women had repelled him. But a stronger force working for the Braganza marriage was the policy of Louis XIV. Louis it was who, in the tradition of Mazarin, desired that marriage and he it was who arranged it. He looked upon Portugal, its still considerable trade and its great colonial possessions, as a counter-weight to Spain, the long-standing rival of the French power. The choice of Catherine of Braganza for a wife to the restored King of England had also for motive the immediate financial advantage it brought to the Crown, which was already feeling the insufficiency of the parliamentary settlement of its income. It brought the town of Tangier to the English monarchy, the port of Bombay in the East, as also a commercial base badly needed against the rivalry of the Dutch in Asia; and it brought open trade with Brazil. But more immediately important was the dowry promised by the Portuguese Crown. It came to more than a quarter of the total income nominally provided by Parliament for the King and to more than a third of what was actually received during all the wrestling between the King of England and his wealthier subjects.

This comparatively small extra margin of revenue made all the difference; it was with Charles as it is with many a private man whose income is insufficient for his establishment – a fraction of that income added to it makes the difference between permanent indebtedness and freedom.

But the Braganza marriage was most unfortunate as a piece of policy from a cause of which the men of 1662 could as yet know nothing. The new Queen was incapable of giving Charles an heir. She suffered from repeated miscarriages, and after a certain lapse of time it was clear that the only legitimate successor to the King would be his brother James.

Now the importance of this proved in the long run enormous, because James was destined – and there again the men of 1662 could not have guessed it – to make that departure in religion which destroyed his Crown and his House. Considering Charles's determination to save the Crown at all costs, he would undoubtedly, had Catherine of Braganza borne him a son, or even only a daughter, have had the child brought up a Protestant. He was not yet far advanced on the road which was to establish an increasing conviction of Catholicism in him, and, at the very end of his life, reception into the Church. As it was, with Catherine of Braganza's inability to provide an heir, direct succession to the King was impossible – short of a divorce; and how the suggestion of divorce did come into the affair we shall see in a moment.

Edward Hyde had grown very unpopular with the populace of London and even with his own wealthy landed class, which had already begun to pretend to the government of England. Being the devoted counsellor he was, and having proved, on the whole, a most successful one in his judgment of the situation when there was first question of the King's return, he was of course given reward. Charles made him Lord Chancellor, a post which meant in those days not a prize for some political lawyer in the House of Commons, but an administrative as well as judicial post immediately second to the power of the Crown. The income which was thus in the gift of the King when he made a man Lord Chancellor was enormous. It was calculated at seventy thousand pounds a year. This meant in the social value of money, comparing those times with our own, some two hundred thousand a year at least of today, and Hyde, as was only natural with the advance of years and his long experience of poverty in exile, had grown at once avaricious and ostentatious. He built himself a palace at the top of St. James's Hill, along Piccadilly Lane. As everyone knows, the people of London nicknamed it Dunkirk House, under the false impression that Hyde had taken a commission from the French King when Dunkirk was sold to the French. It seems certain (through lack of evidence) that he had taken no such commission, but it was quite in the morals of the time to have done so; his financial position as Chancellor would sufficiently account for his expenditure, large as it was.

Charles had also given him the title of Clarendon, after a deserted and ruined royal palace near Salisbury which had not been used for a lifetime. The name is famous in English constitutional history of the Middle Ages through the story of St. Thomas of Canterbury, and was further famous for some very long time through the History of the Great Rebellion to which Clarendon devoted himself at the end of his life. It is much the fullest single document we have on that period. It is written with a great knowledge of men and, up to a certain date, of domestic events in England. It gives the author the advantage, of course, of stating his views, as, for instance, his strong inclination against the monarchical spirit in the Europe of his day and his corresponding inclination for his own class and what had become their new religion.

Clarendon's famous *History of the Rebellion* suffers not only from this class-biased opinion, but also from a certain number of doubtful statements and a smaller number of certainly incorrect ones; but it remains one of the chief historical works in the language.

Clarendon's misfortunes, which came rapidly after the first years of his elevation, have been represented as due to ingratitude on the part of the King whom he had steadfastly served in poverty and exile. That judgment is unjust; it would have been necessary to get rid of Clarendon anyhow. It was perhaps inevitable that the now elderly man should take on too much authority seeing how indispensable he had been to Charles since boyhood; it made him difficult to work with as a colleague and even more to work with as a subject. To an attempt to get rid of him by impeachment Charles preferred asking him to go abroad and, of course, to resign his office. He obeyed, and left England in the latter part of 1667. It is pathetic to remember that his reputation with the masses, and particularly with the people of London, and especially with the sailors in London River led to his maltreatment at the hands of Englishmen during his exile. He was actually attacked and beaten at Evreux by members of an English crew who attributed to him the keeping back of their pay.

The splendid marriage of his daughter Anne and his consequent close relationship with the Duke of York, now heir presumptive, did not save him. Perhaps if anything it hastened his fall for it increased the jealousy of his equals.

He has left on the story of his country a deeper mark than his character or achievements deserve, though his character was temperate and even and his achievements, in judgment at least, were considerable. The popular hatred aroused against him in London at the very end was irrational, as such popular hatreds based on the loud ill-informed rumours of a capital city always are. They were particularly irrational in the London of that day because it was a community growing out of bounds. London was now – in 1667 – no longer small enough to have any united civic sense, nor yet so large as to be incoherent and therefore voiceless. It still had an opinion. How wild this opinion could be, and how changeable, was to be seen from ten to a dozen years later in the excitement of the Popish Plot. But for whatever reasons – most of them were bad reasons – this London "feeling of the street" was violently excited against Clarendon and had he not yielded to it it might have become an arm for use against the Monarchy by that faction of wealthy men which was already becoming dangerous. The enthusiasm of the Restoration had been largely lost by 1667. The Parliament, that double committee of the wealthy, and in particular the House of Commons, after half a dozen years of uncontrolled power was capable of taking things into its own hands and directly interfering with the affairs of the State. It was even more excited against Clarendon than was the popular mass of the city outside.

All this being said, the natural demand for a scapegoat must be counted also. The plague and the great fire had nothing whatever to do with Clarendon, but they had left a mood behind them which did want a victim. The invasion of the Dutch up river as far as Chatham, the burning of the great capital ships and the sound of the enemy guns loudly heard in London itself – all that disgrace was the direct product of the lack of statesmanship in the merchants and embryo bankers of London itself with their financial control of the wealthier classes, and in the work of those classes acting in the House of Commons. The populace can never be expected to know how it is governed, and it was monstrously convinced that the blows it had received were due to the Chancellor.

Clarendon was in the eyes of all a sort of Viceroy, he was the second person in the kingdom, and there came into his fall that element which you find all through English history so long as the Monarchy endures (or at least right up to 1685) the element of what we may call the "substitute victim." While the mere name of King still had such power that men hesitated to attack the Crown directly, they loved to attribute its supposed errors to a bad counsellor. It had been so with Buckingham, it had been so with Strafford, it was so now with a lesser, but very unpopular name, that of Edward Hyde, Earl of Clarendon. Even had Charles desired to maintain him he could not have done so without risking that prime object of his, the security of the throne. Therefore did he persuade the old man – old by the standards of that day – to withdraw and even to leave the country.

There was this further piece of wisdom about Charles's action in dismissing Clarendon. An attack upon the heir presumptive, James, was possible enough in the near future. When that attack should arise the prince's name would be associated with his father-in-law's.

Charles could not, of course, know as yet the nature or the violence of that coming attack. He could not know that it would become what it was through the intense emotions of religion, for James was still stolidly Protestant and Charles himself had as yet only leanings towards the old religion. But certainly if Clarendon had remained in office another four or five years his name would have been as unjustly and violently associated with the conversion of the Duke of York as it had already been with the sale of Dunkirk and the Dutch raid into the Medway.

The next item to remember in the list is the failure of Charles to achieve toleration. That effort was to be made continually by him and his brother until the end of the dynasty twenty years later. It is the one chief character by which the later Stuarts should always be remembered. Charles's effort towards toleration during the first half of his active reign failed not through popular feeling, which had not as yet been aroused, but through the political attitude of the Parliament.

Of organised opinion, by far the strongest force against toleration was that of the Church of England with which the squires were thoroughly intermixed. We have already seen the reasons for this strong feeling, the memories of the outrages suffered under the Commonwealth and the determination that such indignities and losses should not return. But there were other bodies of organised opinion whose action towards toleration must be remembered. There was first of all the dwindling but still active Presbyterian tradition. Even by 1660, only nine years since, a very large proportion of the livings had been in Presbyterian hands, and though many who still held them were willing to conform, a great number of steadfast men preferred to suffer confiscation and poverty rather than do so, and undoubtedly a much larger number retained their Presbyterian attitude at heart though not going so far as refusal to conform.

Now, the Presbyterians in England were in favour of toleration for dissenters – naturally for it would be to their advantage. What is more remarkable is that they extended this bias in favour of toleration to the Catholics.

The system of Presbyterianism – that is of Calvinism – had been throughout Europe, and particularly in these islands, the opposite pole to Catholicism. Calvin's great construction was the construction of a Counter-Church which, in its deepest philosophy (in the matter of salvation), and in its mere superficial structure (in the matter of discipline and church government), was a direct contradiction of Catholic principles. Yet the Presbyterians of England as a whole had lost that anti-Catholic fervour which had distinguished them not a generation before. This was in part due to the fact that their own demand for religious freedom ran parallel to the Catholic demand, but more to the fact that the Catholic demand was feeble and inoperative. The Catholic protest was spread, of course, over a much wider field than the Presbyterian action. The minority which held to Presbyterian tradition in England was nothing like the size of the Catholic-minded minority. But it had held power; it had been highly disciplined and was still largely so; and though it was at odds with the official Protestant religion of the State, it was at least Protestant. It is that which counted in the struggle. Why those with Catholic sympathies counted so much less in strength than in numbers I will describe in a moment.

Another body of organised unacademic opinion was the Independents; and yet another was the less organised body called the Society of Friends, or, popularly, the "Quakers," which both the royal brothers sympathised with, and which set so remarkable an example of constructive social effort in America before the end of the reign.

The Independents, perhaps not very numerous compared with the Presbyterians, had the prestige of association in people's minds with the former government. They had once ruled England in the person of Oliver Cromwell and his associates; many of them had thus become wealthy; many of them had taken active part in administration. Now they were for toleration, not only from expediency but from principle. This was remarkable because not ten years before they had been the loudest in their abhorrence of papist idolatry, and it was religious feeling as much as greed and revenge which had led their leaders to behave as they did in Ireland. But they were certainly on the side of the King in this first half of his active reign so far as the policy of toleration was concerned.

I repeat, until the transformation of the whole business at and after the turning point of 1670, first by the suspected and then by the declared conversion of the Duke of York, the Houses of Parliament formed a front opposed to toleration, because toleration would have freed the Nonconformist bodies. But in the *latter* half of the active reign – after 1670–1674 – the Parliamentary front against toleration faced the Catholics rather than the Nonconformists. It ended by adopting a definite policy of alliance *with* the Nonconformists *against* the Catholics.

How large the Catholic minority was I have described elsewhere. It is a piece of historical truth which should always be insisted upon that one family in more than three, probably one in four, taking England as a whole, still retained some traditional sympathy with the old religion.† But this body of what may be called "attachment to ancestral tradition" was neither united nor organised.

---

† I have given the grounds for this estimate at length in my study of James II. I will not repeat the list here. It is certain that one in eight were admittedly Catholic. The only doubt is on the size of the "Margin," the "Penumbra," the people who sympa-

THE FAIR RUN

In the wealthiest part of society there was a certain knowledge of the Catholic Church, because that wealthier part of society still held a certain traditional culture, and the fears which men were beginning to feel that there might be a considerable movement of conversion towards Catholicism among the gentry, and especially among those at court, were justified. But the definite and avowed Catholic body in England was but half of the Traditionalists, one family in eight. Though willing to accept heavy sacrifices, they were less and less able as time passed to act. They were always torn between their patriotism and their religion, and, of course, this difficulty got greater in proportion as one moved gradually away from the admittedly Catholic body. Many a man who had sympathy with the old religion which had been that of his father or grandfather and of which the full memory was retained in his family, would not on that account go to the length of declaring his sympathy in set terms, nor perhaps feel very much one way or the other.

Moreover, the opportunities for practising the Catholic religion were very limited. A man could hear Mass at the Embassy chapels in the capital, and, surreptitiously, in the private chapels of specially favoured families of standing in country places; but such private chapels were few and scattered. The mass of those who still professed themselves openly to be Catholics could not live a Catholic life. On top of this was the fact that any open profession of Catholicism debarred a man from all the chief fields of public action. The astonishing thing is not that so few as half the sympathisers with the old religion – that is, so few as one-eighth of the country – still openly professed Catholicism; the astonishing thing is that so many as one-eighth should have professed at all!

It is not often recognized, but it is an historical truth of the first moment, that Catholicism under English law was more thoroughly persecuted than under any other law in Europe, and that special persecution of this sort hardly applied to any other Christian body. The Huguenots in France were not only tolerated, they were privileged; and when later the effort was made to suppress the remnant of them, it raised a violent outcry.

---

thized in varying degrees and had family traditions of varied strength but would not risk place and business by open declaration or did not feel strong enough to take up such a position.

In close connection with this question of Catholicism in England and the effort to tolerate it at the end of the Monarchy, is the popular feeling against France. This was based upon the age-long antagonism between the French and the English peoples – an antagonism based on violent contrasts in temperament, but much more on the difference of religion. There entered into it also the proximity of the alien power and its domination of European thought and social habit during this last half of the seventeenth century.

Louis XIV in these years of the '60's of the century was claiming by right of his Spanish wife the inheritance of the Spanish Netherlands, the territory which today we call Belgium. He had raised a large army for the seizure of the towns on the north-eastern frontiers of his kingdom by right of his claim. The claim had got legal basis, but behind Louis's intention was the determination to put an end to the national danger of that open frontier of the north-east, as it was from the Spanish Netherlands that had come for a century and a half those invasions which had aimed directly at Paris and had penetrated deeply into the heart of the country. It was to make this impossible for the future that Louis XIV moved to occupy the Belgian towns and had them fortified, so as to form a wall as it were against further peril.

In doing so, the French King depended upon a sort of alliance with the merchants of the northern Netherlands, that is, what today we call Holland. For the Spanish power was for these also an enemy of long standing as being the power against which they had established their independence.

When Charles declared war against the Dutch his policy was strongly supported by popular opinion in London and by the city, and enthusiastically by the House of Commons. He was voted for the first and last time in his life a sufficient supply, and in this movement for the attack on Holland, wherein the Duke of York acquired such towering fame as Admiral of the Fleet, a great part was played by the animosity which Englishmen felt against the French power. There was even a moment when the English Government allied itself with the Dutch, and later with the Swedes (the ephemeral thing was thus called the "Triple Alliance"), in order to make Louis accept the terms of his Spanish opponents.

The whole thing was complicated and unreal. The Dutch merchants themselves were secretly approaching the King of France for an understanding. The King of France did not seriously want to pursue a quarrel with England – it was all to his advantage that the two commercial and maritime powers, England and Holland, should be in rivalry. Meanwhile, this same King of France was secretly treating with the Emperor for an eventual partition of the Spanish Empire when the reigning King of Spain should be dead. It was not the Triple Alliance which caused Louis to make peace with Spain, it was this secret treaty of his with the Emperor.

But that the Triple Alliance should have come into its brief moment of existence and that it should still be referred to with enthusiasm by our Whig historians does show the strength of popular feeling in England against the French Monarchy. We should always bear that feeling in mind when we come to the next phase, when Charles completed his private understanding with his cousin of France and played the French subsidies against his rebellious Parliament.

There is a last point to be emphasised before we leave this first half of the active reign: before we come to the critical turning point of 1670. The personal attachment of his people to the King (and to the combination of Charles and James in spite of their opposing characters) undoubtedly grew during these years.

We shall see, in particular when we deal with the naval story, how the reputation of the Duke of York grew in those years and what high standing his great victory against the Dutch by sea gave him in English eyes. But the Duke of York was never personally popular either with the people of London or the English people at large. His closed character forbade that; but his brother, the King, was popular, and increasingly popular as time went on. His defects were of just the kind which a populace admires or condones, especially a town populace of a capital. The deserved reputation of a rake was in his favour with them, but that was the smallest part of the business. What counted more was that his courtesy and kindness to all those about him created a legend in his favour which he also deserved and which spread rapidly from his immediate circle to the generality of his subjects.

The King, remember, deeply loved the sea, and that mood was already one with which English were in sympathy. He had taken pleasure in the sea after a fashion they understood; also he was an athlete, a great rider, skilful and energetic, and one might say, industrious at his moments, and (what Englishmen love) skilful at games. His tennis, to which he was devoted, was famous.

All this fitted in with the national temper. But perhaps what did most for the King's popularity was his courage and energy daring the Great Fire Of London (1666). He and the Duke of York worked physically with all their might during that disaster and the public remembrance of their active devotion to the public service persisted.

One can sum up the general situation at the end of this first half of the long passage which Charles made from his restoration to his temporary re-establishment of the Throne, by saying that it was a fair voyage, sailing "full and by."

The passage promised to be as prosperous in the next ten years as it had been in these first ten. Storm was coming but there was no premonition of it. The main event which was to change all was as yet unsuspected when the critical year of 1670 opened. In the preceding year that event had already stirred, but as yet men knew it not.

Catherine of Braganza

AN OIL PAINTING BY OR AFTER DIRK STOOP CA. 1661

THE FLEET AND EMPIRE

T IS DEBATABLE WHAT FRUIT OF STUART STATESMANSHIP AND especially of Charles II's foresight should come first in its advantages to England.

Had the King succeeded in finally and permanently restoring Kingship that certainly would have been the major fruit of his action. But failing this there were side effects of his judgment and command which have affected the whole future of the country and greatly to its advantage; the first of these is undoubtedly the complete establishment of the Navy. What had been tentative and embryonic until the restoration of Charles to his throne became, after 1660, by his own action and that of his brother James (who was the direct chief at the Admiralty), that capital political asset of the British people: a formed and permanent preponderant naval power.

Charles and James Stuart could not, of course, have done what they did but for the strong foundation already laid by their father with his special levy of ship-money, whence, as from one creative act, the whole story of the British Fleet derives. Nor could the two brothers have had, so early as 1665, the fine force then available at sea but for the long training of personnel, the long experiments in naval action, under the Commonwealth.

But all these beginnings of the affair left loose ends. There was no permanent navy in being with its rules, traditions, school of tactic and the rest, until Charles II and his brother confirmed and established the Fleet. The Fleet of England, which was to determine her own fate and the fate of half the world until 1914, was made by these last Stuart Kings, Charles II and his brother James II.

It may be presumed that if Charles had been free to take over the direction of naval affairs himself, he would have been as great a leader or Admiral as our history knows; not only because he had the sea in his blood and the whole habit of it stamped on to his youth so vividly, but because he was an excellent practical designer, because he studied deeply all the problems of the dockyard, oversaw the draw-ings and models and took a passionate interest in every side of the business: and also he knew better than any other public man the all-importance of sea-power to England: he repeated it, emphasised it and maintained it as did no other; and against what odds! But James ran him close in devotion to the trade, equalled him in an appreciation of what it meant to England, and had opportunities which Charles never had of command in action. No one has behaved better under these opportunities than the Duke of York. No one got greater naval fame early in life than he, nor more deservedly, though his experience was so brief.

The United Provinces, with their great market and Bank at Am-sterdam and their highly developed sea-power, were the commercial rivals of England, not only in their imports from the East, wherein they had greatly the advantage over us, but also in their trade with the West Indies, and further in their carrying trade, wherein more than in other departments Amsterdam was the rival and as yet the superior of London.

In the early years of the reign, immediately after the Restoration, the Dutch were in alliance with France. Louis XIV, just beginning his active reign, was envisaging, upon the death of his brother-in-law the King of Spain, the putting in of his wife's claim (which meant in practice the claim of the French King himself) to what had come to be called the Spanish Netherlands; that is, to those provinces which, during the turmoil of the Reformation, had retained their traditions and remained loyal to their legitimate sovereign at Madrid – mainly through disgust with the Calvinism of the ruling great merchants of the Northern Netherlands, based on Amsterdam.

If Louis were to make an effort to occupy and administer the nine completely Catholic provinces of the Southern (or Spanish) Netherlands, an alliance between him and the seven United Provinces of the north and their Calvinistic merchant oligarchy would serve the double purpose of weakening Spain and leaving him free from anxiety on the left flank of his action. If or when, therefore, the trade rivalry between London and Amsterdam should once more lead to conflict between the Dutch and the new English King, as it had already led to conflict between the Dutch and Cromwell before them, England might have to meet the French as well as the Dutch naval power. But

French naval power was as yet ill developed and, further, young Louis had no desire to handicap himself by serious engagement against the new and growing naval power of England.

On this account the First Dutch war of Charles was little more than a duel between the Dutch and English Fleets. In that duel one great action off Lowestoft sufficed to establish the high reputation of James (June, 1665).

In that action he first used his new and personal tactic of the line. This was a capital revolution in the story of naval warfare, and there is no reason to doubt the contemporary and subsequent opinion that we owe this to James himself. Hitherto naval action had been commonly by units – individual actions of ship against ship. James fought with the whole of his command in line, discharging from all his starboard guns as he sailed northward in front of the enemy fleet, then going about and using his port batteries in the southward run. By the end of the day it was a victory and might have been a decision, but for a false order given by a subordinate during the pursuit of the defeated Dutch Fleet in the night, after James had gone below.

For all the long hours of that summer's day he had been in the greatest danger, with friends killed at his very side and his clothes splashed with their blood. He had won; and he amply deserved the reputation of that victory.

What he did *not* deserve, but what his ill-fortune burdened him with, was the still mysterious order to shorten sail during the pursuit.†
There was no decision, but the issue was put off until further fighting should establish the one or the other naval power as supreme.

This first very famous action and victory of the Duke of York does not directly touch on the thesis of this book, but it must be emphasised only that we may remember the great place which the young commander, in his thirty-first year, took in the eyes of his countrymen who were later to be his subjects. After that naval success he was recalled to land, Sandwich took over the command and (to his

---

† During the night after the battle and while the languid pursuit of the defeated enemy was proceeding before a light breeze, an officer of the Duke of York (a member of the House of Commons) ordered sail to be shortened and the enemy so escaped – James was asleep. Why that order was given by a subordinate has never been explained.

bitter disappointment) the naval career of James seemed to have been checked at its very outset.

The reason for the recall has been debated. It is commonly put down to fears for the succession; Charles's Braganza wife had given him no heir and the mortal peril in which James had stood during all that long and fierce naval action certainly made a deep impression on his mother and his brother and on all those who were concerned with the precarious continuity of the Crown. But the succession could hardly have been the only reason. Had it been so James would not have been sent against the Dutch again when, eight years later, it had become quite certain that Catherine of Braganza could give Charles no heir and that the succession plainly depended upon the survival of James.

This glorious re-entry of English sea-power upon the stage bore unfortunately little fruit for the moment. It was contemporary with the Great Plague which paralysed the action of London and halved the living force of England (1665). It was followed by the immeasurable disaster of the Great Fire (1666) and (what was worse in its moral and political effect on the country) it was followed by the disastrous policy of the House of Commons in refusing further supply for the Fleet. This wretched piece of spite or parsimony – and certainly of short-sightedness – led ultimately to the King's reliance on foreign subsidy: for the Fleet was vital to England and as Parliament would not supply the funds for it these funds must be found elsewhere.

In the first flush of enthusiasm for the war, an enthusiasm nourished by the City with its great mercantile interests, its beginnings of banking, and consequent rivalry with Amsterdam, large supplies had been voted over and above the insufficient annual revenue already established. But the Commons had no method in what they did. The rich men who had had to pay the subsidies began to fear further burdens, and though there was as yet no renewal of the smouldering conflict between the Crown and its wealthier subjects, discontent with continued levies of money was sufficient to tempt the Commons to refuse further aid in any amount sufficient for that critical moment. Moreover the desire of these rich men to control government got stronger every year. The Commons were told that if they remained deaf to all appeals the Fleet would have to be laid up. There would even be danger of invasion. But they were not moved (1666).

The result of their attitude was the presence in the next year (1667) of Dutch men-of-war in the estuary of the Thames, and the Medway. The Dutch guns were heard in London. English deserters manned and piloted the Dutch first-raters, because they were angry at the arrears in their pay, and they helped at the burning, by the enemy, of some of the finest units in Charles's fleet.

This shameful and happily unique episode in the history of the Royal Navy proceeded wholly from the strange policy of the merchants and squires in Parliament in refusing supply to the King for the maintenance of the Fleet. It was only while the ships were laid up and the crews largely dispersed that the enemy raid was possible.

This first Dutch war did have one great effect on history, initiated at this time – the occupation of the Hudson and of the established Dutch Settlement known as New Amsterdam on Manhattan Island at the mouth of the great river.

*****

One of the major actions of the Stuarts was the founding, erection and confirmation of the British Colonial Empire.

Many modern Englishmen, caught by the enthusiasm of their time, would say it was the greatest Stuart action of all, for the conception of an oceanic domain throughout the world, of its glory and of its presumed permanent benefits, is still strong in the English mind. For some indeed the word "Empire" has almost replaced the word "England."

Those who think thus "Imperially" exaggerate in many ways and misjudge still more. The strength of England does not reside in such things, but in her financial position, in her now irradicable aristocratic constitution of society and in her Fleet. Moreover, the Colonial expansion of England is but one half, and the less important half, of her territorial basis. The more important part by far is India. But both India and the Dominions arose through, and are functions of, the Fleet.

No matter. That which is called today "The British Empire," as also that larger (and not coincident) thing, "the English-speaking world," is the creation of the Stuart century, of the four Stuart reigns, and in particular and especially is it the creation of the third Stuart reign, that of Charles II.

THE FLEET AND EMPIRE

It would be absurd to say that Charles himself or even his father and grandfather made the thing. It is not good history to regard the four Stuart Kings as the chief conscious factors in that development, but it is much worse history to leave out of English history the capital truth that the Colonial Empire and the English-speaking world in general were planted and grew under the Stuarts. The New World still carries about it the mark of the Stuart time.

In a future perhaps not very remote, Englishmen may see this organism, "The Empire," either in dislocation or decay or turned into something alien and unconnected with themselves. In such a detachment they will be able to judge it better and they will see how truly it sprang from the seventeenth century and how even the occupation of India, even the new colonial system following upon the Napoleonic Wars, are connected with a Stuart origin. For the whole thing centres in the British Fleet and the British Fleet was the creation of the two Charleses and of James II.

So much for the general thing: now for a most important particular point. *The new departure dates from the occupation of New York.*

The strategic key-point, the capture and holding of which made possible a united English-speaking seaboard beyond the North Atlantic and the consequent expansion therefrom inland, was the island group at the mouth of the Mauritius (or Hudson) River, the southern tips of Manhattan and Long Islands, and the opposing shore to the west of them. That decisive event – the taking of what we call "New York" – fell wholly within the personal reign of Charles II, and within the most active years of that reign. It is sketched or attempted, the first blow struck, in 1664. The work is concluded within ten years. By the Treaty of Breda in 1674 the town of New Amsterdam and its dependencies are formally and finally made over by the Dutch Republic to the English Crown. From that day forward British North America and later the United States were assured.

Now why was this? Why does all turn on the acquisition of "New York"?

If you will look at a map of the North Atlantic eastern seaboard you perceive at once that it is backed by a long system of not very high, but yet mountainous, hills. They form, not continuously but as a whole, a sort of wall or barrier. They are not such as to prevent travel through them and political expansion beyond them. They are not a permanently serious obstacle. But the forests with which they were covered in the seventeenth century and the absence of a settled population, the lack of roads, did make of that belt a natural frontier. On the one side was the coastal strip, on the other the vast almost unknown interior.

Add to this main geographical structure the capital fact that, in a time and place where water carriage was far and away the most important means of transport, *the Hudson was the one transverse highway.* Though there were wide sheets of water such as the Delaware Bay stretching far inland from the Atlantic, there was no river, save this one, which could bear heavy traffic from one side to the other of the barrier chain. That one exceptional means of transport was the broad and (in all its last southern half, the deep) stream which its first masters had called the Mauritius River in honour of Maurice of Nassau, their military hero, but which their English-speaking successors called the Hudson after one of the earliest, but not the first, discoverers of that drowned valley.

The bed of the Hudson and its continuation northward through Lakes George and Champlain towards the St. Lawrence not only form a natural highway from the Atlantic seaboard to the interior, breaching the barrier hills, but also a strong line of cleavage, a fundamental division, between the group of territory to the east and north and the continuous territory to the south. The Hudson Valley geographically cuts off what later became the States of New York and those of New England from the States developing from, and continuing, the original example of Virginia in the south.

The Hudson Valley is not only thus the appointed and inevitable boundary between the one territorial group of English-speaking settlements of the Atlantic seaboard and the other – the inescapable dyke dividing north from middle and south – it is also by far the best entry for commerce and for immigration.

All the other American eastern rivers are shallow. The fluvial system of the Atlantic seaboard throughout its 1,500 miles from the St. Lawrence has no other good navigable water-way but the Hudson.

Moreover, New York Bay at the sea end of that waterway, is exceptionally well suited for the approach of transport. It is almost completely landlocked. Once you have got through "The Narrows" you are in full security. Whole fleets of such a maximum draught as then was known can lie in that sheet of water, and the shores of Manhattan were available for wharfage.

All this the Dutch, the pioneers of that time, the most eager and the most advanced commercial group in Europe, had perceived. In the first years of the seventeenth century, from 1609, the young commonwealth of lowland provinces in rebellion against their constitutional government, the throne of Spain, had founded in New York Bay, at the point of Manhattan Island, what they called New Amsterdam. It was regularly organised, fortified and pallisaded under a political authority appointed from the Northern Calvinist Netherlands in Europe and kept in continual touch with what was then the greatest commercial power of the day and might well have become the dominating commercial power of the future.

The few inhabitants of that settlement on Manhattan Island in 1664 were of mixed origin not only Dutch, but Swedish, French Huguenot, with some proportion also of English-speaking settlers from near at hand. But its political direction was from the United Provinces and in particular from Holland.† This town in Manhattan Island was an outpost of the robust and hugely increasing Dutch commercial system, with its newly founded Bank of Amsterdam. By the time of Charles's First Dutch War it had been held for fifty years by the United Provinces and bid fair to establish itself permanently as the main outpost of Northern Europe, upon the American Atlantic seaboard.

Had it so matured, the unity of the infant English-speaking settlements on that same seaboard could never have been achieved. They were already sufficiently separated by varying religious traditions and varying political ideals. With a flourishing well-defended foreign military and commercial centre dividing the one group from the other there could have been no English-speaking colonial system nor any future United States.

New Amsterdam, thus established as the strategical and political key-point of all that shore, was challenged. It was challenged first indirectly then directly by the Stuart power. The challenge succeeded. Hence "America."

---

† It will be remembered that the name "Holland" which is now given to a Sovereign State, formerly the Northern Spanish provinces, originally belongs to one only of these, the wealthiest, centred in Amsterdam.

CHARLES II: THE LAST RALLY

The occupation of New Amsterdam, in the First Dutch war, was not of immediate permanent effect, for it was ratified by no permanent treaty. But in the Second Dutch War, which came with the turnover of policy after 1670 and Charles's new attachment to French interests, New Amsterdam passed permanently to the Kings of England, and was rechristened after the Duke of York, whose name it now continues, attached to the greatest port and city of the New World. When New Amsterdam, already christened New York, became permanently British at the Peace of Breda, one major result of the Stuart maritime policy had taken root: a continuous English-speaking control had been established over the farther shore of the North Atlantic from the Carolinas to Maine.

There came later in Charles's reign another piece of Colonial policy which a careful appreciation will discover to be only second in importance to the capture of the Hudson key line and a foundation for all the large expansion which was to follow. This second piece of Stuart statecraft is a direct fruit of the temperament, talents and judgment of the King; its name is Pennsylvania.

Though this capital development belongs to the later years of the reign, fifteen years and more after the first grasp on the Hudson and nearly ten years after this hold upon the completed Colonial line was established by the Treaty of Breda, we must allude to it here for it is in direct connection with all Charles's work in establishing the English Colonial system.

William Penn received his grant and charter from the fervent goodwill of Charles and James. That grant and charter lie at the root of all later Western expansion of English speech and custom over what was later to be called the United States; and he received it from the friendship and sympathy of Charles II and of James, Duke of York, who was a special supporter of Penn as the son of an Admiral and as one of these Nonconformists whom the two Royal brothers made it their policy to protect.

The reasons that Pennsylvania is thus of the highest importance in the story of the English-speaking New World are both moral and geographical.

Morally, Pennsylvania founded that system of political and religious neutrality without which the coming expansion would have been impossible. Geographically the new colony of Pennsylvania was planted as a gate giving entry to the Ohio valley and thence to the Upper Mississippi beyond.

So much emphasis has been laid in our histories upon the New England states (the colonies which were later to be the Puritan group of States between the Hudson and the French settlements to the far north) that the role of Pennsylvania is obscured. Yet a very elementary knowledge of the map is enough to prove to anyone who follows the story, though it be for the first time, that not New England but Pennsylvania did the trick. The pioneers who gradually extended the influence of the eastern seaboard into the interior, and so built up what was to become the United States, were of every kind and origin and among them can be found numerous settlers and migrants from the states of New England; but the door through which all had to pass, the political society which determined the western movement, was not that of New England with its peculiarly Calvinistic traditions, but that of the broad, wise, and just William Penn: the Quaker who founded Pennsylvania, and bequeathed his spirit to his followers.

The southern colonies, Virginia and the Carolinas, had an economy of their own, more or less connected with which were the societies of Maryland and Delaware. That economy had developed upon lines which may fairly be called aristocratic. The great estates were largely cultivated by slave labour, a thing of specifically English origin, based upon the trade in negroes, seized and carried off to the slave markets of the New World. At the origin of this slave trade stands the name of John Hawkins, who trained Drake and was the head of all that early group. The southern colonies based on slave labour were led and dominated by men accustomed to wealth, to ease, to a European level of culture. They continued in some degree the squires of seventeenth and eighteenth century England. But, more than these, they had felt the influence of French culture and the Cartesian clarity. Also they had wine.

This southern group of colonies it was which presided over the first growth of America and gave the new United States their tone, constitution and direction. But their general unity came from two moves: (1) the occupation of the Hudson river-mouth, and (2) the foundation of Pennsylvania. *Both these things attach directly to the personality and will of Charles Stuart, Charles II, King of England, as also to those of his brother James.*

THE SUNKEN REEF

NE DAY WHEN I HAD LANDED FROM MY LITTLE BOAT IN A HAR-
bour of South Devon I came across a sailor man who discussed with me the loss of a foreign man-of-war which had
struck an uncharted rock. In talking of the wreck he used a
phrase with which I was unfamiliar and which has stuck in my mind
ever since. He said, "She struck a sunken reef !" Of uncharted rocks I
had heard often enough as also those very dangerous obstacles which
do not uncover even at the lowest tides such as the Varne in the
Straits of Dover or the Druid's Mare. But the phrase "A sunken reef"
was new to me. Apparently it was, in whatever place this man came
from, an ordinary term for a danger of this kind.

Now what happened to the great experiment of Charles Stuart,
second of that name, is precisely that he whose leading talent was
that of the helmsman, he who was to steer so successfully through so
many difficult passes, and in all appearance reach his goal at last, failed
– because in the course of that passage he struck a Sunken Reef.

Let us be clear what this disastrous obstacle was. It was not the
passionate hatred then felt (in 1670) by a strong minority of Englishmen for the Roman Church. It was not even the general dislike of the
Faith which was felt by the majority. It was the presence in his own
mind, and in that of his brother James, of an imperative attraction,
the satisfaction of which was incompatible with the accomplishment
of Charles's great political aim in life: an imperative attraction towards
the Catholic Church.

It was not even James's open and loyal profession of what had
become for most men a hostile creed that ruined the great experiment
at restoring English Monarchy. James was driven out after Charles's
death on account of his religion; but he might well have been tolerated
if the long preparatory period under his brother, the reign of Charles
II, had not been filled with an increasing suspicion and fear of Popery.
The reason that the Crown crashed in 1688 was that the more active
and better organised forces in England had determined against Cathol-

icism even in individuals. They had determined against accepting a national dynasty the crowned heads of which were personally attached to Rome. This determination they would not have reached if, for twenty-four years before the death of Charles, there had not increasingly run through the English governing class a more and more active suspicion that Catholicism might become too powerful for their repose.

Those on either side who imagined that Catholicism could become, as late as 1670, once more the main religion of the English were imagining a vain thing. They were talking nonsense; and the better instructed of them were talking insincere nonsense. But what even the better instructed felt and what the bulk of middle class opinion in the towns, especially in giant London (the master place),† did sincerely feel was that something hostile to themselves as they now were and to their now rooted traditions was in danger of remaining permanently powerful among them.

*****

There are three principal steps in the transformation of England from the ancient Catholic Thing of a thousand years, the Thing of Bede and Alfred, of Edward, of the Plantagenets, of the Shrines and the Minsters – of the Mass – to the Proletarian England of today. Each of these steps is of greater moment than any economic, any social or constitutional development; for each vividly concerns the Soul of England, and from the Soul all outer things proceed.

These three steps were as follows:

The first was that accidental, capricious, breach with Christian unity which followed on a violent personal whim and passion, a disordered appetite, in Henry Tudor, legally pronouncing divorce between England and the general life of Europe – the Act of Supremacy, A.D. 1534. The marrow of that thing had been unconsidered, and its consequences quite unforeseen. Henry had fought for divorce with the angry gesture of an impatient man who pushes aside an obstacle upon a mountain path and lets loose an avalanche.

England was, as a result of that disturbance, to become, alone of the great provinces of the West, an enemy to the European Order. But

---

† Three overwhelming factors: money, activity, numbers. London handled the trade and all the banking; in London men met and energised one another as nowhere else, receiving all the news; London by 1670 already meant with its suburbs a quarter of a million, soon to be half a million souls in an England of six million.

for that fatality the Protestant rebellion against Authority would have failed. Only a scattered mass of small communities had so far been dragged into the stream of dissolution, but when England, England the Roman Foundation, lapsed, the balance was permanently altered. The catastrophe was confirmed by the vast spoliation of Church lands in Britain. Efforts at repair were made. A desire for reunion lingered before fading, but the thing was never undone; the wound was never healed.

The second step was Robert Cecil's Gunpowder Plot of 1605–1606. Sixty years and more had passed and the country was now in two parts, one Traditional, the other innovating and revolutionary in its Philosophy; one still Catholic in mind, the other moved by the mighty influence of Calvin. England might have remained so divided – to her political hurt – as France remained divided. Her fate ordered her to be one nation, and the Gunpowder Plot was the turning point in this doubtful balance.

The third step came sixty years later again – in 1669–1673 – when the dread of a Catholic dynasty arose. It was the final act whereby it became ultimately impossible for England now to be of the Faith again. The Catholic tradition had fought hard to survive. A large remnant of the Faithful remained true to their fathers, when the two men who were in succession to be Kings of the English, in days when kingship still stood in men's minds for the effective government of the nation, heard an inner summons to return to the ancestral Catholic home and so destroyed themselves and their line. These two men were the Royal brothers, Charles and James Stuart, sons of the martyred King who had laid down his life for the Protestant principle of separation; for the Establishment; for the National, as against the Universal Church. He had held his authority to be perfect. His sons demanded much more and attained that much more to their temporal ruin.

It behoves us to understand how the two brothers came to this frame of mind; how they separately approached that spell of Catholicism which its votaries proclaim to be Divine and its enemies abominable, while the rest stand by gaping and wondering what the quarrel is all about.

Let it be well remembered that it was these two men between them who changed the history of England through their recall to Rome, as it is with all who feel that command. It came to each in an individual fashion.

It is a personal influence. It gets hold of men and women (as some think to their destruction, as others think to their ultimate beatitude) by the same apprehension as does a romance or some strong mood of artistry; some particular form of music, some particular appeal of landscape. But there is another element, and more profound, therein. The individual soul hears the message as of a voice; the voice of a Majestic Personality. The newcomers are beckoned. They are called, as one may be called by a deep tune or a long regard; yet to each one so moved that demand or persuasion comes with a particular accent attuned to himself alone.

It is no exception, therefore, to find that Charles and James came by different roads to their City of God and entered by different gates.

*****

James, the younger brother of the King, first known as Duke of York, later (when he came to the throne) as James II, had a double effect on the reign of Charles himself and on the history of his country.

So far as Charles is concerned, that is during Charles's lifetime and reign, James was a sort of whetstone upon which the high talents of the elder brother could be sharpened, and that because the older brother was in such strong contrast to the younger.

Both men suffered the Stuart weakness of promiscuity, both of them had the Stuart strength of intellect, at a time when the emotions of ardent greed and a new religious myth were between them beginning to obscure intelligence. Both had that almost violent characteristic of the Stuarts, a passionate and determined patriotism. We would have to qualify the word, of course, in the case of the ancestor, James I of England, VI of Scotland, because he came to England as a foreigner; but his son Charles and his two grandsons Charles and James displayed this almost physical affection for England to the full.

Both were very courageous (though James had a greater opportunity for displaying courage); both were national in their devotion to physical exercises (James, especially – a horseman, forever in the saddle); both were, of course, marked with the same unmistakable concavity of profile which I have ascribed to their Florentine inheritance.

But with this catalogue the likeness ceases, James was far more self-centred, far more cut-off from the general sympathy of his kind and, consequently, far less understanding of men than his brother.

CHARLES II: THE LAST RALLY

There was never a man in the conduct of the English State, from its very origins to the death of the Monarchy in 1688, who had so thorough a knowledge of men as had Charles II. He knew what was passing in their minds. He understood all their frailties and made allowance, if anything too much allowance, for all the turpitude inherent in what is called "Public Life." James never knew what was passing in another man's mind or in a woman's either. He was perpetually showing surprise, where almost everyone else would have guessed long beforehand what was toward.

Two anecdotes will sufficiently illustrate this lack of comprehension in him. When he heard that Anne had betrayed him at the end and that her ridiculous husband *"Serait-ce possible"* ("Could it be possiblt?") had accompanied her flight, he spoke with all the bitterness of sudden discovery, saying that his very child had deserted him. The blow fell upon him unexpectedly and the more violently – though there was perhaps no one else in the Court who would have imagined any other end to the situation.

The other anecdote is this: in the autumn of 1687 there came, after many days of misunderstandings and troubles between him and his wife, a moment in which she refused to eat at the Royal table. She sat there with him, they two apart above the rest, as the rule of Royalty demanded; but she would not look up from her plate or take anything. Her husband was bewildered and alarmed. He took counsel of his spiritual adviser. His spiritual adviser said that probably the lady's sulkiness was due to his continual frequentation of a mistress and abandonment of his own wife. To James this whim of the Queen's was at first incomprehensible. He had thought the situation normal to Royalty. On being assured that things were indeed so and that Mary of Modena was consumed with jealousy, he handsomely made amends. He domesticated himself for a time and to that episode we owe the Old Pretender. It could not have been true of any other man or woman in the palace, that they should have been thus blind to an obvious situation.

But if this contrast between a thorough understanding of his fellow beings on the part of Charles and a complete lack of it on the part of James is the strongest difference between them, there are also many others.

The great talents of Charles were generalised. Their action was most conspicuous in politics, but in foreign politics as well as domestic. They were also apparent in such by-ways as marine construction and interest in scientific experiments. The talents of James were exercised in one field alone, that of admiralty. He was a great English seaman, and it was a misfortune at the time for the country that he had neither a free hand nor a continual and prolonged exercise of naval command. When he had it he exercised it with rapidity, decision and striking originality. We owe to him, as I have said, the line of battle as against individual ship action, the invention of signalling for the control of such line of battle, the formation of a complete and permanent body of naval officers.

Outside this department of admiralty, wherein he excelled, James was a loss rather than an asset.

Again, there went with the narrowness of James's temperament a sincerity in declaration and conduct quite different from Charles's subtlety and genius for negotiation. In a supreme test this was strikingly apparent. When his brother suggested to him a public reception of the Anglican sacrament, the better to conceal his real religious position, James answered in a famous phrase that by the Grace of God he would never do so base a thing. It would have been better for Charles had he been limited enough to make an equally heroic rejoinder.

James was strongly influenced by whatever woman was at his side, particularly by his first wife, Anne Hyde. It was thus that she, by her conversion to the full practice of Catholicism, brought him to the same conversion, in spite of his early aversion to his mother's religion. Charles was never under such female effect. *His* attachment to the Catholic faith proceeded from an experience of cities and of men, a strong sense of reality, and the single use of the intellect – this last an avenue of approach which has brought many into the Catholic scheme. No woman ever influenced Charles, either in this supreme matter or in any other. Never was a character less affected in the larger matters by the advice or mood of women.

As a consequence of this contrast between the two brothers there was a permanent contrast in their popularity. James had no friends. He often thought he had a friend, but always that friend betrayed him. Charles was universally beloved, beloved not only by the crowd of individuals with whom he came in contact, not only adored by his dependents, but thoroughly popular with the mass of his subjects and particularly with the poorer populace of London who knew him best.

CHARLES II: THE LAST RALLY

From all these causes the life of Charles had, on the surface, at least, an increasing mark of success about it; that of James was tragically marked by failure. Which of the two, after the functions of this life had ceased, enjoyed the better fortune we know not; for we cannot follow the adventures of the dead.

*****

Each of the brothers had begun by a mixture of indifference or aversion where the ancient Faith was concerned. Each would have been equally astonished (but in different ways) had he heard in early youth what would happen to his mind in manhood. Each was a highly individual case: but then, every conversion is a highly individual case. The strong English nationalism of Charles I and his two sons took, in the younger, the form of a distaste for French things; and as Catholicism had appeared to him through a French mother and the cousinship of the French Royal Family, he was the more in reaction against it. His hero in that military career to which he had desire to devote his life had been the (then) Huguenot Turenne.

James's closed soul was nowhere more tightly barred than in this prevention against the Catholic atmosphere of France. He was on his guard against it and – most deterrent of all emotions – he felt scorn for it. When the Faith came to him it came to him, I say, incredibly enough, through his wife; it was that astonishing marriage with Anne Hyde which, against all probability, ultimately turned out to be the deciding factor.

I have often wished for the leisure to write an even brief life of that strong woman. Ugly, upstanding, full of vitality and will, she came of a stock and of surroundings the most removed from the Catholic Faith in all England. Anne's father, that Edward Hyde whom we have seen as a chief influence in the youth of the two Royal brothers, was, by all the traditions of his blood and all his own habit, strongly bound up with the new anti-Catholic England. The class to which he belonged (the fairly well-to-do squires), the profession which he had tacked on to that class (the legal profession), had now acquired in all their traditions a rooted opposition to Catholicism. Apart from this the man himself felt a personal dislike of the Faith and at the same time confidence in its ultimate failure.

We have seen how he was one of those who belonged by natural temperament to the Protestant England that was already established and was in process of becoming the thing we now know.

When his daughter Anne had first refused James in his youth she was as much steeped in anti-Catholicism as he was. When the Royal fortunes changed and she had reason for returning to her capture, she and he were still in that strongly Protestant mood – a mood reinforced by patriotism.

She knew very well what she was about when she admitted James to her secret favours. The Restoration was at hand and to dominate him who would be next in succession to the Throne was now well worthwhile. She caught him and held him. When their child was to be born she constrained him to a marriage which would guarantee its legitimacy. All know the story of the way in which his own mother furiously battled to rescue him from such toils, how he himself wavered, how his most intimate friends were put up to slander Anne, how she triumphed over them all. Six months after the landing of Charles and James at Dover and the revolution in fortune which had made the Restoration certain, their child was born. James acknowledged himself the father, and in a little while Anne Hyde, saluted as Duchess of York, had firmly established herself. The Queen Mother capitulated; it was Mazarin who saw the wisdom of that. Her own father got rid of his violent opposition (if, indeed, it was sincere); her intelligence, her restraint, and what one may call her "stance" – her firmness of attitude, physical and moral – confirmed her in her great position.

By the second anniversary of the landing she was the well-established wife of the man who would presumably inherit the Crown of England, because Charles's new wife was soon regarded as incapable of giving him an heir. Her own children, as they were born and died, were the heirs to England. Her two daughters, Mary and Anne the younger, who alone survived among her children. were admitted apparent inheritors of the Throne.

Her moral power over her husband was absolute. Strong as was his own character, hers was stronger. They said that she led him by the nose in everything except his love affairs and certainly her convictions were impressed upon him as his could not be upon her.

Mark, then, this momentous accident. In the late winter of 1667, Anne Hyde being then a woman of thirty-one and having till recently followed with increasing devotion the Liturgy and Sacraments of the Church of England, doubted for the first time in her life the credentials of that Ministry in which she had been brought up and to which she was devoted. It was noticed that she did not communicate. There followed for two years what you may find not infrequently in the story of any conversion, a very great stress of doubt and attractions hither and thither.

When Communion at the Christmas feast of 1669 was taken, as the custom was, by the Royal Family in state, the Duchess of York publicly absented herself. At last she was received into the Catholic Church; but already that cruel stroke which was so soon to kill her had fallen. She died in great agony, of cancer of the breast, three years after the first stirring of her new vision and only a few months after her full acceptation of the Faith.

That powerful soul and body were tried with fearful agony – consonant to her vitality – and even at the end that powerful intelligence was repeating the phrase which haunts all minds – even the firmest – "What is truth?" Yet in the depths of the soul she had no doubt.

He who would understand the woman who set her mark so strongly upon the royal dynasty of England must read that declaration of her conversion which she wrote in sincerity and pride and which remains to us (I will quote it in full):—

Paper Written by the late Duchess of York

It is so reasonable to expect, that a Person always Bred up in the Church of England, and as well instructed in the Doctrine of it, as the best Divines and her capacity could make her, should be liable to many Censures, for leaving That and making herself a Member of the Roman-Catholick Church to which I confess, I was one of the greatest Enemies it ever had. That I choose rather to endeavour to satisfie my Friends, by reading this Paper, than to have the trouble to answer all the Questions that may daily be asked me.

And First, I do protest in the presence of Almighty God that no Person, Man or Woman Directly or Indirectly ever said anything to me (since I came into England) or us'd the least endeavour to make me change my Religion: it is a Blessing I owe wholly to Almighty God, and I hope the hearing of a Prayer I daily made him, ever since I was in France and Flanders; Where seeing much of the Devotion of the Catholicks (tho' I had very little myself) I made it my continual Request to Almighty God, That if I were not, I might before I died, be in the true Religion. I did not in the least doubt but that I was so, and never had any manner of Scruple till November last: When reading a Book call'd *The History of the Reformation*, by Doctor Heylyn, which I had heard very much commended, and had been told, if ever I had any Doubt in my Religion, that would settle me: instead of which I found it the Description of the horridest Sacriledges in the World, and could find no Reason why we left the Church, but for Three the most Abominable ones that were ever heard of amongst Christians: First, Henry the Eighth renounces the Pope's Authority, because he would not give him leave to part with his Wife, and marry another in her lifetime. Secondly, Edward the Sixth was a Child, and governed by his Uncle, who made his Estate out of the Church Lands. And then Queen Elizabeth, who being no Lawful Heiress to the Crown, could have no way to keep it, but by renouncing a Church that could never suffer so Unlawful a thing to be done by one of her children. I confess, I cannot think the Holy Ghost could ever be in such Counsels. And it is very strange that if the Bishops had no Design, but (as they say) the restoring to us the Doctrine of the Primitive Church, they should never think upon it till Henry the Eighth made the Breach upon so unlawful a Pretence. These Scruples being rais'd I begun to consider of the Difference between the Catholicks and Us, and Examin'd them as well as I could by the Holy Scripture: which I do not pretend to be able to understand, yet there are some things I found so easie, that I cannot but wonder I had been so long without finding them out: As the Real Presence in the Blessed Sacrament, the Infallibility of the Church, Confession and Praying for the Dead. After this, I spoke severally to Two of the best Bishops we have in England, who both told me, there were many things in the Roman Church, which (it were very much to be wish'd) we had kept; As Confession, which was, no doubt, Commanded by God: That Praying for the Dead was one of the Ancient things in Christianity: That for their parts, they did it daily, tho' they would not own it. And afterwards, pressing one of them very much upon the other Points, he told me. That if he had been bred a Catholick, he would not change his Religion, but that being of another Church, wherein, he was sure, were all things necessary to Salvation, he thought it very ill to give that Scandal, as to leave that Church, wherein he had receiv'd his Baptism.

All these Discourses did but add more to the Desire I had to be a Catholick, and gave me the most terrible Agonies in the world, within myself. For all this, fearing to be rash in a Matter of that Weight, I did all I could to satisfie my self: made it my daily Prayer to God to settle me in the Right, and so went on Christmas-day to receive in the King's Chappel: after which, I was more troubled than ever, and could never be in quiet till I had told my Desire to a Catholick; who brought a Priest to me, and that was the First I ever did Converse with, upon my Word. The more I spoke to him, the more I was Confirm'd in my Design; and as it is impossible for me to doubt of the words of our Blessed Saviour, Who says the Holy Sacrament is His Body and Blood; so I cannot believe, that He who is the Author of all Truth, and who had promis'd to be With his Church to the End of the World, would permit them to give that Holy Mystery to the Laity but in one Kind, if it were not Lawful so to do.

I am not able, or if I were, would I enter into Disputes with any Body: I only in short say this for the changing of my Religion, which I take God to Witness I would never have done, if I had thought it possible to Save my Soul otherwise. I think I need not say it is any interest in this World, leads me to it. It will be plain enough to everybody, that I must lose all the Friends and Credit I have here, by it, and have very well weighed Which I could best part with, my share in this World, or the next: I thank God, I found no difficulty in the Choice.

My only Prayer, is That the poor Catholicks of this Nation may not suffer for my being of their Religion; that God would but give me Patience to bear them, and then send me my Afflictions in this World, so I may enjoy a Blessed Eternity hereafter.

St. James's Aug. 20. 1670

It was not possible that, with such an example before him, James, being what he was, inflexible in one line of action, and so isolated that a permanent companion would determine the current of his mind, should not have followed her.

That she was dead and that she had died so horribly moved him the more. He had queried, as many another has queried since, the possibility of accepting the Faith without suffering the consequences of such publicity. But when he was told that the thing could not be done, that to be a Catholic forbade concealment he accepted Authority at once and thenceforward never wavered.

We have just seen how, when Charles, intent upon that one continuous task of salvaging the Crown, bade James take the Anglican Communion publicly as a mere form while in private worshipping according to his own new conviction, James answered the proposal with the memorable words, "By the Grace of God I will never do so base a thing."

Charles heard that iron Phrase. Charles in his heart most vehemently agreed. But Charles did not follow. His business of this world was still the more important in his eyes.

Such was the process whereby the Duke of York went through those gates which closed behind him, which shut him out from his own people. Such was the road down which he went to his passion of abandonment, dethronement and exile.

*****

The approach of Charles was, as I have said, quite other. The Faith had first come – the first echo of it – when he was but twenty-one (we saw that adventure after Worcester in 1651): many years before it came within a hundred miles of James.

Yet James passed him in the middle of the race. It was not until the last moment of Charles's life that he bore witness as James had done, nor did he bear witness before the world as James had done but to two or three about his death-bed alone.

Thus was the seed sown by chance at Moseley which was to grow prodigiously but was to bear no full fruit for more than thirty years. Charles Stuart had these arguments in mind during the crossing of the Channel by night on that collier which saved him. They remained taking root slowly in some fashion or other during all his exile.

From the moment of his coming to France and in all that followed another factor appeared in the developing of Charles Stuart's religious experience, it was the factor of travel.

Now this factor is in any spiritual experience, especially in the approach of a modern and Protestant Englishman to the Catholic Church, of the highest importance. We may find it difficult to appreciate that truth today because modern travel is for the most part of hardly any spiritual value whatever; I mean it leads to no expansion of the spirit, it leads to no new inward experience worth having, and this is especially true of modern travel as it is undertaken today by the leisured classes, in which I include our official historians, the academic people.

They may go to Italy, France and Belgium, the Rhine country; they may see the ancient grace of Austria or Spain, and come away with no more knowledge of what the Catholic Church is or has been than they started with, when they left home. The degree of that knowledge when they started was very little over zero and remains on much the same level when they return. I have in mind one acquaintance out of many who acted for England in certain important matters during all the course of the Great War, moving perpetually through North Italy. He came home under the vague impression that a Sung Mass was an office which invariably took place in the late afternoon or evening. It is a tiny detail but illuminating, as it would be if a Frenchman who had spent all his time in England during the Great War went back home under the impression that the English Bible was the Vulgate in its original Latin, or that the Chant of Evensong in Canterbury Cathedral was the Gregorian, or that the Thirty-nine Articles were press cuttings from a newspaper.

Well, the modern traveller moves by road or rail through a foreign country at a pace which permits him to see nothing. He spends the most part of his leisure in cosmopolitan hotels which give him no conception of the people about him. His guide-book furnishes him with names which connote to *him* nothing of the Christian past.

But the man who travelled abroad in the mid-seventeenth century, even when he travelled in state, saw and heard the people; a man who moved continually as did Charles from one difficult strain to another, short of cash, anxious, depressed, saw thoroughly enough the men among whom he moved. He could actually feel and touch in Holland, for instance, the contrast between the Calvinist merchant oligarchy and the Dutch Catholic population – by that time a minority – which lived side by side with them. In France he could see the current of popular life in every town he passed through. He would appreciate among the commercial classes the strength and character of Huguenotry. Even among his grander relations, even under the roof of the House of Orange, Charles would experience many aspects of the Continental world and they would leaven a mind of such intelligence and vigour.

In those long years then, which were the stuff of his early manhood, from twenty-one to thirty, he had obtained through his very suffering and difficulties a special education. It was more than an instruction, it was an increasing knowledge of culture and a knowledge acquired in the very best way whereby such a knowledge can be acquired, the very opposite of the academic fashion: life.

Now it is an invariable experience that a man with wide and manifold contacts among the forces of Western Europe makes real acquaintance with the Catholic Church. Its power of attraction and repulsion is always present with him and strong, and a man so circumstanced sees what may be called the landscape of Catholicism, not only in its unity but in its infinite vitality and variety. Here we get another contrast between the two brothers in what was for each the chief accident of his life.

The Faith came to Charles largely, widely, in multiple fashion; it came to James through the impress of one character always at his side – his wife, and of a will, even stronger than his own strong will. James Stuart in this greatest of human discoveries approached it by a straight path, he saw it through a narrow window; Charles Stuart approached it through the whole breadth of a campaign, he saw it not through any window but in the open, under the main vault of the sky.

Charles, in this capital matter, was vastly more privileged than his brother and yet could not act, or thought he could not act, with the uncompromising directness of his brother. He still hesitated, he still delayed.

With neither of these two men did the growing national hostility to Catholicism weigh very much. I mean it did not in either case deflect their vision of what each had discovered. Charles's reason for concealing his convictions and delaying the act which his conscience cried out to him to perform was political. He thought first of the Throne. He was indifferent to the convictions of his fellow Englishmen, his subjects; and the same was true of James. James was even more indifferent to the anti-Catholic mood of the majority. But that mood was of powerful effect in making Charles hesitate, or rather refuse, to declare himself, and it was of catastrophic effect in ruining the life of James. Whether acting straight-forwardly in the uninstructed mob or in the more cultured Protestant middle classes or acting obliquely and by intrigue through the influence of men like Shaftesbury or Danby, the national opposition to the Catholic Church was the principal matter of the time and we must here pause to consider its nature.

The main element was *national* consciousness, which had been growing ever since the later Middle Ages. Nationalism was not universal as it is today, but it was already, by 1660, the prevailing mood. Many hated Catholicism on its own account. A large proportion of this "many" were so clear-minded as to hate the actual doctrines which they could define and which they opposed; but for most men the root of the matter was the conflict they felt between the national ideal and the cosmopolitan Faith of Europe.

That is why the intense and sometimes violent antagonism of the English governing class to Protestant nonconformity was of a different texture and quality altogether from its opposition to Catholicism.

CHARLES II: THE LAST RALLY

Generations later our official historians (their strength does not lie in historic imagination) speak of these early Nonconformists as though they were modern dissenters and think it quite natural that toleration should have been extended to them – but not to the Papists. In the eyes of most modern Englishmen the Nonconformist, the Church of England man, and, for that matter the most complete sceptic are, if they be Englishmen, all of one stuff, which stuff of course is a stuff of Protestant texture; for England today one may call uniformly Protestant, in general morals as in political outlook. The England of the seventeenth century, even of the later seventeenth century, was of a more varied make-up, but the main stream was flowing strongly against the Catholic tradition and its inheritors.

Another feeling closely bound up with this doctrinal one was the dislike and suspicion of France. The root of this hatred of France so strongly felt in England was, and still is, religious. For France is a main example of that Catholic culture which is in such bad odour with Englishmen. Between the two cultures of Western Europe Catholic and Protestant there is a direct irreconcilable difference in moral values and social habits.

But the Englishman's dislike of the French has another ingredient, almost as powerful as the contrast in religious culture, and that is the contrast in racial temperament. Your average Englishman today is more at home in Protestant Hamburg than in Catholic Cologne, but he is fairly at home in both; he does not feel himself at home in Amiens, and were you to put him among the most Protestant Huguenot society of Nimes he would feel it to be very alien to him.

This native and inescapable, instinctive, reaction of the Englishman against the Frenchman is exasperated whenever the French people are passing through a period of unity and therefore of strength. It is fairly quiescent when the French people are occupied in their favourite pastime of Civil War, latent or actual, because men do not hate a thing when they feel it to be weak as they hate it when they feel it to be strong. France in her miserable modern Parliamentary condition, France during the Civil Wars of the late sixteenth century, was tolerable enough to Englishmen; but France armed and united under one will with Government and people working together is quite another matter, and when a united France proceeds to win victories in the field and capture cities and provinces the situation is intolerable to the Englishman.

Now this moment of 1670–1674, when the Catholic sympathies of Charles and James were beginning to imperil the English Throne, was precisely the moment when French unity was at its strongest, and therefore French power in Europe at its highest.

The reign of Louis XIV garnered the fruits of Richelieu and of Mazarin, and the French Monarchy, worshipped by the whole people, was far the strongest thing in Europe. French administration was the best organised, it was the most central, it was the most prompt; and the permanent peril to French life and power – the German peril – was at its weakest in Louis XIV's day, through the advantage Richelieu had taken of the Thirty Years' War in the previous reign.

There is yet another element to be considered, the effect of London on the religious affair.

It has been well said that the two capitals of France and England, Paris and London, are the motive powers of all our modern history. If London had not been as much influenced as it was by the Reformation, the country as a whole would not have gone Protestant. If Paris had not been as strongly leavened as it was with Catholic enthusiasm the Huguenots might have won their battle.

If you test the thing numerically (a most imperfect test) you may say that not more than one-eighth of London was avowedly and openly Catholic in 1670. London followed here the average of the country. But the proportion of intensely anti-Catholic people in London was larger by far than the same proportion of them in the smaller county towns and far larger than the proportion in the villages which, we must always remember, made up the bulk of the English population at that time.

In London there was perpetual come and go, active contact, between minds, the news and foreign stimulus of a great port, the opportunity for getting together to plot or to organise; and in London there was concentrated wealth. Nearly all the growing credit system was housed in London. The money-lenders flocked to London, whether in the shape of scriveners like John Milton's father or of goldsmiths or of great territorial lords putting out their surplus at usury.

All over England the anti-Catholic feeling was strong; but in London it was of especial strength through its opportunities for concentration; and London radiating its influence, especially over the south and near-west, London's fear "lest the Pope should land at Wapping Old Stairs" (as Swift has it) was shared in the southern ports and along the great roads to the Channel and to the Severn Sea, to Bristol and to the East Anglian marts.

Some have said that a further ingredient in the anti-Catholic feeling of Restoration England was due to the vested interest of those who had made fortunes through the religious revolution of the previous century when from Henry VIII to James I, the Church was looted wholesale. There is both truth and falsity in this statement and it is important to distinguish between them.

There no longer remained between 1660 and 1690 any appreciable strength in what had not so very long before been the acute anxiety of the new Reformation millionaires, lest their new millions should be taken from them. They were now firmly settled, and there was no appreciable chance of their losing the great incomes which they had acquired through the destruction of religion. The orgy of loot which had rushed for Church lands and Church dividends of all kinds had filled the last ten years of Henry VIII (1537–1547). The tide still ran strongly during the next half-dozen years when the rich men who, in the reign of the sickly child Edward, made hay while the sun shone and swept into their pockets chantries and prebends and school endowments, and all the rest of the medieval inheritance.

Throughout Elizabeth's reign – that is right on to the end of the sixteenth century and beyond – the capital wealth of religion was still being looted in great wads. One Bishopric for instance was kept empty a whole lifetime while courtiers battened on its income, and the revenues of every See in England (notably those of Canterbury) were clawed at and snatched at and nibbled at continually to feed the new fortunes of a new nobility.

The estates of those who sympathised with the old religion were sporadically but effectually rifled and whenever an excuse could be found, estates were confiscated for the profit of the new men.

But all this main earthquake in the economic history of England had settled down half a century before the Restoration of Charles II. There was indeed a sort of aftermath of robbery conducted by the leaders of the Great Rebellion, men like Lambert and the rest, but confiscations and seizures by the Parliamentarians, though they were largely religious in excuse, were not specifically anti-Catholic. The Catholics would support every measure to restore landed property to something of its old arrangement for they would personally benefit by such a re-establishment of old titles and claims; but those who benefited by these later thefts were not specifically anti-Catholic – they were simply men who had the opportunity to steal and who therefore stole. Bradshaw, for instance, the Regicide judge, made it his business to dip for his private advantage into the dowry of the Queen.

Of any connection between anti-Catholicism and the Church lands there was, so late as 1660, little or nothing left; but there was a memory, an element of lingering doubt, which was to that effect.

We must remember that the fall of Charles I began with the violent quarrel of the Scotch landlords against him, when he began restoring ecclesiastical endowments which had been robbed from the Established Church in Scotland during his father's minority. The outcry raised by Charles's attempt to re-endow, not indeed Catholic livings, but Protestant Scotch livings, and to do it at the expense of the robbers started the whole business which ended in the scaffold at Whitehall. For that was the match which lit the train: that was the thing which bore fruit in the abortive Scotch War of 1640.

Now this war was not so far from the men of 1660 as the Great War is from ourselves, and the more recent confiscations were of yesterday. Men did not connect the Catholic minority in Restoration England with the threat of losing the wealth they made in the main religious upheaval of the sixteenth century. The Russells for instance (who had combined with their own accumulation that of the Wriothesleys) had no dread of losing their millions through the Catholic sympathies of the later Stuarts. But they did continue a strong family tradition, the core and strength of which was opposition to the Catholic Church at home and abroad.

There is one last thing to be said about the opposition to the ancient creed; those who still sympathised with the ancestral religion were perhaps a quarter of the country, those who actually confessed the ancient creed openly (which we know to have been at least one-eighth) worked at nothing like the potential of their opponents. In judging historical movements we must always estimate the intensity of motive and action as well as its mere numerical extent. If the Catholic-minded minority (and it was a large one) had been fanatical or even active it would have been a very different affair, but they were thoroughly cowed. They had not fallen as low as they have today, of course; they were still in touch with their fathers and in many families continuity with the past was unbroken – but in bulk the Catholics of Restoration England lay low.

Charles, then, could never restore monarchy in England unless he restored it as the monarchy of a people upon the whole Protestant. Therefore, though his mind in its maturity fully accepted the authority of the Catholic Church, to admit publicly his submission to that authority was too hard for him; it would mean the sacrifice of all his life's work. Therefore, that submission must be postponed.

Years before his younger brother had turned to the religion of Europe, Charles was already fully convinced – but would not move. He had seen reality – but he would not openly acknowledge it. He had been touched so deeply that when James after his own conversion urged him to declare himself his eyes filled with tears. He passionately affirmed his conviction. He would in due time act upon it, but not now...not now. So it was in the tenth year of his active reign, so it was to be up to the last extreme of life, to the edge of death, even up to that last scene in the sick chamber amid the royal hangings of Whitehall, when that same Huddleston, the priest of the Flight from Worcester, comes in by a side door and receives the King at last.

It is not for us to weigh the credit and the debit of others in the supreme matters of the soul. We know the obvious rule in black and white; having come into touch with reality, having grasped the truth, we must bear witness to it at all costs. So James did to his eternal honour; but so Charles could not, because the cost was so desperately, so ruinously high. What! Must he give up that to which he had devoted the whole of so militant, so finely militant a life? Must he sacrifice all that intelligent, tenacious helmsmanship? Must he lose the prize for which he had steered that ship during more than thirty years of stress and ceaseless labour?

Yes, that was the price demanded of him – and he could not pay it. Never was a higher price demanded of any man. Let no man say that he would himself have paid it. No such demand was made upon the brother James but on *him,* Charles, the demand was made, and it was too great.

Yet though he did not respond, he lost most thoroughly all that for the sake of which he had refused to respond.

*****

The Craft in her fair sailing had struck a Sunken Reef. She sprang a leak whereby she slowly filled, and it was to sink her.

THE TRIANGLE

FTER THE TREATY OF DOVER THE BATTLE BETWEEN KINGship and private wealth is finally engaged. The pretext or weapon of religion is directed against James the heir to Kingship and therefore against Kingship itself. Kingship could not have survived even as precariously as it did had not Charles used with such talent or genius the cards which fate had dealt out to him and in especial the interplay of French Alliance, Dutch need and the ambition of the plutocracy in Parliament with the shadow of the City of London and its banking power behind all.

Let us appreciate the elements of the high game Charles Stuart had to play during those critical years.

The rightful government of England, which Charles had inherited, which it was the business of Charles to restore, was Monarchy, hereditary to his family. Most Englishmen at the moment of the Restoration would have applauded that object – indeed, all of them except a minority of enthusiasts who still clung to the memory of the Great Rebellion, and a still smaller minority of men who had made their fortunes out of the loot and swindling, blackmail and common theft which always accompany grave social disturbance.

But though the general spirit of the country took Monarchy for granted and accepted its full restoration, there had arisen in fact – and was now part of political reality – a wealthy governing class which had challenged the Crown to battle in the Civil Wars; and had won.

Not only could the memory of that decisive victory never be effaced, but it had changed, without their willing it, the whole spirit of the English gentry, of the lawyers and of the great merchants and money-dealers with whom both lawyers and gentry were now inextricably mixed up. Wealth – in some degree consciously but in a much greater degree unconsciously – challenged the Royal power.

All this is commonplace; repeated here perhaps too often, but to be emphasised whenever this crisis in the story of England is told.

Further, we must repeat that the manner in which the challenge to the Royal power would be delivered by wealth, the instrument that would be used for making that challenge good, was Parliament and particularly the lower House of Parliament: the House of Commons; that is, a great committee of landowners and leading lawyers and other forms of wealth. The reason the House of Commons must thus inevitably act against the Monarchy was that no one can live without an income, and that the King's Government now had no income save such as might be voted by the House of Commons. The old Royal revenue by which the Crown had lived had disappeared. It was replaced by a vote taken in the House of Commons and granting the King such and such an income a year.

That income was wholly insufficient for three reasons:

I.— The value of money was already changing rapidly at a moment when the amount required by the Crown was being calculated. It continued to change. The precious metals purchased less and less, with every decade, of the goods and services which make up incomes, private or public. The sum of £1,200,000 which had been put down on paper as the annual revenue of the Crown admitted by Parliament would, even if it had been fully paid, have had a purchasing power less and less as time went on.

By exactly how much the purchasing power of the Crown fell in the twenty years of Charles's active campaign for the recovery of his inherited popular power, it is very difficult to determine. I have given elsewhere the arguments for fixing a minimum and a maximum to this depreciation of purchasing power during the Restoration years. Even if things had stood for the succeeding twenty years exactly as they were at the Restoration it would have been utterly impossible for the Crown to live on its official income.

II.— But things did *not* remain as they were, and that for the following reasons: (a) the instruments of public action, notably armament, were growing more and more expensive with the development of the arts and sciences and particularly of maritime armament; (b) exceptional expenditure, due to war and preparation for war, perpetually and unavoidably interfered with the regular schedule of receipts and expenses; (c) it was becoming increasingly necessary to the life of England that the large permanent fleet, established by the Stuarts, should be maintained. You will not have sea-power without paying for it; and sea-power – the creation of Charles I and his sons – was an increasing cost. All through the reign of Charles II this is the recurrent trouble. The rich taxpayers in Parliament are all for the glory of sea-power and its benefit to the nation, but they jib at paying the price and they more and more enjoy the opportunity of lowering the kingship.

III.— The revenue of the Crown, increasingly insufficient as it was through decline in the purchasing power of the pound coupled with the growth of necessary expenses, was undermined and ruined by usury. We have seen how, the national revenue – that is the King's income – being so much behind the necessary expenses, the gap had to be filled by borrowing. The money so borrowed came from those who were founding the English banking system at that moment, the silversmiths and goldsmiths, the scriveners and other lawyers who had the handling of other people's money, private investors and so on. The Treasury borrowed the whole time. It stood permanently in debt, repayable at short terms and at a rate of from six to ten and averaging eight per cent. Nothing was commoner than for your possessor of bullion or gold and silver plate, your silversmith with whom valuables had been lodged as security, to get funds from his clients at such and such a rate and to lend those funds out immediately to the Crown at two per cent. higher at least.

No revenue, public or private, can stand the strain of perpetually increasing and recurrent debt at eight per cent. And this usury was ruining the financial power of the Crown for the advantage of that same wealthy class as proposed, more or less consciously, to supplant the Royal power.

As time proceeded the new governing class and its grand committees, the House of Commons and the House of Lords (but chiefly the House of Commons), found themselves, not only in the case of some deliberately, but in the case of others half against their will, pushed and dragged into more and more opposition.

The most important cause of disturbance, the religious quarrel, exemplifies this. I have shown how large was the remaining minority of Catholic sympathy in mere numbers and how its declining moral power was still of effect as well. That power was dreaded mainly because the great majority of the nation was by this time anti-Catholic in feeling and a considerable and very active minority *violently* anti-

141

Catholic in feeling. Such a sentiment was strengthened, of course, by the increasing power of France.

As time went on this feeling was exaggerated by the absence of a direct heir and rendered explosive by the declared conversion of the presumptive heir, then Duke of York. Meanwhile men were aware, more or less acutely, according as they were more or less in touch with the inside of things, that the King's personal sympathies were now definitely Catholic and would almost certainly grow more Catholic. Those who desired to oppose the Royal power, those who were for killing the Monarchy (from Shaftesbury downwards), had this instrument of religious anger ready to hand.

Those who were conservative, national and therefore supporters of the Royal power, nonetheless desired to check it on the religious side.

Nor was the religious factor only anti-Catholic in form. It also appeared as a determination to maintain the Established Church and to destroy Nonconformity. This last issue grew less intense as the reign proceeded: partly because the memory of the Civil Wars was somewhat fading: partly because all over Europe the victories of Louis XIV had made the line of cleavage between Catholic and Protestant deeper than any line of cleavage between the various parts of the Protestant body; partly because the new colonial Empire was largely Puritan in sympathy.

It is true that the Southern American colonies were then the wealthier and that these were in the main orthodox Anglican – save for the experiment of Maryland. But that American Anglicanism was highly Protestant in tone as it is to this day. Indeed, it is one of the most remarkable things about modern America that the stronghold of anti-Catholic feeling is still in the South, though it is there not exasperated by the highly organised Catholicism of the great industrial cities, as it is in the north.

It will be seen from all this that the King, had he lacked genius, would have fallen as a matter of course into the hands of the House of Commons. He would, but for his own dexterity and determination, have become, as he himself bitterly put it, "a mere Doge of Venice." The wealthy would have taken his place (as at last they did indeed), and his great effort would have failed. But Charles did not so easily accept the apparently inevitable. He was one of those characters who, having great secret will power in themselves, appreciate the action of will upon the affairs of men. Spurred by his determination to be free, to be untrammelled and to be King indeed in spite of the rich, he played his hand in the form of what I here call "The Triangle."

Let me explain this term.

All success won through management – that is, through playing upon others; all diplomatic success, all success in negotiation and intrigue – depends upon the simultaneous presence of at least three forces, and the playing of each alternatively against the other two.

This is a universal truth. Where only two main forces are in the field confronting each other, there is no interplay. It is mere shock and the choice between victory and defeat without manœuvre. But when a third party enters, there enters with it the power of a wise man to use it tactically – and Charles in these matters was wise indeed.

The three forces thus in play were the Dutch, the French Monarchy, and the House of Commons. It was the business of Charles, who knew that each was a potential enemy, to play off each against the other two. The whole story of his fine diplomacy from the moment of his accession to his death is the story of that imbroglio.

When the House of Commons proposed to bring him to his knees by interrupting supply, he drew revenue secretly from the French King. When there was danger that this would make the French King his master, he played the Dutch card and frightened Louis with the prospect of Holland on his flank. When the use of the Dutch might have made them too powerful in their trade rivalry and their colonial possessions, he played alternatively the French card and the House of Commons's card. He never allowed himself to fall wholly into the hands of any one of the three. He remained independent of all three to the end.

*****

There is in all this story an element difficult for the modern man to grasp; the very great power of Holland.

Indeed, the high European importance of Holland in the seventeenth century seemed something exceptional and paradoxical even to men of the time.

I say "Holland" because that is the name under which the Calvinist mercantile oligarchy of the seventeenth century came to be called in later times. It is today the name we give to the whole of the seven provinces which were ultimately released from their connection with Spain. We mean by Holland today all that northern part of the Netherlands which is governed from the Hague, which has in its government, and in its leading social classes a strong anti-Catholic tradition, and which is thus distinguished from the Southern Netherlands, the nine provinces of which remained loyal to the Spanish throne and are now called "Belgium."

But the Holland which concerns us in the long piece of steersmanship conducted with such genius by Charles Stuart, the Holland which he played alternatively against the French and against his own usurping plutocracy at home, the Holland which was the third party to the "Triangle," was nothing so large as what we call Holland today. Of the seven provinces which were united in their revolt against Spain and were each so jealous of its independence, only two really counted in the game; Zeeland and that particular district which had for generations been called Holland proper, lying to the north of Zeeland and, like Zeeland, open to commerce and to the sea.

The name Zeeland explains itself. It is a name you find more than once in the various districts of Teutonic speech on the North Sea and the Baltic. It means a coastal district. The name Holland on both sides of the North Sea – on our side as well as the Dutch side – means the "hollow land," the district protected by dykes against the sea and kept artificially habitable in that fashion. These two provinces, Holland and Zeeland, and especially Holland, were the centres of wealth and heads of political power. It was easier for them to affirm and maintain the rebellion against the legitimate government in Madrid because they were a distant outpost. There was present here the same cause which you find in Reformation Germany: the more you were protected against central imperial influence by distance or by geographical conditions the better your chance of maintaining a successful rebellion against the imperial power. That is why at the time of the Reformation you find the mountain cantons and the distant northern cities and districts better able to keep up the religious revolt than the others, for Protestant Germany is divided from Catholic Germany by geographical conditions much more than by any imaginary difference of race.

So it was with Holland. The Netherlands as a whole, from Flanders and Brabant in the south to Guelderland in the extreme north, "the Sixteen Provinces," were at the end of the Middle Ages a mass of industry and civic life, of commerce and of the international carrying trade, which brought with it the currency of all Western nations, founding exchanges. They had formed part of the natural inheritance of the Dukes of Burgundy, whose memory is still so respected in those countries. They had come to Burgundy through an heiress and all the Burgundian land had come to the Hapsburgs through another marriage. Charles V, the great Hapsburg Emperor of the Reformation period, had already found them difficult to govern through their exceptional prosperity and cosmopolitan intercourse. The difficulty took at first largely the form of a simmering religious discontent; part of the universal quarrel then waged with the official Church. But it was really, at heart, a quarrel between great merchant cities with their traditions of local independence and the centralised monarchic system of sixteenth-century kingship, and this quarrel was felt most of all in the system of taxation.

When the Empire of Charles V was divided the Netherlands fell to his son, who also inherited Spain. The Prince of Spain, as he was called (later King of Spain), was by all the ideas of the time the "natural lord" of the Sixteen Provinces, which owed their peculiar economic supremacy to their holding the ports of the Rhine and the Scheldt, the outlet for all the new commerce which was making from Continental Europe for the ocean routes across the Atlantic and round Africa. The exchanges of goods and of precious metals poured like a tide, ebb and flow, into the seaports of the Netherlands, which thus came in direct touch with the Americas and with Asia – all the new trade.

The cost of administering and arming the vast Spanish Empire could only be met with the greatest difficulty on the old lines inherited from the Middle Ages. The trade with South and Central America and Brazil, including the imports of bullion, could not, under that antiquated system, yield sufficient revenue to the Central Government, neither could Spain itself, even when it included Portugal for a whole lifetime of union therewith. The treasury of the Spanish King had no reserves but the Netherlands.

CHARLES II: THE LAST RALLY

Now the taxation of a newly-awakened and newly-enriched commercial society on old territorial feudal lines was a delicate business to arrange. It was almost impossible to effect the transition. The normal revenue of a feudal monarch came from dues paid him by his feudal inferiors at stated times, as, on the inheritance of a lordship. He had no way of getting at the main income of his subjects save by voluntary grant on their part, though there was an indirect way of getting part of it through customs at the ports. Economic friction between the Spanish legitimate Royal power and the local, Netherlands power with its half republican town traditions, was complicated by a violent outbreak of religious revolt.

The main motive was not religious; the main motive was the incompatibility between the old slow insufficient feudal system of revenue and the intense urban life of the Scheldt and Rhine ports and their hinterland. But the new Calvinist teaching excited and focused the discontent. There was a wild outbreak of mob savagery against all the inheritance of the Middle Ages, especially its exquisite statuary and glass and woodwork and its architecture. All was falling into anarchy when the King of Spain dispatched an armed police expedition, small in numbers but excellent in material, which energetically repressed the destroyers and re-established order under the Duke of Alva.

But the small first-class army of that first-class soldier was, of necessity, like every other army of the time, a mercenary force. It had to be paid and paid very high. The money for these wages was raised from Italian bankers who brought it round in ships by way of the English Channel to the Netherlands coast. These treasure ships took refuge from pirates in certain English ports, where Elizabeth, of course, gave them protection as would any sovereign of a settled state give protection to the revenue of a sister state engaged in suppressing anarchy. But that very far-seeing statesman, William Cecil, who was the real master of English policy, overruled the decision of his nominal mistress, the English Queen, and ordered the treasure to be detained. Alva could not pay his troops and they rebelled.

With that the long struggle conducted by the Merchant Princes and the town leaders of the Netherlands to establish their independence of the Central Government in Spain began, as Cecil had foreseen it would begin. He risked the chance of Spain's making war against Elizabeth. It was a very great peril, but he calculated rightly that Spain was more concerned to keep in with England against France than anything else. So, in spite of the outrage done to him, the King of Spain did not declare war and England (and France also, for that matter) was free to intrigue first secretly, at last openly, in favour of this Netherland rebellion against Spanish power. This rebellion, however, was neither universal nor long drawn out. The fact that it was mixed up in the north with Calvinism lost the leaders the sympathy of the popular masses there. There remained a sort of hard surviving nucleus fiercely maintaining the movement in the two northern centres; that is, the now immensely wealthy merchant town of Amsterdam, and The Hague, where local rule was in the hands of the millionaire House of Orange. Amsterdam had grown almost suddenly, in a lifetime, from an obscure northern sea-port dependent on fishery, to become the chief commercial city of Western Europe.

The House of Orange was the other centre of money-power through its immense estates inherited from a dozen different sources, including that heiress from whom it drew its title. In the male line it was the House of Nassau: German princes. William of Orange, having had all his career made by the Spanish Crown, first treasonably intrigued and then, when he felt safer, openly rebelled against that Crown, was outlawed and consequently killed. But the enormous wealth of the family continued in his sons and increased, as did the wealth of Amsterdam (its merchant fleet, now covering every sea, its carrying trade and its great accumulated treasure) as a centre of exchange. It is important to remember that since Spain would not admit the independence of these two small Northern Dutch districts, their ships were free to carry on commerce with the whole Spanish Empire and the Portuguese Empire as well, commerce which the custom of the times barred from all who were not subjects of the same King. Holland prospered by being nominally subject to Madrid, against which it was in rebellion.

The next point in the triangle is Louis XIV and his occasional financial advances to his cousin the King of England.

There are here two matters to be explained, without understanding which the situation has no meaning. The first is the French King's ability to help the English Crown; the second is his reason for desiring – occasionally desiring – to help it.

CHARLES II: THE LAST RALLY

Louis XIV's ability to find spare money for his cousin Charles was due to his larger resources of revenue and the more rational system under which that revenue was gathered.

The population of the three kingdoms, England, Scotland and Ireland, was in the period 1660–1680 certainly more than eight millions and more probably nearer nine. The population of England and Wales, which is known within a fairly small margin of error by estimates made at the end of the century to have been then somewhat over six million, had been growing for some time, probably through the expansion of trade and of the ports, and particularly of London. It must have been considerably over five millions in 1660 and was certainly well over five and a half millions and perhaps over five and three-quarter millions by 1680.

The population of Scotland was very much less. It has been put at about a million and a half, and that is probably something of an under-estimate, for though the Highlands had not yet been ruined, yet no great commercial or industrial development had taken place in the Lowlands. This brings the total population of Great Britain to perhaps rather less than seven millions when Charles was restored to his throne and certainly much more than seven millions at the time of his death twenty-four years later.

What was the population of Ireland? The country had suffered horribly in the Civil Wars but was more flourishing then than it was to be later under the violently hostile London government after the Stuarts had been driven out. It must have had a great deal more than a million and a half people. It probably had nearly two millions, possibly three. If, then, we regard the total number of Charles's subjects in the three kingdoms as fluctuating round nine millions – first less, then more, as the reign proceeds – we are probably not making an error of much more than ten per cent. either way.

The population of France, including the recovered provinces and annexations of Louis XIV, has been estimated with far less accuracy. It was certainly far above fifteen millions. It may have been twenty. Divide by four to get the number of family units (which is the only right way of counting the activity of a country, especially under mainly agricultural conditions) and you get some two million hearths in Charles's realm, and perhaps five in those of Louis.

The contrast is not so great as is generally imagined. The picture of France overwhelmingly numerous compared with the contemporary British islands is a false one. The French soil was more productive and the nature of its produce more varied. On the other hand, English agriculture towards the end of the period was improving faster than was French, and English trade of all kinds was in a far higher ratio to the population than was that of France.

If the two Crowns had enjoyed or suffered the same machinery for raising revenue there would still have been a great gap between them – the revenue of Louis would have been considerably greater than the revenue of Charles – but not so very much greater as proved in fact to be the case. We have statistics on the matter far more accurate than the general estimates of the population and we know that the regular revenue of Louis came to something like five times the real revenue of Charles, including revenue from the Customs. The figures were carefully gone into in Charles's case and in that of his cousin. The English Crown actually received about a million pounds a year. It was supposed to be one-fifth as much again but was so eaten into by the charges of money-lenders (which at the worst went as high as ten per cent.) and by the favouritism of the wealthier classes in placing their dependants, friends and relatives in public employment, that the actual amount received was not quite one million pounds. This is excluding, of course, the slight contribution from Scotland and the precarious payments from Ireland, most of which was spent at home.

The reason that Louis XIV had ready to hand such a much larger revenue in proportion to the area and numbers of his realm than had Charles is due to the method of collection, what may be called "the practical rights" of the taxing power. The French King could on a large scale impose direct taxation at will, after the modern fashion. We today, in any modern country, have long ago reverted to the Roman idea that the executive can take from the revenue of the citizens exactly what it chooses. The pretence that the thing is voted by the House of Commons is kept up, as is the still more hollow pretence that the House of Commons represents the desires of the taxpayers in this matter. But we all know that in point of fact the authorities decide how much we have to pay, and that they take by force the amount they have decided upon. Indeed, it would be impossible to conduct the finances of a modern state in any other fashion.

Now the French Government had not yet reached this ideal state of affairs, but it had gone a great way towards it. The great mass of the population – all that was neither technically clerical nor technically noble – was subject to a direct tax, for the amount of which custom had something to say, but decision by the Government much more. This direct tax was called the "taille," a word derived from the verb meaning "cutting" or "cutting off." A margin was lost to the revenue by the interception of those who collected the taxes – even after the great reforms of Colbert – but there remained a yearly net revenue of some five million pounds.

As a result of all this the French Crown, though heavily burdened with great military expenditure, which grew crushing before the end of the reign, was in the period 1660–1680 in command of a much greater regular revenue in proportion to the area and the numbers of its population than the Crown of Great Britain. The English revenue was a fixed amount settled by a bargain between King and Parliament at the Restoration. The French revenue was elastic and expansible and that made all the difference. The two cousins, Charles and Louis, were in the position of two men in private life one of whom has a fixed income, paid him by a hostile guardian who deliberately designs to keep him embarrassed and furnish him with less than he needs, while the other is supported by relatives who have long admitted his right, as head of the family, to their contributions, and his further right to press for larger payments if necessary than those which he has hitherto received. In such conditions the less embarrassed of the two men will always provide occasional supply to the other.

It must, however, here be remarked that the amounts which Louis provided for his cousin were much less than the general rhetoric of our official history may lead the leader to believe. With the French livre at about 1s. 6d. English, or about twelve and a half livres to the £1, the private subsidy paid by Louis after the Treaty of Dover was two million livres, which works out at more than £160,000 a year – rather more than sixteen per cent. over and above the actual revenue of the English King.

As for the silly legend which makes out that the mass of Charles's revenue was squandered upon his mistresses and his luxuries, it is hardly worth wasting our time upon it. He established his principal mistress in the position of a wealthy English peeress. He made gifts, of course, to the others. But these sums were insignificant compared with the general needs of the Crown for public purposes, for the payment of usury on debt, for the support of the officers and function of government, and especially for the creation and maintenance of the Navy – the one thing on which Charles Stuart bent all his energies and the one thing that those who desired to harry him starved him in to the best of their ability.

So much for the ability of Louis to come to the aid of Charles in the struggle of the latter with the new and increasingly hostile governing class and its committee, the House of Commons.

What as to the motive? Why should Louis have helped his cousin at all? Why should he have tried to help to save the English Crown?

The first and obvious motive was the importance of guaranteeing himself from interference during his effort to establish permanently a strong north-eastern frontier for France. This motive we have repeated and it is obvious. Contemporaries called it his ambition, and he himself spoke of the accompanying victories as his glory. But the essential thing was the shutting of that gate whereby invasion had poured in over and over again from the north-east into Gallic territory.

After that, as a motive, came the desire of Louis for guarding his flank. It is mere elementary strategy and geography but it must not be neglected. Even supposing that he was able to hold his own, fighting forward in the Rhine delta, enemies from beyond the Rhine would find an exposed French flank in the Low Countries until Louis had occupied everything up to the line which follows what is called "Old Rhine": the narrow waterway which drains out to the North Sea in continuation of the great international river.

The French Monarchy had not only a strategical and military object, but was also concerned to liberate the Dutch Catholics. These were not oppressed as the English Catholics were oppressed, indeed there was not anywhere on the Continent of Europe so thorough a persecution of the old religion as there was in England, Scotland and Ireland; but the very large minority of Flemish-speaking Catholics in the provinces governed by the Dutch merchant oligarchy was badly under the weather. When the French armies entered Utrecht vast crowds flocked in from the countryside to hear the Mass, which had been for the moment restored. There are no statistics, of course, but on the analogy of all the other districts in Western Europe where the religious struggle was at work we can safely say that in the early seventeenth century more than half the population of the seven rebel provinces centred on Amsterdam was still Catholic in sympathy, and, as far as possible, in practice. The stories of Holland and England are more or less parallel in this affair. The myth of a purely Protestant Holland which you read of in Motley, for instance, is as absurd as our own Elizabethan myth. There happened in the seven Dutch provinces what common sense would teach one to expect; the old religion dwindled, but it dwindled gradually, and even as late as the invasion of Louis, Catholic numbers were still considerable; certainly a third, perhaps more. But the religious motive had ceased to have very great driving power so late in the day as this. It was still the military and dynastic motive which moved the King of France to attempt an establishment throughout the Low Countries.

There remains one very interesting motive, the motive of Monarchy. How far did Louis help Charles from the feeling that both were kings and from the knowledge that the opposition to Charles was essentially an opposition to kingship? That feeling counted but it did not count very much. National policy had already become more important than European. As a good European, Louis would naturally support Monarchy wherever it was imperilled, but he was far more concerned with the interests of his own dynasty and with the interests of the French people whom he represented. The break-up of Christendom into independent nations which was at last to threaten the general life of Europe had already gone so far by the time of the French wars in Holland that a ruler thought of his country first and of Europe after. The idea of a completely independent nation, not morally bound to Europe nor obeying any common international code of Christian morals, had not yet arisen; but it was on its way. The process has led us to the position which we now deplore.

Louis then was not paying on the whole nor scheming on the whole to preserve the Stuart dynasty. His aim was to advance his own people; that is why you find him occupied, as Charles's peril increases, in keeping the English Throne weak, in bribing the patriots of the

House of Commons with sums which they eagerly accepted, in financing the domestic opposition to the English King.

Such a tangle of motives makes almost undecipherable history. The modern reader is perpetually finding a man acting on one side whom he expects to find on the other, and honest English Liberals of the nineteenth century have wept to find Algernon Sydney – only one in a host of others – pocketing French gold. The younger contemporaries of Macaulay could not make head or tail of it.

But in all the welter – the French Ambassador and his master subsidising the King and also the Opposition, the high-souled spokesman for Parliamentary England taking and even soliciting money from France, the Dutch merchants joining an alliance against Louis XIV, begging for English support against the French invader, and at the same time going behind the English to propose terms secretly to the King of France – one thing runs right through the confusion, obvious and distinct like a coloured thread in a white fabric, and that one thing is the triumphant diplomatic play of Charles II. He always gets the better of this or that or the other opponent in the game of criss-cross which all were playing. He never becomes the instrument of France. He does not in the event of the long wrestling suffer the final yoke of his wealthy subjects in Parliament. He escapes being identified with the fates, good or evil, of Amsterdam.

There has never been a finer game played and it merits what it has never had, a monograph devoted to that one subject alone – the triumph of Charles Stuart over a very network of desperate opposing forces.

That triumph was at the very end of his life complete.... It lasted not two years! You may take the illusory complete restoration of Monarchy as achieved when William Russell's head fell on the block in Lincolns Inn Fields, July, 1683. For a year and a half a year the King of England's head was a head really and fully crowned: but in the first days of the second year the rich rise again, and less than twenty-four months after the death of Russell you have rebellion and Sedgemoor, in another four years the destruction of Monarchy.

GATHERING STORM

I HAVE SAID THAT THE FIRST HALF OF THE KING'S ACTIVE REIGN, the first half of those twenty-one years when he was occupied in attempting a decision as to whether the Throne could be re-established, were upon the whole fair-weather sailing; in spite of the shocks of fire and plague and even foreign invasion due to the folly or avarice – but more to the class-ambition – of the wealthy men in Parliament.

Charles in those ten years had not fully restored the Royal power, of course. The attempt to do so was in any case heavily handicapped, and with the increasing expenses of the Crown would prove more difficult every year. The Government had to find about £400,000 annually beyond the gravely insufficient sum which the Commons had allowed it at the Restoration. In other words, the King's expenditure, of which the heaviest item was of course the Fleet, exceeded by forty per cent. the King's nominal revenue, and by at least fifty per cent. or more the King's real revenue. For the sums received by the Exchequer were eaten into by usury.

The Crown of England was in pawn to the new moneylenders, who were already called bankers. The income of the King was anticipated regularly, and anything from eight to ten per cent. might be extracted from him, according to the severity of the squeeze. It is probable that he also had to meet more than ten per cent., counting commissions and renewals of I.O.U.'s. To such a process there could be no end but the ultimate abdication of kingship and the usurping of its functions by the rich. That is of course what happened in the long run. It is essentially that which we mean when we talk of the "Revolution," 1688–1689. But so long as Charles lived, he planned with all his intelligence, he fought with all his strength, to prevent that catastrophe and to keep the national government in the hands of the national dynasty, and of that Royal office which was essentially representative of the people as the squires and merchants could never be.

The first phase, before the conflict became violent and a matter of life and death, ended with the Treaty of Dover, the secret compact between Charles and his cousin Louis XIV, King of France, which was signed on the 22nd of May, 1670.

The storm did not break immediately upon this transaction. It muttered for a year or two, gathered, and then fell in full strength, so that it very nearly shipwrecked Charles's command. We shall see by what an unexpected reversal of fortune he managed after ten years of increasing peril to weather that storm.

The Treaty of Dover is the convenient and even the necessary point of departure marking off the new state of affairs, the second half of the King's effort, from the first. But that Treaty was not the main cause of the change from fair weather to foul, as it is often represented to be. The main cause, let it never be forgotten, was Anne Hyde's gradual change of religion, debated in her mind between 1667 and 1669, accomplished in 1670 and through its effect upon her husband, James Duke of York, emphasised by her own death in 1671, causing that heir presumptive to the Throne to declare himself publicly a Catholic, and so to present the Money-power and the House of Commons, which spoke and acted for the Money-power, with the fullest opportunity for attacking the Throne.

There was an earlier point of departure than the Treaty of Dover; at least, it was an earlier point of departure for the change in financial policy, though it did not mark, as did the Treaty itself, an immediate reversal of foreign policy. That earlier private, and at first unemphatic, point of departure was the effect produced on Charles's mind by the refusal of the Commons to support the Navy, and the consequent shock of the Dutch invasion, and the burning of the ships in the Medway. It was clear to the King from that moment that some form of supplementary revenue *must* be obtained if England were to carry on as a monarchy at all; with the power of the purse in the hands of the rich Commons and the City of London, yet the executive still in the hands of the King, there was a divided control which could not be stabilised until one or the other of the rivals should prove master. Meanwhile, it was impossible to be king or to arm a fleet or to pursue an active foreign policy in defence of England's Eastern commerce and in the founding of English supremacy at sea without additional revenue from some source. The Crown had already turned the greater part of its remaining capital into income; it had got rid of such fragments of the Royal patrimony as were left, and still it could not nearly meet the bill.

At such a moment came the opportunity for finding new revenue by an understanding with France.

The French King was at the point of initiating a fundamental change in his own foreign policy; he had hitherto used the merchants of Amsterdam as his support against Spain. The claim he had made in the name of his wife for the fortresses to the north-east of the French frontier was a claim based upon her right as part heiress of the inherited Spanish sovereignty of the Low Countries. At first he had proposed to press his claim only insofar as it guaranteed the immediate frontier; for the future, from 1668 onwards, he was determined, at the suitable moment, to extend that claim to the whole of the Netherlands; he would command not only in Flanders but in Brabant, at Brussels, and from Amsterdam itself. The Netherland provinces had been subject to the Spanish Throne, they should in future be subject to the French Throne – that was the plan.

It was not so extravagant in the world of that day as it sounds in the world of our day. The legal claim could be not only argued but established. The consolidation of that claim by force of arms seemed probable enough. What the results upon Europe and upon France itself might have been had the attempt succeeded is conjectural, but we may presume that the addition to the French provinces of the Netherlands, however safeguarded by the confirmation of local customs and liberties, would have been too top-heavy an arrangement for the Bourbon Monarchy to have maintained. It was one thing to round off the frontiers of that Monarchy to the Rhine, as was done at last by the occupation of Alsace, it was one thing to round it off by obtaining under treaty the Jura country, that is Franche Comté, from the nominal rule of Spain; the Rhine was a natural frontier, the Jura was of French speech and of French culture from the beginning of that speech and that culture; it was one thing to establish French garrisons in the towns of Flanders, a mere strip covering the most vulnerable section of the French defences against invasion; it was another thing altogether to take over the whole Flemish population and – far more important than mere numbers of subjects – the vast commercial activity of Holland.

Anyhow, the attempt failed and the effort at uniting the seaboard of the North Sea with a political head in Paris, the effort at recreating in highly organised, definite form, what had been in the early Middle Ages the vague, the very loose feudal tie between the Rhine delta and the Gallic side of the Empire, has not borne permanent fruit from that day to this. There was a moment following on the Revolutionary and Napoleonic wars, when it looked as though the thing might be done. With the fall of Napoleon the experiment then made failed once more.

Louis XIV needed for this policy of advance in the Netherlands even up to the whole line of the Rhine and including Amsterdam itself, the neutrality at least, and preferably the benevolent neutrality, of England. It would be better still for him if he could get the alliance of England against that Dutch mercantile power which was the maritime rival, the commercial rival, the colonial rival of London.

The attempt to obtain such neutrality, or even alliance, had forces working for and against it.

Against it was the unchanging instinct of England against allowing a strong power to occupy the Low Countries. That instinct is as strong today as it was in the past. The strategic reason for it is obvious. It was put epigrammatically by Napoleon, when he said that Antwerp was a pistol pointed at the heart of England.†

Another force working against the new plan of Louis XIV was one which our official history has absurdly exaggerated, but which is in truth of great weight: the religious sympathy between (and therefore the cultural sympathy between) the now Protestant majority of England and the Calvinist Government of Holland. In each country there was a large Catholic minority (much larger in Holland than in England), in each this minority whetted and exasperated the anti-Catholic feeling. The plain citizen of London, he of the middle classes and of the crafts in that capital, however much he might dislike the Dutch, or resent their competition, disliked the French a great deal more. General and ill-defined feelings of this sort are no solid foundation for a foreign policy, but they help to canalise such a policy.

---

† Epigram for epigram, and picturesque over-statement for statement, the same thing might be said later of Cherbourg; and certainly the shape and attitude of the Cotentin is much more like a pistol than Antwerp could ever be. Antwerp might rather be compared to a bomb.

That which is easy to do in line with such sympathies is difficult to do in opposition. We all know how, before the Great War, or at any rate before 1904, the English Government working with Prussia, had the tide under it, and how during the Great War, and since, the English Government and interests working with France have had the tide against them. Nationalism, its ignorance and its violent fevers, had not reached the pitch in 1670, which it was to reach two hundred years later, but it was already very active and strong.

Another force making against alliance or even neutrality, making against support of *any* kind for the French King on the part of England, was the presence of trained, well-read and observant men, who not only from sympathy but from calculation put in their powerful official word for Holland. Chief of these was Temple. He was the author of the Triple Alliance, as it was called, that understanding between England and Holland, later joined by Sweden, the object of which was to limit the advance of the Bourbon power. The Triple Alliance was still in existence, though it was ostensibly pacific and neutral. It was still an obstacle, and though that obstacle had largely been turned by "the Eventual Treaty" between the Emperor and Louis XIV – a secret pact whereby those monarchs were to divide the Spanish Empire on the "eventual" death of the King of Spain, which seemed at the moment so imminent – yet the Treaty was still there on paper. The Triple Alliance was still in existence.

Now let us look at the other side.

In favour of Louis XIV's aim, the neutrality or better still the support of Great Britain, there was in the first place the commercial interest of English merchants and English banks. The merchants were struggling to surpass their Dutch rivals in the struggle for the trade of the Far East and, in a lesser degree, of the West Indies. There was an informal war continuing uninterruptedly between the armed mercantile marine of England in Asiatic waters and the armed merchant ships of Holland. There was a potential point of rivalry in the Cape of Good Hope, which before the piercing of the Suez Canal was the Dutch relay on the journey to the wealth of the Malay Archipelago. In the long revolution of European affairs the evidence of that old struggle is still present: the Dutch colonies of the Far East are today guaranteed by the Fleet of England, but they are still Dutch, they are still a source of very great wealth. The Cape is called a Dominion, but the Dutch language and Dutch traditions are rooted there, and will presumably extend their influence rather than lessen it. The antagonism between the two "maritime powers" (the general common term for England and Holland at the time) was vivid and vital in 1670, and those who desired to work with France in this country, those in France who desired English support against Amsterdam, could depend upon that strong current of feeling.

Then there was the steadfast policy of Charles and his brother for the consolidation of the English speech and political tie on the eastern seaboard of the Atlantic. The symbol of this was the English effort against New Amsterdam which has already been described. We saw on a former page how that effort was crowned with success by a formal treaty in 1674, a treaty which turned New Amsterdam into New York and made certain the political and cultural unity of the sea-line between the mountains and the ocean from Maine to the Carolinas. That treaty would never have been obtained but for Charles's alliance with France: it was the direct fruit of the alliance, a fruit which seemed a minor one at the time, but which has proved to be of vast consequence in our own day, for we owe to it what is called "the English-speaking world."

But much the strongest of the forces making for the new policy of working with France was the determination of Charles to be rid of that internal enemy which threatened the very existence of the English national Monarchy; the Money-power at Westminster. The revenue of Louis XIV was five times his own at home, as we saw; it was even more than three times the total financial resources (supposing he could have collected them all) of the three kingdoms, including Customs duties. As the French Monarchy was not divided against itself, had an excellent and *elastic* financial organisation, was based upon a widespread independent peasantry, and was unhampered by great private political fortunes or a tyrannical usury (although Louis, like Charles, was compelled to borrow, he was master of the money-lenders rather than they of him) as Louis also had a continuous financial administration wholly in his own hands – on account of all these things Louis could subsidise an alliance.

He was in a position to do on a small scale what modern England has done on so great a scale: he could purchase the neutrality or support of other powers. Of this situation Charles could take advantage

– and did. The sums forthcoming to support the English Treasury as an armed ally of France were small, but they made all the difference between the necessary subservience of the Crown to the rich men in Parliament and of independence for the Crown from those rich men in Parliament and from the City of London behind them. When the first secret negotiations were undertaken in 1668 (they were then talked of as no more than a "friendship"), Charles had in mind a sum of one million English pounds. With this he could have entered the way fully on Louis's side, he would have been rid of the galling curb whereat the Parliamentarians were perpetually tugging.

In the event he could never get anything like this support, not even a quarter of a million for each year that the war lasted, he obtained the promise of £150,000 down, in another connection to be described in a moment. The English Crown was also, after the common victory, to obtain the opposing coast, the Dutch islands in Zeeland, following that unceasing policy of a bastion beyond the water whereof Dunkirk had been the latest example.

When a man's total revenue including new Customs duties (much of which were neutralised by Parliamentary interference with French trade) was little over a million a year all told in his own realm of England, and Parliamentary grant in practice much less than a million, a subsidy of £225,000 a year to be obtained only in process of costly active war seems, and was, inadequate. But it did make it possible to pursue an active foreign policy; it did give the King just that elbow-room which he needed in order to be King at all, even for a precarious moment; for the King is not King unless he orders the foreign affairs of the nation.

The agent of this great reversal in foreign policy was Charles's younger sister, Henrietta. She was a perfect agent for the thing that had to be done. The King loved her passionately. If it be true, as it is true, that no woman had any influence on him, yet his affection for this darling child – as he remembered her, and as in character she still was – would certainly move him, had he needed moving. But, of course, he was ready enough.

She was the sister-in-law of the French King, married to the wretched younger brother, effeminate and viciously effeminate, and jealous of her into the bargain – jealous even of her absence for a few days. In those few days, a single week, she had seen her brother and had concluded the secret Treaty of Dover. That jealously-guarded instrument promised the war subsidy for England as an ally whenever the moment should come in the judgment of Louis for launching the attack on Amsterdam; that small but at the moment decisive supplement of income which would allow the English fleet to be fully armed and manned, and even some slight land force to support it in the attack upon the Netherlands. But there was added another promise, to which we shall return – for it is of the first moment. Henrietta and her brother said their good-byes. He accompanied her half-way to the French coast and returned disconsolate, for not only did *he* love *her* – and what else had he ever had to love, save England, kingship and the sea? – but *she* loved *him;* and who else had ever loved him? Only his poorer attendants. Who of his own world had ever cared whether he lived or died? That fearful thing the isolation of the soul, descended upon him again.

*****

The time has come to note that other still smaller supplementary subsidy.

The French King was to pay his first cousin, over and above the war subsidy necessary for supporting in part (in small part) the arms of an ally, a further sum of rather less than £150,000. This was to be paid at the moment of the English King's choosing, just as the larger war subsidy was to be paid at the moment of the King of France's choosing; and that much smaller subsidy, a lump sum, was to come six months hence, but it was earmarked for a very strange object. It was to provide Charles with funds for adding to his very small standing army (some 6,000 men), for the purpose of keeping order if rebellion should threaten in the problematical and presumably distant occasion of Charles's openly professing Catholicism.

Now what was the origin of so singular a proposal? What would be its probable or possible upshot?

As to the upshot, we can answer at once, for all our history is there to provide the answer. Charles was never to declare himself Catholic: he was to be received into the body which he already knew to be the unique guardian (and infallible) of reality and truth, only when it was certain that he had come to death, and that by such an action, utterly private, unknown to his subjects, the throne would not be imperilled.

It is as certain as anything can be that when this clause was written down in the secret treaty which his sister took back with her to be put into the custody of Louis, Charles with his clear mind, long views and tense will, had not the remotest intention of pursuing the policy proposed. Who then proposed it? It cannot have been Louis himself; he presumably knew that those words would appear in the secret thing, but he himself must have been as certain as Charles was that they would be implemented by no overt action. Nothing could have been more disastrous to Louis XIV than to increase the already violent internal divisions of his new ally. He was a man given up wholly to a broad political plan, as was Charles. It was his, step by step, under a very heavy strain to be demanded of his subjects, to consolidate once and for all the defences of the French quadrilateral: what the great founder of modern French power had called "the square field."†

That was the business of *his* life: he was to restore, to rebuild, consolidate, Gaul; just as his cousin was to restore, rebuild and consolidate the national monarchy of England. Of the two cousins, Charles was to die thinking that he had succeeded, whereas almost immediately after his death it was proved that he had failed; Louis was to die thirty years later, having indeed as by a miracle preserved the fortified frontiers he had created: they were to stand inviolate for a hundred years – but no more.

No, Charles did not initiate or give any moral value to that presumption of early public conversion: to imagine otherwise is to contradict the whole of his life. Neither did Louis initiate it. To the very end he fought hard to prevent the strengthening of Catholicism in England, because such strengthening would weaken the power of England as a support for himself. He stood for the Catholic culture, he despised the moral chaos outside that culture, but his prime motives were national and dynastic. He certainly connected Catholicism with monarchy, but the whole world knew, and none better than Louis himself, that English monarchy was not to be restored but rather overthrown by any emphasis on the ancestral faith of the English.

The one person who could sincerely have written those words or demanded their insertion was Charles's beloved and beloving sister herself. She would act with the lack of judgment to be expected of

---

† It is as a fact a pentagon: but let it go at that.

her intense affection, coupled with her intense faith. She knew that her own brother, to whom her soul went out, was as certain of the Faith as she was: she had no capacity for judging the impossibility of the vision she had entertained. She would, I verily believe, have imperilled the Throne (it would be juster to write *destroyed* the Throne) for the sake of that one soul; just as many a woman in private life has caused a conversion which has ruined her husband's private income and destroyed the worldly chances of her own children.

But to say that "Minette" – the pet name of family affection, the name of early childhood – initiated that strange clause is not enough. Charles, though he certainly would not act upon it, permitted it. Louis, though he certainly would not have acted upon it, permitted it. What was the motive of either man? Each a very great diplomatist, each an intensely determined far-seeing and subtly weaving master of policy.

Their motives were very different. Charles must have all the money he could. He would get this money without action. It was money for words. Even with that addition, he would have in the first year of the proposed war barely a third of what he had hoped for, and certainly not enough, not nearly enough, for the first stages of the campaign. But it gave him breathing space, it gave him some months of freedom. And one who was living under the tyranny of usurious debt needs even temporary freedom as a drowning man needs air. In such very brief intervals of real kingship one opportunity or another might arise for striking some blow, of achieving some act whereby the coming of true kingship could be advanced.

So much for Charles's motives, they should be clear enough to anyone who knows the time and the man.

But what of Louis's motives? We can answer that by judging what followed.

The Treaty of Dover was signed on the 22nd of May, 1670. It had been kept dead secret. But four Ministers signed with the King, Arlington, Clifford (a very strong and combative Catholic himself), Arundel and Bellings. Louis was now in possession of a document which he knew could be held over Charles as a pledge of policy. Further, he could be certain that certain responsible statesmen were privy to that document, as well as the King their master. What is more, he must have known, with his means of information, and his judgment of men, that another exceedingly important person would have had wind of what had happened. That other exceedingly important person was Ashley, Ashley Cooper, later to betray his master and to be remembered with infamy, not without awe, under the title of Shaftesbury. It mattered nothing to Louis that those who were privy to the Treaty of Dover would, through their special position, have the whip hand of their master. What mattered to Louis was that this piece of paper gave *him* the whip hand. If anything, he exaggerated the anti-Catholicism of Englishmen in his day. He thoroughly understood the crippled and ambiguous position of the English Crown. He knew as well as any man in Europe what the fate of that Crown might be if he used his secret knowledge against it.

When you put all those things together you understand, I think, the Treaty of Dover, not only in its main motive and foundation (the acquirement of English support for the French attack on Holland), but in this one odd detail of the "Catholic subsidy" which, small as it was and almost fatuous as a proposed but quite impossible policy, was of very great value as an instrument in the hands of an ally who was also a rival.

As for Minette, hardly had she got back home to her unhappy marriage-bed when she suddenly died in great torment, believing herself to be poisoned by the chief of the infamous men who surrounded her infamous husband – and for the vilest of motives.

She was wrong, poor woman, her death was natural. It resembled that of her sister-in-law, Anne Hyde, in its abruptness, in its agony; and I have often mused upon this singular coincidence, that the two beings most directly concerned with that religious rock on which the English monarchy struck and ultimately sank, Anne Hyde and Henrietta Stuart, were struck down in the same awful way with the same awful rapidity, immediately after the step by which each had so profoundly affected the destinies of England.

*****

Meanwhile that stirring within the Court of St. James's, within the private circle of the King of England, that lighting of the match which was to blow up the monarchy at last, was suspected.

First, a very few, then others, then more, knew that the Faith had appeared in their midst.

Those who could foresee the necessary consequences – Ashley Cooper could foresee them best – were beginning to trim their sails. The chances of success for an attack upon kingship and all its kind were taking on a new and very different life from what they had hitherto done. A real battle was opening between Charles and the revolutionaries, for the revolutionaries now held a trump card: the secret treaty and its "Catholic clause."

We all know how these things leak out, even in our own day when secret matters of state are kept much more secret than ever they could be in that older time. I have myself heard with my own ears a public man boasting abroad of an approaching capitulation to an enemy in the midst of a great war (it was a policy he favoured). He made the boast volubly, at his own table, and marvelled that any echo of it should have reached further than those who sat by him. Yet there were two or three servants in that big room, and they were neither dumb nor deaf; and outside that big room there were throughout Europe men ready to pay for what those servants could tell.

Confidences are whispered by the most loyal to the most loyal, and by these to others very loyal again, until twenty, thirty, fifty, men and women know what has been said. When it is something that has not only been said but *done,* the circle spreads wide indeed, and so it did here. With the new Catholic leanings of Anne Hyde, the new orientation of her husband's mind through her influence, those best informed, most secret and most treasonable, were standing by for attack.

The central matter, then, of the "change over" pivoting on the Secret Treaty of Dover is not political but religious. It was not alliance with France that was perilous to English monarchy and to the special task of Charles, it was the increasing conviction that Charles and his successor would be papist.

Since men can but conceive of the past in terms of the present – and this is the fruitful source of most bad history – modern Englishmen can but believe that the matter of papistry was subordinate to the popular fear and popular dislike of Louis XIV's expanding power. But to the men of the time the dominant thing was the fear of a Catholic Throne. The adjuncts to the main quarrel, the surroundings of it, all had their importance; the effort to get a new wife for Charles, the closing of the Exchequer, were grave matters, but overshadowing them all was the fact already known to an increasing number that the heir presumptive, brother of the King, would publicly admit his Catholicism, and that a few already knew, and more surmised, that Charles was at least in sympathy with the old religion.

On this ground the attack on the Throne could now be delivered with confidence, and was so delivered. Because James proposed in a second marriage to wed a Catholic princess Parliament protested. Because James was papist they would exclude him from command at sea, losing the best man the nation had for that purpose: at least, the best among those who were by the custom of the time eligible. They would exclude him by a new general law forbidding anyone to hold office under the Crown who did not take the sacrament in the Anglican form and repudiate on oath the doctrine of Transubstantiation.

The whole atmosphere changes. There is even talk of proposing the eldest of the King's bastards, Monmouth, as heir to the Throne. All that mood which was to end in the proposed exclusion of James from the succession was alive and strong before the opening of 1673.

Another great battle had been fought at sea against Holland; it had had none of the conclusive character which had attached to the action in the first part of the reign off Lowestoft. There were heavy English losses – as there were also heavy enemy losses – but under the very light western air on that misty day the two fleets drifted towards the enemy coast without anything approaching a decision, and James, in command for the last time, brought back eastward a fleet almost as badly crippled as was that of his opponent.

Henceforward the King through the open conversion of his brother, his own suspected approach to Catholicism, is vulnerable and a permanent target. It was in part a counter move from his side that he should set up as his principal, or at least most prominent, minister, such a man as Osborne (later Danby), a man openly and almost exaggeratedly anti-French, and certainly, though less violently, anti-Catholic. But the event which marked the change most deeply and showed wealth to be now equal or superior to the King was the defection of Shaftesbury. That abandonment and betrayal is outstanding in the story of the man himself, in the full light it throws upon his mind, but its interest lies not in the personal study of Ashley Cooper but in the general study of the even battle between Charles and the rich men who were determined to bring down the Monarchy.

Ashley Cooper, later Shaftesbury, was the first of those whom Charles had chosen as ministers to support the Throne. He had been made Lord Chancellor, which meant an extra income (added to his own vast inheritance) of something equivalent today to more than £200,000 a year.† He was, through his talents, through his fortune, and through his capable continual intrigue, much the most considerable of the men who spoke and acted for the King. Yet when it came to debate on the Test Act, Shaftesbury threw all his weight against the Duke of York, against the declared policy of Toleration. He had been Chancellor so recently as November of 1672, the discussion of the Test Act fell in the following spring. In the next November, after a year's tenure of the supreme office, he was dismissed. Henceforward, in the midst of all his twistings and turnings, he kept clearly before his eyes the undoing of the Royal house and of the Royal power.

Shaftesbury should be taken henceforward as the typical figure of wealth withstanding monarchy. What were his motives?

They were, I think, three.

First, he was a man who betrayed for the sake of betrayal. He had early learnt the fear which a man inspires if he can manage to be persistently disloyal and yet to persuade men that his support is worth having. He had ratted furiously, and one might almost say consistently, throughout the whole of a life now well on into the fifties (he was born in the summer of 1621). He had joined Charles I at Derby as a very young man, he declared himself strongly Royalist, yet he deserted that cause, ratting to the Parliament at the opening of '44; he had supported the regicides after the murder of Charles, and then he became one of the few men whom Oliver feared, and possibly he designed to marry Oliver's daughter. He changed over again to support the Presbyterian faction, so that the Protector vowed that he was the most difficult of all men to manage: an understatement. Then, with Oliver dead, you find him deep in intrigue with Monck; he fills the Restoration with his name, appears as we have seen almost lieutenant of the King, and then rats again in this fashion upon the Test Act. But this time he ratted for good. After he had been dismissed (with such violence of comment) from the Lord Chancellorship he had opportunity for return, even French policy might have supported him, but he refused.

---

† Seventy thousand in the money of 1670; for social value among the higher classes, multiply by at least three.

CHARLES II: THE LAST RALLY

What was behind this final decision to remain in opposition and to undermine his former master? It was in great part spite and pique, but it was more a feeling that he was the typical and chosen leader of his class against kingship. In that matter Shaftesbury is the villain (or hero) of the piece.

Immensely wealthy though he was, we must not ascribe his power mainly to his wealth. That wealth being territorial gave him greater weight in the west and south, particularly in Wiltshire and Hampshire, but the wealth would have been nothing save for what he built upon it by a talent for political intrigue and for the management of men through such intrigue. In this talent he had no equal, and has had none I think in all modern political history.

Shaftesbury is one of those men whom it is impossible not to gaze at fixedly with a sort of false admiration in spite of their villainy because that villainy works in an air of the highest intellectual power and of the widest experience – even of the most acute judgment. The man against whom he had pitted himself, the King, was his superior in all these qualities, and, morally, so immensely his superior that it is between them a contrast like that between black and white. Charles had called him, and justly called him, the worst and the wickedest of his subjects; but even Charles could not take his eyes off so admirable a player of the game. It was a game of treason, of avarice, sometimes of cruelty, a game always shot with mean hatreds and degraded by complete contempt for honour, but it was a game played by a master hand.

We shall understand Shaftesbury best by watching Kneller's portrait, the fine dark eyes, the delicate mouth, the subtle fingers of the hand. It is a matter of permanent satisfaction that such a man died disappointed and defeated. Men of that stamp more commonly achieve through public life what they will: hence the peculiar odour of public life.

I cannot leave him without mention of two anomalies. The one we know through the always useful testimony of another contemporary, also treasonable in temper, Burnet. Through Burnet we learn of Shaftesbury's "dotage on astrology." And the second point is his continuous attachment to Locke.

There would be much more to say of Shaftesbury if he were the matter of these pages instead of the subject of a passing notice. He was an excellent scholar; he *spoke* Latin, and that gave him prestige with foreign men. He was one of those many famous figures who, by surmounting a heavy handicap of ill-health, do but the more exalt themselves: he was a thorough invalid, suffering at last from an incurable tumour which perpetually discharged; he had perhaps never an hour of full physical health in all the last twenty-five years of his life. It was probably this physical defect in him which made him so conspicuous a power in spite of his feline character; for feline men, like every one of the cat tribe, can fight. He had no devotions; he had perhaps no affection; he certainly had no faith. And nonetheless, I leave him with regret. His picture makes the onlooker feel that he had known the man.

With 1674, on the approach of autumn, matters stood thus:

The King had fought one pitched battle, and lost it. He had made an open and emphatic declaration for religious peace; the Commons having refused supplies unless they were given the right to persecute, Charles yielded to them and to their insistence on persecution.

On the other hand he did not abandon his cousin the King of France in foreign policy, though he would not run the risk of still deeper indebtedness by war.

As against the Money-power Charles had won hands down in one very important action: the moratorium which he had imposed upon the repayment of capital debt. The bankers had thought to hold him entirely in their hands: he and his council had, early in 1672, provided what was vitally necessary to the Fleet by stopping the repayment of principal of the bankers' debt and continuing only for the moment a six per cent. interest thereon. Shaftesbury, though he had not yet betrayed and deserted, did his best to support the money interest in this.

Lastly, Charles won for good the once doubtful issue of the colonies. After that year, 1674, the Atlantic seaboard was united and secure.

The King had done well to avoid either abandoning his cousin and ally, Louis, in his Dutch War, or engaging himself so deeply as to run the risk of ruin – which, as it was, threatened him enough. What would have happened if Louis had been completely successful in the Netherlands we know not. England might have had to oppose, but the King of France after overrunning nearly all Holland with the largest army raised since the Middle Ages, after crossing the lower Rhine and occupying the ill-kept fortresses of the Dutch merchants thereon, had failed of his objective. There had happened to him what so often happens in war: *one* oversight had robbed him of full victory.

The Dutch merchants were in terror and all for capitulation. Young William of Orange at The Hague, bent on ultimate kingship, was screaming in factitious anger against a defeat which he could have done nothing to avoid, and was talking bombastically of abandoning Europe for the East. It was at such a moment that the French commanders, having been in possession for more than twenty-four hours of the sluices, failed to hold that decisive point and retired from it, not understanding what would follow. What followed was the flooding of all the low land and the saving of Amsterdam.

Thenceforward Louis might and did advance and was in three or four years the signatory of a victorious peace, but he had not destroyed the Dutch oligarchy or its bank, nor had he occupied the northern provinces in their fullness, nor completed his mastery of the Netherlands.

He was never to obtain it. The war had turned upon that one moment of negligence, or misapprehension, at the sluices on the dyke which contained the Zuider Zee and runs eastward from the great port, the heart of commercial Holland.

That one local strategic error counted as much for the future of Europe as did the accident which you may read and understand in Foch's lectures on the art of war, where he speaks of how von Moltke blundered against Bazaine's advance guard which he had taken for the rear guard, and so learnt that fate had put him unwittingly between the two main French armies. Hence Sedan, and all the orientation of Europe following upon that battle, until the great war – and after.

WHIGGERY

T IS AT THE RISK OF AN INTERRUPTION IN THE COURSE OF THIS study that I put here the consideration of a certain force which in its growth foreshadowed the English Political Revolution from a Monarchy to an Aristocracy, and in its maturity was the fruit of that change.

The battle raged round the heir to the Throne and his firm religion. But the force of which I speak, now in 1674 almost born, and soon to be baptised with the name we know, was, as it were, the concrete national form of abstract anti-Catholicism and of that which was here in England the special political result of anti-Catholicism – class government by the rich.

This force is known to Englishmen themselves by the half-humorous term of "Whiggery." It is a social thing quite unknown outside England. It is among the most English of English products and without a comprehension of it no man can really know how modern England was made or what modern England is. It was essentially Whiggery that destroyed the English Monarchy in that monarchy's last phase, after the Crown had been undermined by the whole series of seventeenth-century transformations from the last Tudor kingship to the nominal rule of Dutch William. It was essentially Whiggery that supported Shaftesbury and inspired Russell. In 1688 is Whiggery enthroned.

Since this great change from kingship to oligarchy – from the people represented and governed by one Great Person to the people governed, but hardly represented, by a comparatively small group of rich men – is, in its largest aspect, a victory of Money-power over its only serious rival in large societies, Monarchy, men who do not know England may easily confuse Whiggery with mere plutocracy.

To do this – and it has been done by many a foreign historian and onlooker, including so great a judgment as Napoleon's – is like mistaking port for alcohol. Whiggery is full of plutocracy; it is based upon plutocracy. It connotes government by the rich. But it is far, far more particular, individual and national, local and, as it were, personal, than mere plutocracy.

When an Englishman who knows his own country and its past, talks of the "Whigs," there arises in his mind at once the image of a special kind of Englishman who gave its tone to the English governing class as a whole (but especially to the dominating section of that class) from the revolution of 1688 almost to our own day. In our own day there is a strong survival of Whiggery, very vital and likely to endure, even though it be somewhat changed in quality as time proceeds.

Whiggery is a combination of two things which have no rational connection but which happen to have coalesced in England, and in England only, under the accidents of English development from the middle of the seventeenth century to nearly the end of the nineteenth century. Those two things are:—

1. All that is meant by the Liberal theory of the State: freedom of the individual, an inviolate rule of law secure from personal interference; the equality of all citizens before that law; a necessary patriotism without which no abstract principles could preserve the State, and, with this patriotism, a strong conviction that the nation thus loved and served is in every respect superior, necessarily and essentially superior, to all others. There is the first element.

2. The second element is something quite other and nearly contradictory. It is the conception that the wealthy are the natural leaders of the community. On this account their wealth should be as permanent and stable as possible. On this account they must be dignified by sundry titles, often high-sounding. It is inconceivable to the spirit of Whiggery that men not enjoying the best advantages of wealth should preponderate in the commonwealth. To this conception of wealth as the natural and inevitable conductor of society there is added that without which class government could not arise – the worship of wealth both on the part of those who possess it and on the part of those who do not, and more on the part of the latter than of the former.

Now if you will consider these two principles, they will be found as little common in nature as oil and water. It would seem impossible to make them mix. The foreigner (by which opprobrious term not only Whigs but all their fellow-citizens denote the inferior alien) has now for generations been baffled in the attempt to understand how that mixture could conceivably have taken place, or rather, how that mixture can have actual existence. He sees it is so in England and the more incomprehensible does it make England to him.

Consider the two principles separately. On the one hand, equality before the law, the flower and product of that mystical doctrine, the equality of man, which is dimly recognised in the souls of all but which we inherited, in its full definition, from the civilisation of Greece and Rome and especially from that civilisation's conversion to Catholicism some fifteen hundred years ago. On the other hand, the conviction rather than the pretension, the instinct or appetite rather than the claim, that wealth not only must, in the nature of things, but *should,* for implied moral reasons, conduct the State.

There is here an active contradiction in definition, but more than that, there is an incompatibility of stuff. It does not seem possible that men defending and even worshipping the ideal of an equal law should, at the same time, hold this strongly inherited religion of Mammon. Yet the marriage has been consummated and has borne fruit, and its still well-established child is the English governing class. Two dissimilar things have come together and have made a third. It is the practice of nature in every department, animate and inanimate, to administer change in this fashion and to preside, by such a generation, over the course of development in every field. Dissimilar chemical elements unite in some mysterious way which no man understands (and least of all those who call it in one generation an "atomic" process, in another an "ionic"), and behold, you have a third substance, utterly unlike either of the two from the combination of which it proceeds. Take at a normal temperature the gas oxygen and the gas hydrogen. Under certain conditions a chemical spark will make them combine into something that is utterly unlike either gas or any gas, to wit, water. Or see how two pigments, a yellow one and a blue one, will produce with careful selection, a third pigment by mere mixture, and this pigment is green. The yellow sand and the blue sea give you a third quite different thing, the colour of the forest. I will give but one more example, which as it is drawn from politics, may help those who do not know England to understand this English thing called Whiggery.

CHARLES II: THE LAST RALLY

You may notice in the neighbouring but hostile culture of the French, a combination of two dissimilar things: a passion for strict deductive conclusions, following from admitted first principles and therefore absolutely true, not to be denied, compelling acquiescence – and, on the other hand, a mere association of ideas or even a mere association of words, a process which has no more to do with logic than Mammon has to do with human equality.

The same Frenchman who has proved, or rather affirmed by an implied syllogism, that every individual should cast one vote and no more than one vote, will angrily deny this right of voting to that half of the herd which is of the female gender. The same Frenchman, who will affirm religion to be a purely private matter whereon no exceptional laws may impinge, will actively support a policy forbidding a particular religion to be taught by men and women devoted to it and acting in common. He thus contradicts himself from an association of ideas in either case, and yet self-contradiction is what he most detests.

A man observing England from the outside and coming across Whiggery in its great historical examples of the eighteenth-century nobles, and of many a modern statesman glorying in the strength of England, will, I think, without exception fall into one of two errors: he will either think that Whiggery is an ideal republicanism living by the principle of equality, or he will denounce it, as did the great Irishman, in the phrase: "Bloody, base and treacherous Whigs."

It is neither to be praised or denounced. It is to be appreciated.

Had I the space, and my readers the patience, I might print fifty pages of clinching anecdote wherein is visible the nature of this hybrid creature, the Whig. I might tell you the story of that old gentleman in Sussex, who denouncing the looseness of young women in these, our post-war times, said in my hearing (with some vehemence), "Such things were unknown in my youth," and then added softly, as though musing, "except of course, in the old Whig families." Or one could recite the example of that excellent retrograde of about a century ago, who after a speech proclaiming the inviolable rights of the free Englishman to his home, was reproached for turning a number of poor tenants out of doors, and replied with beautiful simplicity: "May not a man do what he likes with his own?" The same man would have harangued by the hour against the vileness of the Russian relations between lord and serf. He could not discover his own parallel because a cloud of Whiggery lay before his eyes.

It was essentially the Whig spirit which defended the French Revolution in the case of some extreme enthusiasts among the wealthiest of English families. It was the same spirit which, with some excuse, defended the rebellion of the American Colonies. It was, above all, the spirit which was irreconcilably hostile to active personal monarchy and which yet desired to preserve the title thereof. It was Whiggery which killed the English Crown, as one might murder a living man, but which set up the symbol thereof as one might set up the statue of a murdered man.

How did this strange, most vigorous and exceedingly national product arise? I will reverse the right order in the answering of that question and talk first of the name, which is unimportant, and next of the thing.

The *name* "Whig" contrasted with the word "Tory" first appeared long after the *thing* had become of high importance in England. "Whig" was the nickname given at first, I believe, to those enthusiasts north of the border who rebelled violently against the authority of the King of England and Scotland because that authority clashed with their extreme religion. There were connected with such rebellions, as with all rebellions, various extravagances and crimes. "Whig," therefore, was used as a term of opprobrium, as one might say "you dirty rebel". "Tory" was similarly used in the third of the three kingdoms, Ireland. It was the nickname there given to men in conflict with English law and the society it had set up in the English effort to conquer Ireland. Outlaws, bandits, raiders, these were Tories. So the men who appealed to law and civic equality against the traditional kingship of England denounced their more conservative opponents by the name of "Tories," as who should say: "You irrational supporter of violence; you mere superstitious follower of ancient names and forms."

But I say that "Whiggery" the thing, was full grown and active long before the name "Whig" had come above the surface. The name "Whig" (as an appellation given to one who stood for that new English mixture of liberalism and money-power, following on the quarrel between money-power and monarchy) was not heard in political discussion, I believe, until the violent dissensions between petitioners and abhorrers, during the effort to exclude the Duke of

York altogether from succession to the Throne. But the Whig theory of the State, the Whig social practice, the Whig mind, consciously and unconsciously at work, you have appearing in the seed or embryo before even Elizabeth is dead. It is tumultuously growing during the Civil Wars and behold, against all expectation and all logic, it is mature and triumphantly established in practice, within half a dozen years of the Restoration.

That strength of wealth in the Commons of the Restoration Parliament, those claims to power by squires and rich merchants, advanced, as it were, instinctively and without definition and increasingly acted upon, even during the first decade of Charles II's activity, were essentially Whig. Whiggery, like everything else, went through its stages of development. It was conceived, was born, was nurtured, grew and came of age. We may dispute as to the exact date of its majority, but it was more than a boy – it was almost a full grown man – when the crisis of 1670, the Treaty of Dover leaking out, came to stamp it for good and gave it a character which it has not yet lost. All the violent, nearly successful attacks on the King, especially the Popish Plot, were Whiggery, Whiggery, Whiggery. The unscrupulous, determined, and convinced further rebellious drive against James II was Whiggery roaring for a prey; and the Revolution of 1688 was, as I have said, Whiggery triumphant and enthroned.

Let those who see the intense and comic contradiction between the liberal theory of Whiggery and the mammonite practice thereof remember that Whiggery led England to her highest summit of political power, and that when its chief representatives confused patriotism with the ideas of their own class, they could advance the plain fact that they had both created and exalted modern England.

When I say that Whiggery made modern England, I must modify that statement by one obvious exception. The great modern European nations have none of them been made by any one spirit to be discovered in them during modern times. They all proceed from a common foundation of Greek and Latin culture and of that Christendom into which the ancient pagan civilisation was baptised. There is, moreover, in every great European nation a mass of qualities especial to itself, which are superior to, and broader than, the political forces which may have formed them in their social or constitutional structure. Still it is true to say that Whiggery was the *chief* formative of what we call today England. Its traditional opponent, Toryism, with its lingering respect for monarchy and even for feudal memories may be cited as a sort of foil or contrast to Whiggery, but Whiggery was the master throughout. It was conquering, before it appeared above the surface towards the end of the first decade in Charles II's reign; by 1674 it had taken on a personality unmistakable; it had by 1681 a name of its own, by the end of the century it bid for complete power and throughout the eighteenth and nineteenth centuries on even into the twentieth, it led the dance.

Now Whiggery in its very considerable achievement used two main forces. It wrote modern English history and it established a religion of what it called "the British Constitution," to which by ceaseless iteration, it pledged the political mind of the whole country.

As to how it wrote English history, everyone who has read that history in any textbook of the last two hundred years and more may understand. Every Whig presumption, every Whig doctrine is taken for granted by our historians. Those who are in reaction against Whiggery are useful as exceptions or oddities, and they are quoted as such. They do not affect the general truth that Whiggery took the story of England and told it in its own terms, suppressed what it would, told what lies it felt inclined to tell, and at last made them all pass – the suppressions and the falsehoods – as current coin. It caused men to take for granted what was true about it; such as, for instance, the fact that it established a reign of law (but a law of its own kind very different from the moral code of Christendom), or the fact that its devotion to wealth increased the wealth of the community. But it also made falsehood take root, as in the pretence that Parliamentary oligarchy is democratic.

There are in the last two centuries many outstanding protests against Whiggery, many powerful literary monuments which rebuke it – for instance, Bolingbroke's "Patriot King." Disraeli, with his acute alien vision and honesty of purpose analysed it adversely, and his analysis was successful; but he did not, any more than did Bolingbroke before him, affect the great volume of the thing. He diminished in no way, for all the volume of his protest and for all its verve, the bulky political stuff of Whiggery, whereof the England of his time, as of earlier and later days consisted. The man lived in the very atmosphere of Whiggery, and his efforts at satirising what was over-

Whig only resulted in a sort of sentimental caricature which was just as Whiggish as could be, permeated with that same humbug of false lineage and very real adoration of wealth which made the Whig what he is. Nor would Disraeli have dared to attack the "Constitution"; he would perhaps have been intellectually incapable of conceiving a political England built upon other lines.

As examples of the way in which English history has been written by Whigs and how their thesis has thoroughly permeated the scholarly, as well as the popular, mind, consider such a major instance as the monstrous legend that James II was planning the *forcible* conversion of this country to Catholicism. One might as well say (and there were men found to say it) that the dull Radicals of Joseph Chamberlain's day were planning to set up an egalitarian republic. Or consider the still more monstrous legend which will have it that the title to the English Throne is parliamentary. Or consider the way in which, all through our textbooks, the phrase "English people" is used, as though it were identical with Whiggery. The revolution of 1688 is acclaimed as the action of the "English people." The second Dutch War, because it is fought in alliance with Louis XIV, is repulsive to the "English people," although not ten years before, the whole mass of England was in a fever of hostility to the Dutch and their commercial power. It is Whig history which has represented the English House of Commons as being primarily a mirror of this same "English people," though it took away their land, forbade their association to combine against the evils of nascent capitalism and maintained the grossest iniquities in popular suffrage and the grossest corruption in administration.

Whig history would have it that the Habeas Corpus Act was something of a divine sort, whereof foreigners were unworthy. Whiggery pretended to have secured for the subjects of the great Whig families an independence unknown to the free peasants on the Continent and for the publicists of the English eighteenth century (or of today for that matter) a freedom of expression which is unknown outside this island. Again Whig history will have it that the continued misgovernment of Ireland was due in some way to the exceptional incapacity or exceptional dishonesty of the Irish people.

Whig history took on various forms and nuances. It is not homogeneous, and that is its strength. It produced, for instance, by a slow process of incubation, the hero worship of Oliver Cromwell. It also produced that very different form of hero worship, or at any rate, of idolatry – the late Victorian legend. Whig history made it impossible for the average English educated man to understand the Middle Ages, save as a sort of picturesque pageant which had nothing to do with his own development. When it found in the Middle Ages anything which could be twisted into some contorted resemblance of the modern things which it proclaimed, Whig history lied without restraint. Simon de Montfort became in its hands, not a vehement, somewhat superstitious Catholic French noble, but an English middle-class Protestant and reformer. Whiggery did not give him those epithets but it implied them, and while it was about it, it made Alfred of Wessex something uncommonly like the squire patron of a Sunday-school.

Like all official history,† Whig history, as it approached the term of its natural life (it is still vigorous but its decay is manifest), sank from level to level in the community. Today it is still the orthodox history of the elementary schools; it is defended, though with increasing difficulty, in the national universities; but its native ground still remains the great mass of the lower middle class, and there it is of greatest effect in those historical novels with which we are blessed or cursed. A future generation, perhaps the next, may watch with interest the appearance of some real piece of historical fiction wherein our fathers shall be made to behave as they did behave; the effect will be startling.

Meanwhile we may note as one last example of the way in which the Whigs have affected the teaching of history in England, the really remarkable instance of Lingard.

Lingard was a Catholic priest. He was also by far the most learned historian of his day and on top of that, he was the first writer to base a complete history of England upon original documents. He originated, he set up, the whole method of modern historical writing in this country. You find his statements, his citations reappearing perpetually (without acknowledgment) in the writings of his successors. A first-rate example of this is the application of the word Senlac to the Battle of Hastings. It was Lingard who made that error, taking

---

† Its publicist in the mid-nineteenth century was Macaulay, in the twentieth it is his relative, Sir George Trevelyan.

the place name which he found in Odericus for something both contemporary and Anglo-Saxon. Now there is no better way of proving the dependence of writers upon an authority than spotting the way in which they repeat his errors. Lingard made hardly any errors; he made this one error and behold it is repeated a thousand times in every textbook put in the hands of every child; and, if we don't take care, the very name of Hastings may be forgotten.

But there is a second thing to be said about Lingard, in illustration of the effect which Whiggery has had upon English history. Lingard, not only as the most learned but the foundational English historian of the nineteenth century, has come to be boycotted. You hardly hear his name; you still more rarely hear his true position described. Most educated men today have not so much as heard of it. Now that piece of suppression is a triumph of Whiggery. *Yet Lingard himself was soaked in Whiggery.* It was the atmosphere of his time and he could not escape it.

While Whiggery has thus presided over the teaching of general history and the making of its own strange doctrines taken for granted throughout the country, it has especially presided over constitutional history. The great Teutonic Myth which sailed triumphantly down the stream of modern English constitutional theory until it struck the rock of the Great War was Whig from beginning to end, for it was essentially Hanoverian. It begins with the presentation of an invasion of this island by swarms of Germans arriving in small boats across the North Sea. They bring with them the whole character of the English people and a special dose of original virtue. They destroy the towns of Roman England; they exterminate its population; they settle in the places they have laid waste and from them all that England is today derives. The "English Hundred" which was unknown until within a century of the Conquest, is ascribed to a German military usage mentioned by Tacitus, noticed by him seventeen centuries before the English Teutonic Myth was invented, and never heard of again until within a century of the Conqueror. Its origins in Merovingian Gaul are suppressed.

In the matter of parliament the theme runs riot. The origin of the medieval parliament in the Pyrenees is never heard of. It is traced to a corrupted lineage which relates it unnaturally to local usages that can be twisted into connection with pre-Conquest times and even to sundry habits of modern German-speaking Swiss. The plain and natural story of the medieval parliament as it is found, first in the French southern provinces, later in the northern, and last of all, under the Plantagenet Kings of England, is put aside behind a screen, as it were, so that no one shall know that it is there. Local customs which are common to England and to the Western Middle Ages everywhere are spoken of as uniquely national. The whole story of English law and government is warped to fit in with the framework of Whiggery. Whether we shall ever get that story out of its cramped and distorted state may be doubted, for by the time we have done so, the interests in these things, with which Whiggery has dealt on its historical side, will be dead.

But what will not die for a long time will be the essentially national tone of Whiggery. It will survive by its virtues and especially by the virtue of patriotism. Were England to suffer some major and permanent defeat, it is probable that this great business of Whiggery would go under for ever; but so long as England is prosperous and proud, prosperity and pride being the twin pillars of Whiggery, Whiggery will stand; and who would wish it otherwise?

At any rate, there you have Wiggery – and Whiggery was that with which Charles was already wrestling when there came that other conflict closely connected with Whiggery, but dealing with principles far more ancient and far more fundamental, the violent issue of royal Catholicism.

THE WOMEN

IT IS THE PARADOXICAL TRUTH THAT IN DEALING WITH THE MAJOR historical business of Charles's reign, which is his great effort at restoration, that point in his private life which is most popularly known and which our official history has both ridiculously exaggerated and misread plays no appreciable part. All our Whig historians magnify the amours of the King and make it one of their central features in the period, and, of course, popular history has not only followed them, but has so underlined the looseness of the Court in private that the essential public business is lost sight of.

Yet the truth is simple enough. Charles was a man who began very early in life a series of promiscuous adventures with women. He continued them during his exile and poverty. When he was back on his throne he changed that random and futile excess for the more regular but still quite irregular connections which might almost be called the norm of that period in the lives of royalties. You get a succession of conspicuous mistresses, some of whom may not have been mistresses at all, and most of whom certainly were. Children are born to him whom he recognises and ennobles after the pattern of his cousin of France. He had already by one of the least reputable of his wandering chances had the handsome son (Monmouth) to whom he remained all his life so deeply attached. The others born after his coronation he could not make less in rank than the eldest born.† And one of the things that has most helped to perpetuate the false reading of women's political influence upon the King is the presence throughout English history after his time of the duchies which date from that harem. Harem is the word and by the use of it we are the better able to understand the central point, which is that men so circumstanced are nearly always indifferent to the advice, let alone the initiative, of the women with whom they associate. It was so with Charles, and

---

† Eldest of those recognized in public. We have already made mention of that first son, born before his exile in his 'teens.

when we understand that, we see what Louis XIV himself and his ministers never saw – that they were wasting their time in elaborate intrigues to deflect English policy by the use of the women.

It was not only Louis and his envoys who went wrong here; it was the mass of men at home about the King. We have letters written to and from Europe all based on the conception that this or that new influence would supplant some older influence, whereas in point of fact neither an early nor a later mistress had anything to do with the international position and the international plans of the King. I shall quote at the end of this brief section the capital instance which proves this thesis up to the hilt. But for the moment let anyone ask himself which of the train produced a clear effect upon policy? He will find no such agent and no such act. In petty things, small appointments and so forth, the women naturally have their influence, in major things they have none.

The explanation of this is not far to seek. The influence of any women upon any man is dependent upon some small, strong, personal touch. It is usually at its greatest where the man is consistently faithful to one woman and is or has become deeply enamoured of her, as had been the case with Charles I. But even in his case the Stuart sense of kingship and of duty to the nation did not allow Henrietta Maria to have her way in that with which she was most concerned, the religion of her sons. She brought up her daughter a Catholic. After her husband's death she made some attempt to influence her youngest son, but during her husband's life she had no say in this one matter which most concerned her and on which she felt most deeply. She was not without effect on the King's political actions, but the chief of them were quite independent of her – for instance, the surrender of Strafford. Strafford was sacrificed by Charles I because the Archbishop of York had advised his Monarch to that effect. We know how violent were the Queen's feelings in the matter, but it was not those feelings which lay at the root of the tragedy, it was Charles's devotion to the Church of England and to the authority of its prelates. Laud was in prison, Williams was the next in ecclesiastical position, and the chief personage in orders to whom the King could turn in what was for him essentially a case of conscience. Williams had judged that "one man should die for the people" and his decision it was that was followed.

CHARLES II: THE LAST RALLY

In the affairs of Charles II there was nothing of all this. Ecclesiastical advice he certainly never dreamt of. Neither did he dream of seeking, following or even receiving the advice of any one of the women about him. Conjecture and rumour, second-hand gossip have done their best to ascribe some slight effect to Lady Castlemaine, but there is no substance in those rumours and conjectures and second-hand relations. No one can be so silly as to ascribe the least powers of the sort to Ellen Gwyn or to her fellow actress. As for the very handsome but monstrous Mancini, to whom he was tied by early memories and whose high rank he respected (no one could respect anything else about her) it may be doubted whether she was his mistress at all; it is certain that so far as the conduct of the State was concerned she might as well never have come near the English Court.

It is so with every one of the famous group from the greatest to the least, but if you would have the most convincing instance of all, you have but to concentrate upon the position and continuous converse of Louise de Keroualle.

If there were one woman who might have had something to say in matters of State it was Louise. She was, very early in the game, the first figure among those who surrounded Charles with their attractions during the second and decisive half of his public life as King. She was, early in the progress of that period, the *Maitresse en Titre,* on the model of those recognised in the contemporary Courts and especially in the splendid example of Versailles. She was more of a confidante and of a close companion by far than any other woman whom Charles met after his brief poignant vision of that younger sister whom he adored.

It was as one who had come to England with that younger sister Minette that she affected Minette's brother. Louise was the one link of memory he had with that beloved being so suddenly and dreadfully called away by death. Moreover, Louise de Keroualle was personally more pleasing to Charles and more permanently so than any of the others. It is not in her appearance – she was somewhat insignificant and languid and in a fashion immature – that we can discover the secret of this. It must have been in the superiority of her manner and in the reasonableness of her temper, to which I think we should add a growing and real affection for her royal lover. It is her whom we shall see in the last supreme moment, anxious and eagerly painstaking for his shriving and for his final acceptance of the truth which he had always seen but which the highest worldly motives had forbidden him publicly to confess.

If, then, there was one woman of whom, with any other man, one might have been almost certain that *she* would have taken over some direction of his mind, it was Louise. He never permitted her the least approach to such direction. He was lavish in his generosity with her and he was certainly grateful to her for a comradeship and conversation which he could find in no other of her sex, but from political action he debarred her altogether.

She had taste in the arts, not profound but sufficient, and admiration of taste was another quality which Charles had inherited from his father. That the monuments and the furnishing of those two reigns, Charles II and Charles I, should have been so exquisite, that we should have had in them such best examples of building and of collection and such appreciation of letters, was not an accident of the time. It was especially a creation of the Court.

In this, then, also, Louise fitted well enough with the humour of the man whose constant associate she was, but she fitted in with no intellectual occupation of his, least of all with the highest of such occupations: the occupation of kingship, the conduct of the nation.

The test of all this, a test at once so obvious and so strong that it is shameful in the most prejudiced even of our official historians to have missed it, is the marriage of Princess Mary to the Prince of Orange in November, 1677.

Charles had had sufficient acquaintance with the House of Orange. His aunt, the widow of the last prince (father of William), the daughter-in-law of that most un-Dutch Dutch hero, of that most irreligious religious hero, William, ridiculously called the Silent, herself daughter to Charles I, was a woman with some of the Stuart virtues, especially tenacity, and some of the Stuart character, but the son whom she posthumously bore to her husband had little or nothing of the Stuarts in him, least of all their loyalty.

His uncle had had more opportunity for acquainting himself with that eccentric and morose character than had many of his contemporaries. He had been under the same roof as Charles during his puny and peevish boyhood: not an occasion for winning his admiration.

CHARLES II: THE LAST RALLY

As William grew to manhood – such manhood as he had – he fell into that vice for which he was later notorious throughout Europe, and on which we further have the decisive testimony of Burnet.

For Burnet's mean soul, which revelled in betrayal, even the betrayal of those to whom he owed most, composed and wrote down the sentence which should never be forgotten, Burnet it is who tells us – though it needed not much telling considering the wealth of foreign rumour upon the subject and the condition of William's last years, notably the position of Keppel – that William suffered from this, shall we say "weakness," and that he was especially careful to conceal it: in which effort, like most of his kind, he failed. William had already been considered for alliance with the English Royal Family. The opportunity had been missed. It was not till now, when the young man was already in his twenty-eighth year, that the subject was renewed.

It will be remembered that James, Duke of York, had had by his wife, Anne Hyde, two daughters among other children, who, unlike the other children, survived, Mary the elder and Anne the younger. Mary at this moment was fifteen years old, and therefore by the custom of that day marriageable; Anne was still a child. Since it was now certain that Catherine of Braganza could never give the King an heir or an heiress, Anne and Mary stood next in succession after their father to the English throne. Though the rule of succession save in the direct form of father and son was not quite clearly fixed, Mary would presumably be in due time Queen of England, unless a son should be borne to James by his second wife, Mary of Modena. At this moment, the late autumn of 1677, no life intervened in the succession after James save that of his daughter Mary and that of her sister, the child Anne, who would come next if Mary had no children.

Now in connection with these two Princesses we must note once again that major matter, the determination of Charles to render as secure as possible the throne for the greatness of which he lived. He had appreciated from the beginning that it was essential to the preservation of legitimate and hereditary monarchy in England that the individual on the throne should be Protestant. This was not because a large majority of the nation was strongly anti-Catholic so early as 1660, but because an official Protestant tone had been given to Government and the whole State and to English society in general for now so long that there was no going back on it. Moreover, the very large minority that was intensely anti-Catholic was especially strong in the three sections of society which counted most in opposition to the Crown: (a) the great landed families, the core of whom had been established by the Reformation, (b) the craftsmen and merchants of London, and (c) the liquid wealth which London controlled, the new banking system. The older traditions, half-Catholic and all royalist, threatened all these three things, and the Crown could never stand permanently in opposition to those three.

Charles, having made up his mind between his conviction of eternal truth and his passion for that local, temporal, royal office which he had inherited and would spend his life to re-establish, having decided for the immediate and very high worldly aim and put off the satisfaction of the other to the last possible moment, worked continuously in his tenacious and single-hearted fashion for the success of what he had chosen.

He could not prevent the conversion of Anne Hyde. He had great sympathy with that powerful character and even if he guessed which way she was going he would have known that no interference of his could have moved her by an inch. He was perturbed by the personal conversion of her husband through her influence and still more through the shock of her death. We have seen how he tried to soften the effect of James's religious connection by keeping it secret and how that proved impossible from the very nature of the Catholic Faith. But one thing he could do (since kings in those days still had real power), he could insist on the two heiresses, the Princesses, being brought up in the Protestant National Church of England. This he did. It was a cruel thing for their father, but he had to submit because his brother, their uncle, was King.

These children seem to have been trained in an especially anti-Catholic manner. They were too young to have any sufficient knowledge of their mother's religious experience. Moreover, the transition of that mother from a devout sort of Anglicanism to the fullness of the Faith had been brief. There were but a few months at the end of her life during which she was fully of the Roman Communion. Therefore you do not find in the career either of Mary or of Anne any clear leanings towards the ancestral creed and practice. With Mary, indeed, that would be most unlikely, for she had neither sufficient vitality nor sufficient brains to approach any complete philosophy (such as is the Catholic) if it happened to be unfamiliar to her. More might have been expected of Anne, who was, on the profound and acute testimony of Swift, "the only really good woman he had ever known." But Anne was equally separated from any such tendencies. The policy of her uncle had thoroughly succeeded in presenting to the nation two soundly Protestant figures as direct inheritors of the throne.

But there still remained the question of their marriages. On whom the choice should fall (it would have, of course, to be the King's choice) would depend the security of the Stuart dynasty almost as much as upon their own profession of religion. As yet in 1677 Anne was too young for the problem to arise. The medieval custom of early solemn marriage engagements, which had been so fruitful in consolidating the mediaeval kingdoms, was dead. But Mary in this year was, as we have seen, already old enough to be given a husband. Who should that husband be?

The great kingdoms of Europe, the great thrones rather, were still Catholic in tradition and inheritance. The Emperor was particularly attached to the ancient foundations of Europe, whereof indeed he was the representative. The united crowns of Spain, with their vast territory, were conspicuously Catholic. The French Monarchy, once more magnificent and increasingly powerful, though highly national, was a champion of the Catholic culture. The Protestant Courts in Europe were as yet petty and divided things. To one of them, indeed, that of Denmark, the English Royal Family was to turn when it sought a consort for Anne. But that was in the future. What of the moment? To whom should Mary be given?

It was a vital decision and in the main a decision between a policy parallel with that of France and a policy which would ultimately be opposed to that of France. Louis XIV ardently desired and half expected (though with reserves) that his own heir should marry Mary Stuart. Such a connection would have made the already dubious attachment of English neutrality or even alliance more secure.

The moment was critical. Decision could hardly be postponed. If Louise de Keroualle had any influence on English policy, this was the all-important moment in which to exercise that influence. Had it been true that her daily familiar association with Charles, who spent his leisure with her at the end of the day, would suffice to affect his decisions, *this* decision on the marriage of his niece was the one for which the French mistress was clearly designed.

And the decision was taken the other way!

Those who do not understand Charles or his position, or even what monarchy meant at the time, have tried to put the thing down to Danby. Certainly Danby had a fine and active hatred of France. Certainly Danby was both active and of great weight with his master; but as certainly Danby was not here the principal; the initiative came from Charles.

Consider the outer circumstance. The King of France was approaching the height of his continually ascending power in Europe. He had failed, indeed, to grasp Amsterdam and thereby to consolidate himself in the full inheritance of the Netherlands. But with the Emperor increasingly menaced from the east by Islam (which in half a dozen years was to besiege Vienna itself), and with the Germanies fallen into that mass of small governments and townships which was the result of the Thirty Years' War, Louis could still confidently go forward and look to the Rhine as his ultimate frontier. We are but three or four years off the absorption of Alsace.

It was the moment when the King of France could begin to emphasise to the utmost the national character of the Catholic Church in his dominions. The other great rival to his house, the Spaniard, was manifestly in decay. Out of all the kingdoms surrounding his realm, England was at once, for the moment, the most important and the least certain. For all these reasons the French Crown had at the same time the power to press, and the need for attaining, the English marriage. Its envoys believed that it had an instrument available for this end in Louise. Louis himself believed it.

They were living in a fool's paradise. Even had Louise interfered she could have done nothing, for the King of England had made up his mind and that Stuart fixity of purpose which in his brother was so open and stubborn as to defeat itself, in Charles underlay, out of sight, but made untearable, every major plan; as a network of fine wire, interwoven below the surface of a cloth, will make it untearable.

William's fortunes were in peril. His military incapacity had borne its natural fruit. It was the right moment to hook him.

He was sent for to appear at his uncle's Court, was affianced, wedded, and had taken off the unfortunate Mary to Holland, all within a month, the marriage taking place on the 4th of November of that year, 1677.

It is easy, for us who know all that followed, to discourse on the error of this decision. The Orange marriage destroyed the House of Stuart. Four years after Charles's death, barely a dozen after the fatal wedding, the Prince of Orange answered the summons of the Money-power in England, of the great landowners in especial, invaded Devon with his motley army of foreigners, marched on London, was joined in bulk by the gentry who held commissions under his father-in-law, saw that father-in-law out of the country and occupied London. The National Kingship of England was at an end, and its destruction will always be symbolised by the name of Orange.

But if we put ourselves back to the date in which the marriage took place, if we put ourselves into the shoes and the skins of 1677 we shall see that all calculable prevision argued for the policy of the King.

Here are the main considerations:—

1. He kept the balance just at the most dangerous time between the three elements of the triangle upon which all his policy turned: he countered the preponderating influence of Louis. He attracted what was becoming or had become the chief Dutch element, and he half-bewildered, half-silenced, the opposition at home.

2. He made the succession secure, so far as could then be judged. Not only was his niece, Mary, the heiress of his Throne, but her cousin William of Orange was after Anne and James the next heir. By the union all danger of ultimate foreign claim was apparently eliminated.

3. He made, did the King, by this decision, public "act of Protestantism." You could not have picked out of all Europe a name more representative to the average Englishman of anti-Catholicism abroad than the name of Orange. The more extreme the English Protestant, the more he thought of the House of Orange as a champion against the Catholic culture.

4. He was by this marriage preparing a Court which should be amply supplied with funds: and funds were what the English Monarchy had lacked. It was the immense wealth of the House of Orange that had given it its place and power, and though that wealth was personal and, in spite of its magnitude, only a fraction of total national revenue, it would make a very great difference to the stability of the English Throne.

5. Side by side with this was the financial alliance or support of the Dutch Money-power. It is true that this was a rival to the rapidly increasing commercial strength of London. It is also true that William represented that faction which had been so long opposed to the financial magnates of Amsterdam. But the main battle between the two maritime powers was over and presumably over for good. It was fairly safe to envisage a future in which, in the long run, the English Fleet would be permanently superior to the Dutch. England could now ally herself with the other maritime power and would soon need no longer fear it.

What Charles did was the best that he could do, within the range of vision granted to him. He could not see the future nor can we see our own, though we now see his. The essential matter in a study of Charles's character and of his effect as a political figure is the basis for the decision he took. The essential thing is our conclusion as to whether it were at the moment and with the only elements at his disposition, wise or otherwise. It was under such standards wise. It was also disastrous and mortal – for it introduced the enemy into the citadel.

Yet let this be remembered, that if Mary of Modena had not borne to Charles's brother that unexpected son, three and a half years after Charles's death, all might have gone well. Upon the death of James, Mary would have entered upon her natural inheritance, the English Throne. Her husband from Consort might presumably have been made King; the religious feelings of the English majority would have been satisfied and this without the necessity for a continued persecution of the minorities.

In other words, what killed English Monarchy was not the conversion of James II before he came to the Throne, nor even his loyal and unflinching adherence to his Faith, it was the birth of the Old Pretender.

There is one more thing to be said upon that marriage. It was the sacrifice of a human being; to make any girl, even the lethargic and hardly competent Mary, the wife of such a man as William, was to sacrifice her.

From the moment of his marriage he was insufficient. The King had jested with him and bade him "do your duty by my niece." It was not in him.

CHARLES II: THE LAST RALLY

Yes: Mary was sacrificed: not that she greatly cared one way or the other. But Royalties are compelled to such acts, and most marriages in that special world are sacrifices of some kind.

This brief study is not concerned with the career of William III and is not mainly concerned even with the motives of his public actions. Insofar as these regard England they belong to the next reign. But it may be as well to conclude with some judgment upon the fellow to whom Charles had united the fortunes of the country.

The major element in that character was a determination to achieve a guaranteed monarchical position. The House of Nassau, especially after it had inherited, through the women, the principality of Orange in Southern France, still more after it had held the administration of the wealthiest province of the Netherlands, reposed for its importance, as had the Medicis centuries before, upon the enormity of a private fortune. This superiority, coupled with certain personal talents, had put the Medicis into the forefront of Europe and right among its Kings. It had given them a sort of kingship in the rule of Tuscany. It made them the wives and the mothers of Valois and of Bourbons. It made them Popes. It might, where inheritance was through the women, have given them at last some great national throne.

The parallel between the House of Orange and the House of Medici was enough to tempt any man, and the temptation was all the stronger in the case of William III because he could have nothing else to distract him, save his private vices. He was a thoroughly bad general. He could not hope for military glory. His bungling at the Boyne is perhaps the best example of his incapacity in arms. He had no gift of speech or of letters. He thoroughly displeased even his own strange companions, and as for women, one cannot conceive any woman feeling a natural attraction towards such a one. The void in his life could only be filled by the satisfaction of a titular ambition.

That ambition was *not,* as has been too often repeated, a desire to see the King of France humbled. The proof that it was not so is that when a final victory was possible before the end of his life, William, having already become a King, refused to support the last and decisive policy of others against Louis XIV.

He had no special devotion to those who were becoming through a prolonged and well-defended independence the Dutch people. He was not a Fleming by inheritance or by habit or by anything in his character, but he did know that on his leadership of one Flemish faction and his command of the Flemish armies he could reach what would virtually be (and what by the action of his marriage and treason actually became) a throne.

All around him and his family had been those great thrones by whose occupants William the Silent, his son Maurice, the considerable General, Maurice's elder brother, the head of them, after the death of his father, and now the third William the grandson of the Silent, were treated as equals: as inter-marriageable equals.

William III wrote, thought and spoke in French. He had nothing National about him. Not even that Dutch nationality which was not yet in full being. All his life was narrow and personal in the extreme. His ambition was not national or religious in motive but wholly egoist. He was determined to be a king.

He lacked the capacity for companionship. But he was tenacious. He had not the virile and spiritual tenacity of his uncle Charles II or of his grandfather, Charles I; but he had a sort of gimblet tenacity which was not to be despised. He bored into a thing and held it.

Also he had this advantage which has served so many men who have desired a high place in this world, he was unscrupulous. He would lie freely and as freely break his word.

There is one last thing to be said about him which has nothing to do with his qualities or his odd defects. He had luck.

Every man who regularly ascends along whatever worldly path must have luck, and William had it continually. It was lucky for him that de Witt was murdered and torn to pieces in the streets which it was William's duty to keep orderly. He may not have known what was toward but he took advantage of it. He had luck in the vacillating decision of Russell at the Hague. He had luck when the plan to assassinate him failed in London as it had not failed with his grandfather at Delft. Especially had he luck at Heurtebise, when the army which could have annihilated him was held back. He obtained all that luck combined with a continuous purpose could give him. That was not much, for he never had joy.

FULL GALE: THE POPISH PLOT

FTER THE ORANGE MARRIAGE FELL THAT FULL AND VIOLENT attack on the House of Stuart, the Popish Plot.

The Popish Plot was in itself only a mixture of absurdity, cruelty and violent excitement soon exhausted. Because it touches on the vital nerve of religion, it has made a most vivid mark on the reading of English history. It has been related in detail a hundred times, and there is nothing new to be said about it so far as the mere chronicle of it is concerned. It would be quite apart from the purpose of this book to go over it again here.

But what *is* to the purpose of this book and of all history in connection with the Popish Plot is the evidence it gives of the way in which it imperilled the Throne, and of Charles's power to carry on through heavy weather. It is an extreme example of the limits to which he would go to save the dynasty and the national monarchy.

The main points of that episode so far as we are concerned – that is, the main points directly connected with the character and policy of Charles II – are as follows:—

1. The evidence which the Popish Plot affords of the intensity of anti-Catholic feeling in a large proportion of the nation, and especially in London. It shows why the succession was in peril and it greatly increased that peril.

2. The evidence it affords of that gravely misunderstood matter, the size of the Catholic body and, under the later Stuarts, of the sympathisers therewith in the mass of the nation.

3. The question of its origin and especially whether Shaftesbury, who certainly guided it, also created it.

4. The example it gives of the extremes to which Charles was prepared to go in his compromises with morals and even with honour: the extreme limit of the sacrifices he was prepared to make for the one object of his life and reign, the maintenance of the English

Crown. The Popish Plot provides the special and critical case of Stafford whose execution I have already pointed out as forming, with two other matters, the grave moral blunder of the reign.

5. (Much the most important point.) The effect of the Popish Plot excitement and terror on the Catholic Church in England. It was the final and mortal blow from which English Catholicism never recovered.

Let us consider these points in their order.

1. The intensity of anti-Catholic feeling in general and particularly in London. I must here beg the reader to pay particular attention to what I may call the "terms of reference."

When I speak of "the violence of anti-Catholic feeling" I do not mean by this that England *as a whole* was filled with violent anti-Catholic feeling. Quite the opposite. It is demonstrable that sympathy with Catholicism was far more general and on a larger scale than it has ever been since and that neutrals were, as always, numerous in their varying degrees. What the phrase does imply is that the potential of anti-Catholic hatred, where it existed, was very high. To use a metaphor from modern electric science, the voltage rather than the amperage of anti-Catholicism was extreme. Its vigour rather than its volume was remarkable. Moreover, this intensity of feeling was especially concentrated in London, which led England.

What had moved the hatred of Catholicism to such a pitch of intensity among those many Englishmen who felt it thus was, of course, the combination of national feeling with the immediate apparent threat of a Catholic succession; added to which was the special circumstances of Louis XIV's recent military successes in the Low Countries. For the Low Countries were essential to England.

But though these main causes of the violent hatred of Catholicism, which rapidly grew to be a sort of delirium, are clear enough, what is not to be accounted for so simply is the insane fanaticism of the moment.

The Popish Plot was not, as has often been said, unique in the history of England for its fury. It was parallel to more than one episode of very strong sectional feeling in the general story of England. When such extravagant emotions have been roused, especially by war or the threat of war, the national temperament of the English leads itself to excessive nervous reactions which are part of that strong visual imagination distinguishing the national character.

There has been a special temptation to regard this exaltation in the matter of the Popish Plot as something exceptional because such a theory permits of a special interpretation very congenial to our official history. If the public delirium of the Popish Plot be regarded as a thing wholly exceptional, a sort of brief collective madness descending suddenly upon great groups of the population, then one can pretend that the fears of the mob were groundless and so proceed to repeat the false thesis that the Catholic numbers in the England of 1678–1681 were very small and the Catholic body almost insignificant.

On this account one textbook after another presents the Popish Plot as a unique anomaly: a thing happening without parallel in our annals and quite irrational.

Now, the reality is just the other way. The intensity of the excitement was, of course, exceptional and the causes of it insufficient. But England in 1678 not only still counted a very large number of Catholic-minded people, as has been pointed out more than once in these pages, but had still surviving in its society *a living tradition of the old Faith*. That is the central point to hold.

It was nearly a hundred and twenty years since the last open practice of the Mass had been stamped out. But it was only a long lifetime since the tide had turned and England had begun to be more and more Protestant. A good half of the population were traditionally Catholic before the Gunpowder Plot, and the Gunpowder Plot stood to the Popish Plot as something little more remote than the Franco-Prussian War is from ourselves. It was not nearly so far off as the Indian Mutiny is from us, and we all know what vivid memories the period of the Crimea and the Indian Mutiny have left behind them.

All the older people at the time of the Popish Plot could remember how, in childhood, the survivors of an earlier generation had talked of the Catholic Church as omnipresent, and how many of that former generation persevered in calling themselves Catholic. There appeared thirty or forty years ago a well-written and lucid apology for the theory that the Popish Plot was real: that there had been a conspiracy never fully revealed, for advancing Catholicism by authority and by force at that moment in England. The thesis was extravagant

196

and the book unconvincing, in spite of its ability, but there underlay that picture the truth that Catholicism, though defeated and weakened and unpopular as being anti-national, was still in 1678–1680 a living force in England, such as it has never been since.

Moreover, the great political Power abroad at the moment was the Catholic culture of France at the very doors of England, and France had just been occupied in a long and half-successful attack upon that other Protestant centre, Holland.

London was the focus of the whole affair, of course; and what is not always appreciated is that, but for London, the Popish Plot would never have been the important thing it was. It was a fire lit by and nourished by *London*, the heat of which radiated from *London* everywhere. Now why was this?

There were many reasons for London's special position in the great religious quarrel from the opening of the English Reformation onwards. In the first place, London was not only a seaport, but far and away the largest seaport of the realm. It received and sent out more shipping and did more foreign trade than all the rest of the country combined.

This meant two things: first, that it was open to foreign influences, new foreign ideas and movements. That was why, at the origin of the Reformation, London contained so large a proportion of Reformed preachers and missionaries of the new idea. In the second place, it had the opposite effect of making London much more alive to unpopular foreign influence and adverse to it, than was the average English town. The Londoner met more foreigners, and it is the almost invariable rule in international affairs that the populace particularly hates the alien with whom it comes into actual contact. In all countries the populace hates aliens; but it is one thing to hate in general foreigners whom one has never seen, and another to hate the foreigner whose grotesque actions and absurd dress are thrust upon you continually. Over and over again people in London have fallen into a murderous mood against foreigners of various kinds. Long ago it had been the Spaniard; now, in the late seventeenth century, it was the Frenchman.

Then, again, London was the place, out of all England, where men and ideas met and activated one another thoroughly. It was the centre of things after a fashion which could hardly be conceived today. Major happenings in the Low Countries or Northern France were known in London within, as a rule, forty-eight hours, and were being discussed all over the town before the end of the third day. Only exceptional storms could prolong that brief delay, but the average county town, even near the ports, for the most part waited much longer for its news and, as a rule, took much less interest in it.

But a last condition was more important than all of these. London was the financial and commercial centre. In London were the funds and the agents who could pay and who, with capital at their disposal, could organise. Since a great part of the excitement was artificial and deliberately fostered, this financial element counted for a great deal. The instigators and agents of the Terror called the Popish Plot had paymasters; and those paymasters kept their balances in the City of London.

A minor point, but not unimportant, is the fact that London alone possessed Embassy Chapels where Mass was said, and the Queen's Household had the same privileges. In London, therefore, out of all the English towns, was the Catholic Church physically and visibly present, and the more an object of mistrust and hatred from such actual presence.

The immediate neighbourhood of London was also the seat of Government. The King's palace in Whitehall and the palace of St. James, Parliament and the Courts of Law normally meeting in Westminster Hall, St. Stephen's chapel and the neighbouring Upper House – all these were available to the London mob when Pym had been doing his work against the national monarchy in the previous generation, but could only do it through the clamour and intimidation of the street roughs. No such crowds could be gathered with an effect of this kind in any other point of England.

2. Now, let us touch once more on the numbers which Catholicism could muster in the England of the later Stuarts. I have repeatedly given the general figures, not only here but in other books on the period; but it will help the reader to understand the excitement of the Popish Plot if the proof of these numbers is briefly tabulated again here.

It was, of course, a time without a census and with very few official figures of any kind. But we have various indications which all converge upon the same conclusion so often given – that about one English family in eight was openly and avowedly Catholic at this time, and *some much larger number* in general sympathy with Catholicism, by a sympathy varying in degree.

Of proofs there is first of all the common sense of the position. A spiritual influence permeating all Society for a thousand years is not wiped out in a moment, especially if those who are concerned in suppressing it have no strong convictions of their own but are only considering money and politics, as was the case with the directors of the English Reformation from the Seymours to the Cecils, father and son, and from the Cecils to the great landed gentry of Charles II's time with the Russells (the chief of the Reformation millionaires) at their head.

It is common sense that England, being soaked in Catholicism in 1560, and hardly yet moved against it ten years later, should be, as all contemporaries agree, at least half Catholic numerically in 1600. The later estimates correspond exactly to such a gradual, not abrupt, decline. You get from a fifth to a sixth of the governing classes, as represented by the commissioned ranks of the rival armies, Catholic during the Civil Wars. More than a third of Charles I's officers were admittedly Catholic, and that is why its opponents talked of Charles's army as a Papist Army. The Papist numbers, of course, declined; but they declined slowly till the very end of the business.

Four years after Charles II's death, ten years after the Popish Plot, when James II was on the point of losing his Throne (1688), Louis XIV urged him to abandon the defence of his Catholic subjects as being no more than a tenth of the population, for it was the whole object of Louis at that moment to dissuade James from supporting the Papists; he did not want to have a divided England as his ally.

Since Louis was putting the figures as low as he could, it is reasonable to regard this "one-tenth" of his as standing for at least one-eighth in reality.

More than one-fifth of the House of Lords was Catholic, and one-seventh was so strongly Catholic as to be willing to risk exclusion rather than abandon their position. Again, when inquiries were made by James shortly after his brother's death among those whose social position entitled them to be Justices of the Peace, there was found to be an even larger proportion of Catholics. Nor let it be supposed that this proportion would be especially high among the well-to-do classes. It was rather the other way. It was the well-to-do and the landed people who suffered most from the penal laws and were most tempted to conform with the national Protestantism around them, for they were burdened by fines, and an open declaration of their religion cut them off from public services and from many forms of public income.

We have yet another piece of proof. When those who would not renounce the Faith were made to leave London, often at ruinous cost to themselves, the number who were willing to suffer rather than keep silent, turns out to be about one-eighth of the estimated population of the day. It was during the business of the Popish Plot itself that this decision was taken to turn out the Catholics who would not apostatise.

As we get in this last generation of the Stuart period about one-eighth for the Catholic body still openly professing its religion in England, what are we to allow for the broad margin of those who sympathised, but who for various reasons, would not declare themselves? Those who, by family tradition or personal experience or mere effect of neighbourhood were touched with Catholic feeling? That margin, of course, cannot be estimated even in the rough way by which we come to our one-eighth for the open and professed Catholics. But on the analogy of every other process of the kind where an old opinion or habit is in decline and has left relics of its former standing behind it, we can safely put this marginal belt at something approaching in numbers the decided and openly professed – and persecuted – minority. If one-eighth of England was willing to suffer as Catholics then suffered, rather than explicitly abandon a forbidden and persecuted religion, it is fair to assume that not far short of one-quarter, perhaps fully a quarter of the whole population, stood in varying degrees of sympathy with the ancestral creed. After all, its traditions were round them on every side; it was still exercising a powerful influence upon men whose fortune permitted them to follow what social practice they chose, and its nomenclature, its ancient ornament of statuary and the rest were still present, its effect on language and to some extent upon popular letters; though these last were filled with extreme opposition to Catholicism, they also retained the memory of Catholicism in many a verse and ballad. The same is true of many a local custom.

In general, one may say that the terrorism of the Popish Plot is largely explained by the very considerable remaining numerical strength of Catholicism in the England of that day.

3. Now, how did the Popish Plot terror originate? Whence sprang that extraordinarily violent humour? Who or what lit the fire which raged so hot and murderous during those brief two years? It is a roaring furnace in the later days of 1678; just dying down, but only just beginning to die down, in the middle of 1680. How are we to account for its starting at all?

We must begin by remarking that no man sets down in black and white for posterity the things which of their nature should be kept secret. We know that Robert Cecil, later the first Earl of Salisbury, was in some way connected with the Gunpowder Plot; but he nowhere wrote down for the benefit of history: "I, Robert Cecil, am going to start a plot for blowing up the King and the Houses of Parliament. I will nurse that plot, and at my chosen moment I will reveal it and thereby destroy my opponents and greatly exalt my own position." That is presumably what happened, but we have no document and no direct evidence. It would not be in the nature of things that we should have. In the same way we have no document saying "I want to have good popular backing against the succession of the Catholic Duke of York. I must get up a violent *anti-Catholic* mob excitement against him. So I think I will start a Popish Plot. (Signed) Shaftesbury." But in this case, unlike the case of Cecil in the Gunpowder Plot, probability is against the supposition that one powerful man or even a group of them *created* the public madness. Such things do not proceed after that fashion and the Popish Plot had all the characteristics of those popular explosions which, for lack of any rational train from cause to effect, we call "spontaneous."

The principal facts are elementary history. A fanatical clergyman, being approached by or approaching a notorious villain, by name Oates, the latter makes depositions of a plot before a magistrate.

Oates had in his vagabond life got his bread for a time as a student among the English Jesuits abroad, and had been turned out for his vices. He now began an elaborate tale, which grew more and more elaborate as time proceeded, describing how he had become acquainted with the plans of the Society for murdering the King of England and massacring the population at large. And, upon such a foundation, rebuilding a Catholic supremacy.

The magistrate before whom this mass of nonsense was deposed was found dead shortly after. It is to this day uncertain whether he was murdered or committed suicide, but the latter thesis is much the more probable.†

A vast clamour arose that the magistrate had been murdered by the papists, but what clinched the affair was the discovery of Coleman's letters. Coleman was a Catholic of wild judgment, loyal to his employers, the Duke and Duchess of York, for whom he worked as secretary, and quite naturally openly and notoriously on the side of the Duke and all that he stood for. Having been inevitably denounced, as the anti-Catholic tide rose, his papers were seized, and among those papers were letters to Père La Chaise, the confessor of Louis XIV. In these letters Coleman zealously preached the opportunity for restoring Catholicism in his native land. He put it strongly and not quite sanely, being a man intense and unbalanced emotions, and of course there was read into his exuberant follies a regular plan for the subjection of Protestantism in England by Catholic France. After that all went merrily. Coleman suffered the fate of a traitor. Coleman was half hung; he was cut down, mutilated, disembowelled, quartered, beheaded, etc., and he was followed by a train of others who did not themselves know of what they were accused. There was no supported evidence against any of them whatsoever, only untested affirmation.

One might, if one were fanatical, convince oneself at a stretch that fanatical Coleman not only thought it possible to reconvert England, but looked forward to that happy event coming quickly. But the accusations, the so-called "informations" laid against the priests and others by Oates and his crew were supported by no corroborating evidence whatsoever. The Chief Justice accurately reflected the lunacy of the time when he said that no evidence was needed; he could

---

† He was of a very nervously morbid character and subject to fits of grave depression. It was proved in the autopsy that he had eaten nothing for forty-eight hours before his death.

believe the guilt of the prisoners without evidence. In the same way we can find today anti-Semites (as the silly name goes), who think that a man's being a Jew is evidence against him for being also anything else you like, from a murderer to a pickpocket. It is strange that the reason of Man should thus sometimes suddenly depart from him, not as when an individual goes mad, but massively and by thousands. But so it is. We have all seen it happen in our own day. Who does not remember the Russians coming through England during the Great War – some of them apparently with Russian snow still on their boots? Who does not remember the corpse factory in which the Germans boiled down the bodies of their dead during that same period? People believed those things firmly, as firmly as ever man believed that the moon is made of green cheese. Readers of *The Times* believed in the Piggott letters long after poor Piggott had made away with himself, and leaders of men in Europe today are as firm as a rock on the point that an innocent General Staff at Potsdam and a peaceful, blameless Government behind them were suddenly set upon by the ruffianly French in 1914.

We have so many examples of popular lunacies in every country that we ought to accept, without astonishment, as a mere objective historical fact, the insanity of the Popish Plot terror.

Not only is there no need to seek out individual creators of it, of whom Shaftesbury would seem the most obvious, but it can be affirmed that the conditions rendered an individual creator impossible. The thing could not have been done by one man or by a small group of men without large, organised machinery for the purpose and a lengthy and considerable preparation of which there was certainly none. The public excitement over the Royal conversion, the intense public feeling against France and Papistry, in London especially, were the conditions for the explosion, just as an unstable chemical combination forms a condition for explosion. A shock or a spark does the rest. The death of Sir Edmond Berry Godfrey, the magistrate before whom Oates had made his first depositions, is sufficient to account for what followed, and Coleman's letters are much more than enough to account for the storm that arose.

What we certainly know as a piece of history without need to conjecture is that Shaftesbury did all in his power to inflame public feeling and to promote the popular madness in the streets of London. He personally procured and paid informers, he followed their actions, he marshalled and directed them against the interests of the Crown, because the whole thing turned upon the attack upon the heir to the Throne. Shaftesbury was not the original and single criminal, but he was the major figure throughout. He took immediate advantage of his opportunity and boasted of it with that cynicism which was one of his main characteristics: a natural concomitant of his high intelligence, vanity, cruelty and political spite.

Let us, therefore, lose no more time over the exact measure of Shaftesbury's responsibility. It is enough to know that the odds are against his having begun the thing, and that we have open and clamorous testimony to his nourishing and continuing it.

4. On Charles's own behaviour during the Popish Plot terror, reams and reams of Whig history have been written, in none of which is the matter understood. Yet it is not difficult to understand! Charles's attitude, his actions, his silence, were all one compromise exactly in line with whatever he had done from the moment when he first began his almost impossible task of restoration.

The whole episode has really only two essential and distinct points about it, which are: (1) Why did he sacrifice Stafford at the end of the abominable affair? And (2) in what degree was this death of an innocent man justified?

We must begin by understanding that Charles had, in all such affairs, one fixed principle to which, with the fortitude of his character, he adhered unfailingly throughout all the quarter century of his effort. "I will let the law take its course."

It is not easy for us today to understand that that principle is a fundamentally immoral principle and bad in politics as well as in ethics. There is nothing sacrosanct about man-made law, about the traditional procedure of Courts of Justice, about the decisions of lawyers. They may be silly or weak, as any other human doings may be silly or weak. The whole business of kingship is to correct the folly and evil of Society, particularly routine, and, by the sacred office of the Crown and its ultimate authority, to over-ride mere form. But it is self-evident that this ultimate function of kingship can only be exercised rarely and upon very grave occasions. Kingship is there as a safeguard. Its duty is to do what under our present oligarchic or plutocratic system of government is done by exceptional legislation.

FULL GALE: THE POPISH PLOT

Even as I write (August, 1939), there has been passed by Parliament at Westminster a law, to have effect for only two years, whereby the Police and the Home Office may arrest and deport a resident in England unless he be of twenty years standing, without trial and without reason given. This has been done to meet the exceptional conditions of the secretly planned explosions conducted by Irishmen in reprisal for the occupation of their northern counties by British troops. Normally, it would not be possible to expel a man or destroy his business without a definite charge preferred and proved in open court.

Exceptional action of authority is sometimes necessary, and it is the very function of a King to provide it on such occasions.

Charles himself attempted, as far as he could, to use the exceptional powers of a monarchy for the mitigation of the injustice done to masses of men by religious excitement. He was only stopped from doing the right thing in this by the determination of the rich men in Parliament to master him through their money-power.

Yet on this occasion when, if ever, justice was clamouring for kingly action, no such action appeared. Charles allowed men whom he knew to be innocent to go to the horrible torture, mutilation and death which followed upon an accusation of treason. He did more. He permitted public officials to pay informers out of public funds which were, nominally at least, part of the royal income. He signed death warrants for what was the legal murder of men whom he knew to be innocent. There is no commoner and no more just accusation against him than this of his behaviour during the Popish Plot Terror.

Had he a reason? Had he an excuse?

He had an excellent reason, which all those who care to understand his life, character and policy can find simply enough. He could only maintain the Throne by accepting what later came to be known as "the constitutional attitude." He could only remain King and thus perhaps re-establish real kingship in the long run, by giving to the servants of the Crown, especially the lawyers, and more particularly the judges, an exceptional and privileged position which they had not in any other country at the time. He could only remain King if he accepted during the moment of the Terror the monstrous illusions of the London mob. To remain King, and by remaining King to re-establish real kingship at last, he allowed the iniquitous verdicts to go forward without interference.

CHARLES II: THE LAST RALLY

So much for his reason. There can be no doubt about it; it is perfectly plain. We know well enough why he acted thus immorally. He sacrificed here once more something eternal called Justice to something temporal, his patriotic aim.

But had he an excuse? In other words, was the degree of his immoral action kept within such bounds as to make it tolerable in practice? Public men (let it be repeated for the hundredth time) are compelled to do evil continually; but there is a limit which they should never pass. Did Charles pass this limit in the matter of his yielding to the violent tornado of the Terror?

I think the answer is to be found in this reply: He did exceed the limit, he exceeded it when he permitted the execution of Stafford at the very end of the affair. By his condonation of injustice in that extreme case I think he should be judged. In all the rest of the affair he could plead that the setting up of the monarchy again was so essential to the country which he governed, that anything could be pardoned him in the pursuit of that object. The sacrifice of Stafford went too far. I could even wonder (fancifully enough) whether, when his deeds were weighed before the Ultimate Tribunal, it was not the death of Stafford which turned the balance and decided the Divine powers to take away kingship at last from his House.

Consider the conditions. Stafford was an old man. He was entering his seventieth year. The accusations laid against him by the informers were manifestly worthless. A few months' delay, perhaps a few weeks' delay, would have saved the poor old fellow's life, for the tide had already turned, the fever was exhausted, and men were beginning to recover their sanity. Moreover, Stafford was the last of that long list of innocent victims. He came, not in the heat of the violent fever, but at the close of it and in its stillness, and Charles might have pardoned Stafford without too much strain. It is true that Russell, in his capacity of head of the potential revolution, leader of the rich men who were attacking the Crown, spoke against the aged peer with as uncontrolled a cruelty as had been known at any period of those brief months of violence. When Russell was secure of the verdict against Stafford, he clamoured for all the abominations of a high-treason execution. He wanted this descendant of the ancient nobility of England, whose fathers were great in Europe centuries before the Russells had been heard of, to be hung, drawn, mutilated, quartered, butchered after the strict legal fashion. This Charles would not permit, and it is to his honour.

When Russell himself came to die for real treason, not for an imaginary, false offence, Charles murmured that he had given the traitor more mercy than ever that traitor allowed Stafford, for Russell was to die a simple and honourable death, beheaded, but not strangled nor mutilated nor barbarously butchered.

I know not whether the modern mood will allow any consideration to lineage, but I confess that it weighs with me. It seems to be particularly disgraceful that the man thus sacrificed should have suffered without any consideration of his place in the highest lineage of England. Of course, such things must not weigh in matters of life and death. But the betrayal of a Howard – and Stafford was a Howard – the shameful death on a false accusation of one who belonged to the premier family of England, does seem to me something exceptionally evil, and counts against the reputation of the King. Others of the Howards have been put to death for treason upon insufficient grounds. The most notable was that young Protestant Duke of Norfolk, who should have married Mary Queen of Scots; Fox's pupil, whom the Cecils put to death under the nominal authority of Elizabeth, his cousin. She at least, unfortunate woman, had tried hard to save him, but Cecil was too strong for her. Howard stood in Cecil's mind for the old nobility and for a parallel to that chance Tudor woman who was maintained as the figurehead of the new Reformation millionaires. Therefore, he had to go. But even that Howard of the sixteenth century did not die under circumstances so damning to those who condemned him as did this Howard of the seventeenth.

Those who care for the picturesque and tragic detail of the national story may read with deep pity the surroundings of his end. He had, of course, denied, as all the victims of the Popish Plot Terror denied, the monstrous falsehood and the accusation brought against him; but what is most touching in the affair is his plea for some little rest before death. He was an old man, he said, who under the strain of his imprisonment could not sleep, might that not afford him relief? For the continued loss of sleep is a terrible thing. His plea was not heeded. When the time came for him to die, he met death well indeed. There was no complaint then, nor any plea for mercy. He had not enjoyed the love of his fellow men, not even of those of his own blood; but perhaps his isolation had given him a particular spirit.

He was not the very last of the victims of the Terror. A man of a certain holiness – which Stafford certainly could not claim – Plunkett, the Archbishop of Armagh, was the last of those human sacrifices. He preserved his holiness, and his memory is still a strength to the Irish.

5. The gale had blown itself out, the wreckage it had left behind strewed the ground. Its worst effects, or at any rate its worst considerable effects, were not those which had been most apparent. It is not the cruel and disgusting death of so many innocent men, nor even the compulsion of such a man as Charles to stoop to such perhaps necessary ignominy; it is not even the horrible spectacle of public mania which should most detain us when we read of that episode in the establishment of modern England.

No: the main thing about the Popish Plot, its accompanying Terror and its murders, lies, and enormous extravagance of evil was this – that it gave the death blow to Catholicism in England.

The ancient religion did not sink immediately upon the conclusion of this chapter in the book of the English story. Another ten years were granted to it, even perhaps twelve or nearly twenty; for it is debatable whether Catholicism were finally extinguished in England by the revolution of 1688 or by the failure of the legitimist efforts of 1691, and even 1715. But, wherever we put the terminal date of the Faith in England, in whatever year we set up its monument as to a thing dead, the mortal blow was certainly delivered in those few months from late 1678 to early 1680. The Catholic Church as it had been in this island never rose again. That is the profound interest of the time and of the act.

Until the Terror of the Popish Plot, the Catholic Church in England had remained, though defeated, yet a living thing in continuity with the English past. The Faithful had been for long at issue with their fellow citizens; they were politically vanquished; their worship (and it is astonishing that in the absence of it so considerable a body of them should have survived) was atrophied and almost forgotten.

But their inheritance still held. The Catholics still knew themselves to be the best of England and, what must seem strange to any modern Englishman, they still felt that they were the real England. When we appreciate that, we can better understand how so many of them were deluded into believing that the Faith might yet be restored. The ancestral Faith was still their secret possession, though they could hold it only in a sort of confused memory without practice to support them. Under the shock of the Popish Plot and its profound consequences, the old English Catholicism disappeared, because all hope of revival was gone. A lifetime later men retained some sentimental memory of what it had been; less than two lifetimes later – that is, in a hundred years – even the memory had gone. By 1780 one family in a hundred at the most kept up a sort of nominal Catholicism, by tradition. Ireland's spiritual support of the defeated had itself been doubly defeated. English priests of the eighteenth century went about as laymen. Certain practices of religion were, indeed, later tolerated again; they could henceforward be of no effect.

There did come in, as we all know, but by other channels, a certain new form of that which had perished in the last years of Charles. The French immigrant priests in 1792 revived the last dying embers. Through them there was preached in the University Church of St. Mary's that pivotal sermon, now forgotten. Young Best – also forgotten – preached the doctrine of sacramental absolution and set all Oxford by the ears before Newman was so much as born. Then came the offer to introduce the Catholic religion into the body of the Established Church itself and to claim continuity, the effort which was first associated with the name of Pusey and then more forthrightly with the name of Newman. Then came the Irish famine and the flood of immigration, which was essentially alien and planted the Faith in the industrial towns of North England, where it attained to new life.

But the slight, though vivid, action of the French immigrant clergy was on a tiny scale. What has been called "the Oxford Movement" more than half a lifetime later, though counting more on the scholarship and social position of its champions, had, without any great increase in numbers, a considerable effect upon the minds of those who led the nation. Some even imagined that a new spring had welled forth. They were deceived.

There was, indeed, to come an established Catholic hierarchy in England, but it appeared as something from without. Its enemies could claim that it was a mere "Roman Mission," and the great bulk of its adherents were of Irish descent or connection. There was, of course, identity in doctrine but there was not continuity between the age-long religion of the English, that which had made England, and the Catholic revival of the nineteenth century.

So the situation remains. The Catholic Church, here surviving up to the Popish Plot, was in descent from, and in touch with, the whole national story. It was a fragment of England apparently doomed and with difficulty maintaining its life, but it could claim to be not only native, but more really native than anything around it. The Catholic Church today in England is of three parts. There is a small, distinguished traditional group of old families and local units (especially in the North), who pride themselves on their fully national claim; but they are very few, and as they pride themselves on their national claim, so they cannot but take on in some degree that national tone, the very core of which is opposed to Catholicism.

There comes next a far more important body, not perhaps in numbers, but in effect – particularly in intellectual and moral effect: the converts. Of these there has been a stream surprisingly steady ever since the mid-nineteenth century. It may be doubted whether the recruitment has kept pace either with the increase of population or with apostasy and forgetfulness; but decade after decade one group of considerable names after another stands out to maintain the strange efficacy, in a society which is strongly opposed to them, of both Catholic philosophy and Catholic morals.

The third section, overwhelmingly the most numerous – so much more numerous that some think that it cannot but absorb the whole of its co-religionists at last – is the section of those who are, either by direct descent or by connection, Irish.

That is what the Catholic body in England has become, in contrast with what it was under the later Stuarts; and the turnover in which the old thing disappeared with no chance of the new things coming for more than a century, was the blow of the Popish Plot.

HURRICANE AND HARBOUR

THE DYING-DOWN OF THAT GALE, THE QUIETENING OF THAT "Terror," was but an entry to a final and more violent phase and a concluding hurricane which the master just rode out: just, barely. It is often so with a perilous passage; the worst gusts are at the end.

The assault of the rebel elements against the Crown fell into two successive movements. First came the intense effort to destroy monarchy by destroying the succession, for legitimate hereditary succession was the soul of English kingship. Next came the desperate last chance of treason and assassination; both efforts failed. They failed as to murder by chance, as to treason they failed against the superior intelligence and helm-play of the King.

Everything was in favour of success for the rebellion, yet he out-manœuvred it and left those very rich men defeated − but that was not the end of the affair.

The second phase was the more perilous. If they could not destroy the monarchy by destroying its heir's rights of succession, if the one man standing up to them was more than their match, if his courage and patience and deep comprehension of motive enabled him to come out of the contest as he did, far stronger than he had entered it, there was yet one resource left to the Whig battalions and their leaders. That resource was assassination, or, failing so complete a solution, at any rate the removal of the King and the setting up of a usurping council and puppet of their own. This was the very last effort and in its turn it failed. The monarchy put the chief and most powerful conspirators to death, and the execution of William Russell, the leading culprit, though not a true leader, marked victory. Thenceforward the King was King. The sound of the axe on the block in Lincoln's Inn Fields on the 21st of July, 1683, was like a signal announcing full victory. Henceforward the King would be King indeed.

Had there been reserved for Charles such length of life as his vigorous frame, his constant exercise and his sobriety warranted, there might conceivably have arisen a throne firmly restored. Such an issue was improbable, but it was possible; what made it out of the question was that sudden ending of the life on which all depended. Not eighteen full months after the execution of Russell, Charles himself was dead; and that lawful succession which he had secured was to fall into the hands of a man who would refuse all compromise with his Faith as with his honour. Against such a man rebellion had its will, and treason, too, and with the triumph of that last rebellion English monarchy came to an end. All the great work of Charles was to be ruined and go void. Wealth was to triumph.

To understand the battle for hereditary right and for the legitimate heir to the throne, the main point to seize is that one which the bulk of our history, as written since the Whig triumph, slurs over or leaves unmentioned altogether; it is this: the House of Commons, wherein the Money-power resided and which had become the standing and mortal opponent of the King, was built up in a fashion which made it representative not of the English people but of the wealthier among them, and especially of the very wealthy. *This was because the great bulk of the members were borough members.*

Those who falsify our history make play with the words "House of Commons" and "representation" in order to muddy the waters. Their readers imagine that a consultation of the country was taken and that it yielded a majority against the King. There was no such consultation. There was no majority of Englishmen against their King. The county members, knights of the shire, came nearer to what we call representation today than any other elements at Westminster. They were based on what remained of the yeomanry. Every freeholder above a very low level, every permanent possessor of so much as a few acres of land, could vote for the knight of the shire. Their numbers were diminishing, for the Money-power had attacked the peasantry as well as the King and was at last to destroy the peasant. But they still survived.

The peasants, then, the free peasants, counted somewhat in elections still. They could vote. This does not mean, of course, that all did vote; as a rule only a small proportion did so or could do so under the conditions of the time, or even desired to do so; but, anyhow, these voted in the counties – which were England – and through them there would be an increasing support for popular monarchy.

But the boroughs, much the greater part of the Commons, were another matter. The franchise in them was of all sorts: a complete welter.

Here you will have a county town where every householder, or nearly every householder, could have his say. Much more often the charter which made the borough a parliamentary unit gave the power of election to a small minority of well-to-do men, the Corporation. Then again the boroughs were not real boroughs, some were towns or townlets, but many were villages or even less than villages.

The borough members, even more than the counties, were in the pockets of the magnates; they stood for wealth, the more powerful because it was indirect. It would have been better for English kingship if the Money-power had been unquestioned and open. Then at least the issue would have been clear. As it was, the Money-power purchasing and dominating the borough voting, falsified the result. When the last struggle should come the King must lose unless he could reform the corruption of the boroughs.

A thing apart from either boroughs or county vote was the vote of London. Here there was a system inherited from the guilds of the Middle Ages. The trades of the capital were incorporated in associations built up still, for the most part, of the actual craftsmen or shop-keepers. The names of those old corporations, still quaintly surviving, but having for the most part lost all trace of their old function, sufficiently explain the system. You may be entertained today with great display of gold and silver by the Fishmongers in their very fine great hall, but you will be the guest of men who sell no fish. You may be entertained by the Merchant Tailors, a very wealthy body devoted to great public service; but your hosts will not know much about the cutting of cloth. The Goldsmiths will more nearly continue their ancient spirit, for at their table you still gaze upon some of their splendid wares, but even these men may know nothing of bullion or of the fashion of gold by way of art. The city company of which I am proud to be a member was among the latest to preserve something of its old reality. It is called "The Inn-holders" and boasts a very charming hall, full of the Caroline spirit. They were, until almost within living memory, not much more than one hundred years ago, charged with the duty of overseeing and keeping at a right standard the hostelries of London. But today they have no such realities about them. Had those realities survived I could not be a member, for I hold no inn.

Well, London, in this later part of the seventeenth century had a large and true representation. It did not, of course, cover anything but a minority of the population, but it covered a much larger proportion than you would find in any other category. There was heavy polling and the real political results were ascertained according as the majority fell.

CHARLES II: THE LAST RALLY

Now these voters in London, it is interesting to note, were, during this last campaign of the King, almost equally divided. One of the chief features in the last days of the struggle was the slight preponderance of the loyal half among those who exercised the suffrage of the capital. It was the capture of London by the King's friends which turned the scale. The margin between the two factions was a narrow one. For years Shaftesbury could depend upon immunity in his treasonable schemes because he could be certain of sheriffs who were on his side and it was the sheriffs on whom depended the Grand Jury. Already a King's man had been chosen for Lord Mayor. That was in the November of 1681. In the next month, December, when the elections to the Common Council took place, the jury which had acquitted Shaftesbury was undermined; more than half of it was lost to the Whigs. The loyal Lord Mayor claimed the old custom of nominating one sheriff. In the June of 1682, after the old gang had used every form of intimidation, there was a sufficient majority to place the loyalist sheriffs in power for good. They would not take up office for some months. It was at the very end of September, 1682, when they thus entered, and, side by side with them, the new Mayor was to be elected, who was a King's man as well. Charles had been out of London; when he came back he found the City his own.

In the first part of the fight, when the issue was the right of the legitimate heir, James, Duke of York, to succeed to the Throne in due course, Charles played a game which was perilous indeed, but successful. He had dismissed that old interminable Parliament, but the new assembly served him no better, for the boroughs were not reformed. It seemed useless to continue the effort. So long as the boroughs remained what they were each successive Parliament would give majorities in the Commons for the King's enemies who were already called by the label of "Russell's men" for William Russell, that heir to the wealthiest of the great families, was the symbol of the attack upon the Kingship as well as the best known name in the attack.

It is singular to read the extreme to which Charles went in his playing of his fish: the length of line he reeled out to rebellion seemed quite inordinate. He was willing – in words at least – to give up everything but the bare nominal right of his brother to be called King after his own death. He was willing to deprive that brother of every active power so only that the essential title of Kingship should be maintained. These sacrifices which were known as the "expedients" seemed on the surface to be a complete admission of defeat; what would be left of that principle of monarchy for which Charles had lived and fought if the effective executive was in the hands of a committee of magnates? But though there is no written paper to tell us so, it is clear that Charles was playing that exceedingly doubtful card, "risk of the worst." He was gambling on the folly of his enemies, on the possibility (which, with his unerring judgment of men, he knew to be rather the *probability*) that the enemies of the Crown, encouraged by his concessions, would kill themselves by an exaggeration of their offensive. It was the tactic of opening the ranks so that a hostile charge shall be tempted to press forward to its own exhaustion.

The last Parliament had been summoned but it had been summoned to meet at Oxford so that the organised mob in London should not come into action. It was Shaftesbury's mob; a minority, of course, as all mobs are, but their leader was confident of what their violence could do. Hence the change of venue by Charles to Oxford.

The gathering of the forces for that Parliament had about it all the atmosphere of civil war. The millionaire Whigs had brought their dependents in arms. Their ribbons were seen flying and the throng along the London Road, pouring up over Magdalen Bridge on the opening day (21st of March, 1681), savoured of a riotous army. The Exclusion Bill which was to crown the Whig victory, which had been passed by so large a majority in the old corrupt House and which the Lords had thrown out so unexpectedly, was going forward again here in this new Oxford Parliament – the fourth since Charles's succession. It would certainly pass the Commons again and a new dissolution would, with the corrupt borough vote still in being, give no relief. The angry Whig leaders would not meet Charles by an inch. They would have Exclusion and nothing but Exclusion; and behind them was something more; it had been determined to make Monmouth heir, to claim his legitimacy and to give him the succession to the Throne.

That 21st of March, 1681, the moment when the English monarchy was on the very edge of falling, was a Monday. For a week from that day the Exclusion Bill was to be brought in again.

On the eve of the Bill's introduction, that is on the Sunday, the 27th of March, the King, collecting his Council, heard them support him in the policy of yet another dissolution. But that policy must be kept a dead secret for the barrel of powder was ready to explode. On the morrow, on that very Monday when the issue should have been joined, 28th of March, Charles in his robes and wearing his crown, took his place upon the Throne and summoned the Commons. They were jubilant with a roaring jubilation, for they made sure that this meant surrender. What they heard at the crowded doors was the King commanding his Chancellor to dissolve Parliament yet again. He was rid of it for ever. There should be none other until he had reconstructed the crazy machinery and cleaned up the impossible welter of the borough vote.

That very heavy blow, the sudden dissolution, did its work because the country was with the King. The rebel magnates were appalled but dared not move.

There arose, after an interval of a very few days, a very flood of public reaction towards the Crown. Charles urged the current by his public declaration which was read to the congregations in churches throughout the realm. He told his people all that he had done to meet the threat of revolution, how he had offered every guarantee for the "security of the Protestant religion"; in other words, how he had abandoned his brother's claim to almost everything in kingship but the name of King. He patiently detailed all the extravagances of Shaftesbury's men and Russell's men in the Commons, their open breaches of legality, their arbitrary imprisonments and the rest. Protestations of loyalty began to pour in from the myriads who "abhorred" the attempted bullying of the Crown. The whole party came to be called "abhorrers" and they had the tide under them. There was nothing left but direct and open high treason; the murder of the King for the setting up of the wretched Monmouth as usurper. Short of that nothing could stop the reform of the boroughs and with it the breakdown of the faction and its artificial borough monopoly in the Commons.

What followed is familiar to all acquainted with the elements of the constitutional story. Certain obscure plotters, some of them fanatical remnants of the old Republican tradition, conspired together. One of them (perhaps an original, much more probably a hired dupe), who had held a commission of Cromwell's long ago, was prepared to do Charles to death. His coach was to be fired on as it passed the spot known as the Rye House on the road from Newmarket to London.

Whoever was behind that piece of "activist" work, there appeared behind them another more formidable group centring round the name and presence of Monmouth, having, as always, for its principal name William Russell; Essex was among them. No one will ever know how much or how little this larger conspiracy of treason had helped to design the murder planned. That it designed the deposition of the King by force is certain. The palace was to be seized.

Charles would not kill Monmouth, his well-loved son. That was left for the next reign. It was a weakness, and the Crown was to pay dear in the next reign for that weakness. Monmouth was spared. But on the 12th of July, 1683, the Grand Jury found two bills against him and a score of others, among whom Russell and Essex out-topped the rest. The wretched Howard of Escrick, Shaftesbury's man, had sold his colleagues. He had turned King's evidence and so saved not only his own neck but what remained of the Majesty of England.

On the 13th of July, the very morrow, the verdict of guilty went out against Russell. Already, in the Tower, Essex had killed himself.

For a few agonised days the vast wealth of what may justly be called the foremost family in opposition to the Crown not only pleaded but *bid* for the life of Bedford's son. Money was their point; for money they spoke; they were the Money-power.

They would pay lavishly for a reprieve. Charles answered with the exact truth: "It is his life or mine." Therefore a week and a day after conviction for his crime, William Russell mounted that scaffold on the eleven-acre green by Lincoln's Inn so near to his own London land; the scaffold with black cloth all about it and the masked headsman standing by prepared.

He died with dignity and courage. In a very few years avengers of his death would arise.

*****

These things having been done there followed a year and half a year of calm. It seemed as though Kingship had won its battle and as though Charles might now pass a quiet afternoon of life having achieved his task. The craft he had so well handled had turned the breakwater-end and slipped into smooth water out of the howling seas and was at rest.

Note

Here are some examples of boroughs and their ridiculous distribution. Bedfordshire has no less than nine, while Cambridgeshire has only one – the town of Cambridge – and Chester has only one, the town of Chester. Cornwall, one of the most sparsely inhabited counties in the kingdom, has no less than ten boroughs. Derbyshire has only got Derby town itself, while Devon actually has eleven boroughs! Leicestershire has only one. Hampshire has twelve, Sussex has nine, Warwickshire only one. Wiltshire has no less than fifteen, including that famous fraud, Old Sarum.

King Charles II

An oil painting attributed to Thomas Hawker ca. 1680

DROP ANCHOR

In this chapter I follow the scholarship and research of Mr. Bryant save in the matter of the moon's age and the like.

He who would know England should come up London River by a flood tide, under the morning sun: on a spring tide, bearing upwards in the swirl from the sea upon waters that run inland all the forenoon, and reach the City at last, bringing to London the salt and the life of the sea.

Upon Friday, the 6th of February, 1685, Charles Stuart lay in the article of death, while such a morning tide swept by....†

He had been struck down at the opening of that week. Already his age had come upon him, but now there had fallen that which comes at the end of age, the failure of the body to maintain its task, the breakdown. It had seized him suddenly, after the long interval of quiet he had earned for himself, after the first full holiday he had ever taken since he took up the heavy task of ruling and of dominating his foes. He had already felt the years; he must sleep after his meals; his powerful stride, though still vigorous, was moderated; he fell into the habit of repetition; he preferred repose. There had come upon him, as there come to all men when the life of the body begins to fail, sundry disagreeables – but nothing which should cause him, or those about him, to expect an end. Then, suddenly I say, the approach of the end was manifest.

It began with a stroke or fit, wherein he stumbled and fell. Before it was relieved his distorted features and upturned eyeballs had struck those about him with the immediate terror of coming evil.

The thing passed, but manifestly its last effects would not be long awaited. On the second and the third day, he lay powerless and at times slightly confused in mind. There was still some doubt. By the Thursday there was none. It was clear that the call had come.

---

† The moon was twelve to thirteen days old and high water at London Bridge about midday.

CHARLES II: THE LAST RALLY

The February dark had already fallen some hours. No light lingered in the western sky up the river. The curtains of the very tall windows, the heavy luxurious palace curtains of Whitehall, were drawn; a fire burnt in the large grate and some few tapering yellow candles of wax cast shadows through the splendid room. Under their light the tapestries and hangings, the rich embroideries about the bed, and the heavy gilded mouldings of the time were caught by that subdued light and by an occasional fitful spurt of flame from the sea-coal fire. The little spaniels which Charles loved so well, stirred and scratched. A great crowd of the Court pressed outside the doors, and the first of them had come into the room itself. Kings, when kings were kings, must die as they were born, in public; for they were not individual men but the State itself – the Nation incarnate. All must be witness to their coming and their going.

Two Bishops of the establishment were there among the rest: the soft and quiet Compton of London, who was later to plan a trap for Charles's successor in the matter of the Seven Bishops, a man of birth, representing the influence of wealth in his profession; the other, the virtuous, sincere little Ken, now recently of Bath and Wells, with his high penetrating voice. They adjured the dying man to partake of one last Eucharist in the church of his baptism, the communion whereof he, the King, was chief and supreme governor; for he was England. The elements of bread and wine had been brought and were present on the table, all was ready. From the pillows came a courteous murmur that there was time enough.

Now, among the men who thronged close at hand, was that one woman who had been more of a companion for him than any other, though in her also he certainly had missed companionship, Louise de Keroualle, Duchess of Portsmouth. Long acquaintance breeds a sort of rooted affection in any circumstance, even in circumstances such as those which had brought him and her together. She was but one of a hand's count among those, the women, who had surrounded him and meant to him at heart hardly anything at all, but she came first and certainly she loved him; even somewhat more than did all those who were familiar with his presence love him. Through her he remembered Minette who had brought her to England and to his side. Also this woman knew by her own hereditary practice and habit, by the tradition of the dead woman, the beloved sister, gone nearly fifteen years, what was passing in that motionless but still functioning mortal mind, and amid her tears she rose to find the French Ambassador, Barillon. She said that the King must have a priest and that soon; now; at once – for time pressed and, with it, so did Death, advancing.

Barillon found York, and that tall dark brother, his face less moved than most, fell on his knees beside the bed and asked whether he might send for one that would reconcile Charles with the Faith he had known but put off, and administer those Sacraments whereby the Christian soul is armoured against its awful passage. The dying man murmured in reply, "With all my heart...." It was well past eight o'clock in the evening. The clocks in the room (there were many) ticked the passing moments, and soon one or another of them would chime. York had risen and had bidden all retire save two men whom he kept for witnesses and pledges, two peers: Feversham (who was the Huguenot, Duras) and Bath. Protestant, they were guarantees to the Bishops; but loyal, they would keep their counsel and would not betray what was toward.

There was a small side door into that high royal room, a door that gave into the death-room by the wall, near the head of the bed. Through it came in – oddly muffled in a long cassock and wearing a wig so that he might have been one of the clergy of the establishment – came in who, and what? The man, the priest, whom Charles, after the Battle of Worcester, had met during his visit at Boscobel, that very same man with whom he had stood in the small, bare, hidden chapel of that Catholic house; the same man in whose presence he had taken up and preserved for reading that short exposition of the Catholic Faith which had sown the seed of all that was to follow.... When such coincidences are suggested for the stage they are suppressed as being too violently improbable, too mechanical a repetition. When they appear in fiction they are ridiculed for a clumsy trick, but in life itself such a coincidence, such a miracle, is to be found. All have known one or another such happening. Are they designed? James, who stood by, said to his brother: "The man who saved your life has come to save your soul," and Charles was able to murmur in his failing voice, "He is very welcome."

CHARLES II: THE LAST RALLY

Ever since the stroke had fallen the doctors had submitted the King to torment upon torment, not sparing him hot irons upon the head, and perpetual bleeding. Scarcely had he strength for the last whispered syllables, for the last gestures. Huddleston the priest, the man whose presence now spanned nearly a quarter of a century of time, uniting the strong, towering, swarthy boy of twenty-one with the man now dying in his fifty-fifth year, knelt in his turn by the bedside and asked him if he would indeed be received into the Faith. He assented eagerly (if one may talk of eagerness when all was so weak), he confessed in full, and in his confession mourned that delay which had postponed to the very last moment what should have been done (but at the risk of all!) years and years before. He called on the mercy of Christ as God.

The Blessed Sacrament had arrived, belated – for it had to be brought from the Queen's Chapel. As it passed, there passed by a Presence transcending altogether the presence of England and Kingship, of arms, of companionship, and memories of the sea. There was passing by and had arrived That which had made and judges them all.

Factus Homo: Factor hominus: factique Redemptor,
Corporeus judico corpora corda Deus.*

Charles Stuart in this supreme visitation did just that which the great Lorenzo, the ancestor of long ago, had done in the same final effort. He struggled to rise and to receive God kneeling in his bed. He did just what was done by his cousin, Louis XV of France, a century later, who also struggled to rise in his last Communion, and said, "My great God comes to me." Charles was bidden cease the effort, for kneeling was beyond his strength. The priest disappeared again through the low side door. York summoned the courtiers and once more they crowded in. Nearly an hour had passed in those whispered and hidden rites.

---

* "Made Man: Maker of man: and also man's Redeemer; incarnate I judge bodies, as God I judge hearts." From the inscrpition around the mosaic of Christ Pantocrator in the Cathedral of Cefalù, Sicily, built, under the reign of the Norman King Roger II, beginning in 1131, one year following his conquest of the island. —Ed.